From Local Champions to Global Masters

# From Local Champions to Global Masters

A strategic perspective on managing internationalization

by

**Paul Verdin**

**and**

**Nick Van Heck**

palgrave

First published 2001 by
PALGRAVE
Houndmills, Basingstoke, Hampshire RG21 6XS and
175 Fifth Avenue, New York, N.Y. 10010
Companies and representatives throughout the world

PALGRAVE is the new global academic imprint of
St. Martin's Press LLC Scholarly and Reference Division and
Palgrave Publishers Ltd (formerly Macmillan Press Ltd).

ISBN 0–333–94730–4 hardcover

This book is printed on paper suitable for recycling and made from fully managed and sustained forest sources.

A catalogue record for this book is available from the British Library.

Library of Congress Cataloging-in-Publication Data

Verdin, Paul.
  From local champions to global masters : a strategic perspective on managing internationalization / Paul Verdin, Nick Van Heck.
    p. cm.
  Includes bibliographical references and index.
  ISBN 0–333–94730–4
    1. International business enterprises—Management.
  2. Globalization—Economic aspects. 3. Competition, International. I. Heck, Nick Van. II. Title.

  HD62.4 . V467 2001
  658'.049—dc21

                              2001036099

Editing and origination by
Aardvark Editorial, Mendham, Suffolk

10  9  8  7  6  5  4  3  2
10  09  08  07  06  05  04  03  02

Printed and bound in Great Britain by
Creative Print & Design (Wales), Ebbw Vale

*To Charlotte, Emily and Anne(-Marie)*
*who, in the midst of globalisation turbulence,*
*have always helped me,*
*each in their own way,*
*to keep my feet on the ground*

P.V.


*To my local champions, Guus and Marijke*

N.V.H.

# Contents

*List of Figures*                                                            ix

*Preface*                                                                    xi

*Acknowledgements*                                                           xvi

Introduction   **Beyond Globalization and its Myths**                        1
               The myth of globalization                                     3
               Beyond the myths                                              9
               The position of this book                                     10
               The structure of this book                                    14

**Section 1:   On the Benefits of Internationalization    19**

Chapter 1      **Internationalization: The Only Way to Go?**                 23
               We have to internationalize or die                           25
               Internationalization is strategic                            27
               Bigger is better ... only a few players will survive         29
               We have to take positions now, it is now or never ...  all bets
                   are off tomorrow!                                         34
               There are only a few interesting targets left                36
               Eat or be eaten                                              37
               Our competitors are already doing it                         39
               Foreign competitors are entering our home market             40
               Our home market is saturated ... our home market is
                   too small                                                42
               We are just following our clients – they are international   44
               We need to be where the market is                            47
               It is key to have global access to clients                   50
               We have to be international from the start                    51
               It is too risky to depend on the home market alone           53
               Summary: where is the beef?                                  54

Chapter 2      **The Conelearn Framework**                                   57
               Cost advantages                                              60
               Network benefits                                             68

# Contents

| | | |
|---|---|---:|
| | Cone and international strategies | 71 |
| | Cone in the European landscape | 90 |
| | Learning opportunities | 94 |
| | The Conelearn framework: beyond the internationalization slogans | 98 |

| **Section 2:** | **On Organizing for Internationalization** | **103** |
|---|---|---:|
| Chapter 3 | **On Entry Modes into Foreign Markets** | **107** |
| | Target markets | 107 |
| | Entry modes | 111 |
| | A strategic reflection on entering a foreign market | 116 |
| Chapter 4 | **On Organizational Structures and Blueprints** | **118** |
| | Show me your organization chart, and I will tell you what strategy you have | 119 |
| | Which dimension to push? | 122 |
| | Beyond the centralization–decentralization dilemma | 128 |
| | Implications for headquarters and subsidiaries | 131 |
| | The role of regional headquarters | 133 |

| **Section 3:** | **On Managing the Process of Internationalization** | **135** |
|---|---|---:|
| Chapter 5 | **Managing the Implementation Process** | **139** |
| | Identifying internal barriers | 141 |
| | How to overcome the barriers? | 149 |
| Chapter 6 | **Beyond 'Implementation': Managing the Overall Agenda** | **158** |
| | The whole is more than the sum of the parts | 159 |
| | Beyond the Cartesian logic | 163 |
| | Beyond the grand plan | 166 |
| | You will never be the same company again | 168 |
| | Internationalization should make a real difference | 172 |
| | It is a never-ending story | 177 |
| Chapter 7 | **From Local Champions to Global Masters: Conclusion** | **180** |
| | Why globalization is NOT happening in your company | 181 |
| | Globalization is strategic | 187 |

| | | |
|---|---|---:|
| *Notes* | | 189 |
| *References* | | 193 |
| *Index* | | 206 |

# List of Figures

0.1    The why–what–how loop of internationalization                                    12
0.2    The structure of this book                                                       14

1.1    A web of internationalization slogans                                            24
1.2    Road map of internationalization slogans                                         55
1.3    Countering the internationalization slogans                                      56

2.1    The why of internationalization                                                  59
2.2    The Conelearn framework                                                          60
2.3    Generic learning curve                                                           66
2.4    International strategy prototypes                                                 73
2.5    Globalization potential in the Cone(learn) framework                             74
2.6    The globalization potential                                                      75
2.7    The globalization limits                                                         77
2.8    International playing field                                                       77
2.9    The international playing field across the value chain in the car industry       81
2.10   Dynamic analysis of the international playing field across functions             86
2.11   International playing field: example of Gillette Mach3                            89
2.12   Conelearn framework: what are the benefits of internationalization?              99

S2.1   The what aspects of internationalization                                        104

3.1    The Conelearn framework and selection of target markets: which markets
       to enter first?                                                                 110
3.2    The Conelearn framework and entry modes: which entry mode to use                114

4.1    Conelearn framework: how to balance formal and informal coordination?           130
4.2    The Conelearn framework and the role of subsidiaries                            131

S3.1   The how of internationalization: managing the process                           136
S3.2   Managing the iterations in the why–what–how loop of globalization               137

5.1    Internal barriers linked with the real globalization potential                  141
5.2    The importance of involvement in development and implementation phase           151
5.3    Shock therapy versus slow and steady                                            156

7.1    Why is globalization not happening in our company?                              182

We could perhaps say
that the town square was replaced by the world arena.
The old town square had also buzzed with voices,
bringing now different wares to market,
now different thoughts and ideas.
The new aspect was
that town squares were being filled with wares and ideas from all over the world.
The voices were buzzing in many different languages.

# Preface

For quite some time now, business and corporate strategy discussions have been in the grip of 'globalization'. After a period of moderate attention in the 1980s, the phenomenon came back with a vengeance in the 1990s to start leading its own life at practically all levels and corners of business and society. Propelled by a buoyant stock market, international political developments and technological innovations, including the growth of the internet, it seduced many a company to engage aggressively in adventures into 'foreign markets' and 'internationalization strategies', whether through greenfield operations or, more dramatically, through mergers and acquisitions.

It stimulated the feeling that all of a sudden big moves were needed and possible. In Europe, the Single Market Programme in 1992 and the launch of the euro currency in 1999 added fuel to the 'globalization' fire, and affected the (need for) international strategies of organizations, far beyond EU borders. And so, by the turn of the century, globalization strategies were no longer the monopoly of a small group of multinational corporations, but perceived as a *'conditio sine qua non'* for any company that wanted to survive.

## Our mission: a reflection on your mission

At a time when almost everyone, everywhere, is being confronted with globalization and internationalization, there is more than ever a need for reflection on what it means, whether it is a good thing, and, if so, how it should be done. At the same time, there is increasing evidence of serious problems, even debacles and disasters, that have been brought about by this same phenomenon and there is, therefore, an even stronger need to identify and avoid the many pitfalls and mistakes that can be encountered on the internationalization path.

This book is intended for managers, as well as business or financial analysts, investment bankers, policy-makers, researchers and other observers or commentators, as an invitation to, and a companion for, reflection on the pressures and processes of internationalization that they are facing or actively involved in, in their own business and corporate context.

Of course, it is never too early to engage in such a reflection and evaluation, before major mistakes are made and billions of dollars are wasted in missed opportunities or actual budgets spent. And it is certainly never too late either, when the first symptoms of trouble are showing up on the radar screen or when all hell has broken loose and your company seems to be on the verge of disaster or bankruptcy. Or you might be in the middle of it, and you would like to take a moment and sit back, reflect on the lessons and learnings from what you have achieved or missed so far, and envision the future course of your movements and strategies.

We started writing this book long before most people seriously engaged in business were willing to take a breath and think for a moment – sorry, sir, we are too busy internationalizing! The recent turn of events, however, led by a change in economic conditions, the turbulence in financial markets and the overextended expectations regarding the 'new' economy, have shown the need for such reflection and re-evaluation to be even more pressing.

From this mission to provide an invitation for critical reflection, follow the implications for the approach and style of this book: it is intended to be questioning, probing, provocative, brief and focused on what we found to be the ever-returning key strategic questions, situated in the context of a simple but structured framework. In so doing we are running the risk of appearing simplistic and incomplete at times. This is a price we will gladly pay if we succeed in our main ambition: to push your thinking forward and help you to develop your own insights, questions or new ideas in the specific context of your own international management and strategy challenges.

The reason for this goes beyond the usual commonplace that our role as teachers, consultants or researchers – we actually prefer the term 'learning partners' – is 'to raise questions, not provide answers' and statements such as 'if we really knew the answers, we would not be here' or 'we would not give them away just like that'. What we really mean is that it is our firm belief and conviction that nobody else can or should give you the answer for your specific case.

Thus this is not a 'how-to' book or 'complete guide to' internationalization, nor a textbook or academic treatment of the most fancy research ideas in the field of strategic or international management. Nor is it probably the kind of book that we expect most readers to read cover to cover in one go, or even to read in a linear way. We have even attempted to adapt the structure of this book to accommodate such 'eclectic' reading (see p. 15).

## A long (hi)story

This book is the result of a personal experience, turned into a research topic. It started almost 15 years ago when the first author, having spent many years in the US, returned to Europe (via Spain) in the wake of the then enlargement of the EU and the high expectations of the internal market programme and 'Europe 1992'.

His initial reaction on returning to Europe was one of surprise: he had forgotten all about the complexity of the European scene. An initial 'culture shock' (returning to Europe, not leaving it!), and frustration about the slowness and complexity of the internationalization and integration processes then underway, became a stimulus for a new line of research. This focused on the European convergence and cross-border integration question across a variety of industries and sectors, such as: truck manufacturing (in the wake of deregulation of trucking and the European transport sector); temporary labour services (in view of deregulation and harmonization of European legislation); and the international mutual fund and unit trust businesses (in the aftermath of the European UCITS directives), and their implications for the need and opportunities of developing successful cross-border and pan-European business strategies. From a rather 'external' perspective or industry-level approach, it moved towards a more corporate and business-level analysis and ended up focusing much attention on the company-specific and internal processes required and (not?) taking place within companies to address the perceived need for cross-border strategies and structures.

The initial research was started at IESE, the International Graduate School of Business at the University of Navarra in Barcelona in the late 1980s. It continued at INSEAD (Fontainebleau, France), at the Catholic University of Leuven (Belgium) where the cooperation started with the second author, and at the Solvay Business School (ULB, Brussels). This led to the development of a series of in-depth sector and company strategy case studies and related articles on the issues of internationalization facing a variety of players, from traditional 'national champions' to established multinationals, predominantly from a European perspective. (Details of all these case studies are provided in the References at the end of this book.)

In the course of this research, we were invited by Video Management NV/SA (now part of *Financial Times* Knowledge) to develop one of these internationalization stories, which we had studied in the context of the Tractebel Chair in European Management Development at the Catholic University of Leuven, into an in-depth illustration for a professional management video under the title *From Local Champions to Global Masters.*[1] True to our 'inductive' or 'bottom-up' approach, the preparation of this video led to the development of this book.

## A contrary view

The experience of our decade-long research generated a healthy degree of scepticism and even 'methodological bias' (*doute méthodique*, as the French would say) against too simplistic views and overextended expectations about the real needs and opportunities, benefits and organizational potential of companies to successfully internationalize in this highly dynamic but still very complex and diverse world.

It was no surprise then when our main conclusions and experience gained in this area collided head-on with the common, simplistic generalizations, propagated by the popular press and encountered in many business circles, on the implications of the introduction of the euro. These were at best unrealistic, at worst downright misleading, or diverting attention from the real underlying issues in developing truly international and integrated markets and strategies.

All big events, such as Europe 1992, Euro 1999, the internet and so on, seem to be creating, and capitalizing on, a (false?) sense of urgency, whereby in-depth analysis, informed judgement, consistent and coherent process management with attention to detail and nuance (where most of sustained value creation in business should come from) fell out of fashion and seemed to have been left to an ever-smaller group of ever-more frustrated professional managers, value investors or lonely academics.

Our insights and conclusions on the complexity of international business development across Europe, however, seemed to become more and more relevant to other parts of the world, as other regions, while attracted by a similar vision of cross-border integration, seemed to be facing equally if not more diverse and complicated business environments and management issues. Even the most successful 'global' companies seemed to be facing renewed problems, either because they never really were as global or integrated as they aspired to be or as the outside world was led to believe, or, so it seems even more recently, if they did succeed, they came to see the limits of the simple model and already started implementing significant deviations of their initial globalization models, often still role models for other 'less advanced' players in this 'globalization race'.

In the pages that follow we hope to offer you a moment of reflection and a modest contribution to the development of some new insights as to where it is we thought we were going, where we should be going and how we can avoid getting stuck in the process in this ever-changing environment.

# Acknowledgements

We would like to thank the many colleagues and researchers, both inside and outside universities and business schools, who stimulated our thinking through their research, cases, teaching and personal feedback. We are also grateful to the participants in executive seminars and the MBA students, who gave us their critical comments and helpful suggestions.

In particular, contributions, feedback and suggestions to parts of this work were generously made by Dr Alice De Koning, Post-Doctoral Research Fellow, Stockholm School of Economics, Stockholm (Sweden); Professor Dr Wim Vanhaverbeke, Technological University, Eindhoven (the Netherlands); James Howe, Global Pricing Manager, DHL International, Brussels (Belgium); Frank de Haan, Managing Director China, Roca (Spain); Mette Stuhr, Management Development Manager, Danisco, Copenhagen (Denmark); Dr Kenneth Freeman, Senior Director, Financial Operations, ThromboGenics, Dublin (Ireland); and Ann De Jaeger, Managing Director VideoManagement/FTK, Brussels (Belgium) whose constructive and creative role in transferring our work from research to video, also contributed significantly in enabling us to write this book.

In addition, we would like to acknowledge the substantial help given in the production of this book and the supporting work by Danielle Gilliot, Research Associate, Catholic University of Leuven; Venkata Subramanian, Doctoral Fellow, Solvay Business School and Patrick Verghote, Doctoral Candidate, Catholic University of Leuven.

We also thank our publishers, particularly the Publishing Director, Stephen Rutt, for his continuing support and commitment to this project.

Financial support from the following sources is hereby gratefully acknowledged: INSEAD R&D; Doctoral Programme, Solvay Business School (ULB); Tractebel Chair in European Management Development, Catholic University of Leuven; Services of the Prime Minister of Belgium, Inter-university Poles of Attraction Programme.

Last, but not least, we wish to thank our respective families who have had to put up with the many disturbances that a project such as this inevitably caused.

PAUL VERDIN
NICK VAN HECK

# Beyond Globalization and its Myths

Is it necessary for us to make the case for a globalizing economy, and internationalizing corporate activity? Do you need more arguments to join the camp of the apostles of the global economy? When did you last argue with your organization, client, or shareholders that your company needed to prepare for the global competitive arena? Most people can see how quickly country borders are evaporating. Companies double their geographic reach overnight and serve customers as easily in Mexico as in Australia or South Africa. The letterhead of most companies lacks the space to list their worldwide offices and branches.

The era of deregulation, technological developments, regional economic integration and converging consumer behaviour has set new rules for success and formulated fresh strategic imperatives to become a winner. If you want to participate – or triumph – in the global economy, international growth is the name of game:

> More and more companies, whether small or large, young or old, recognize that their choice is between becoming global or becoming extinct. (Marquardt, 1999, p. 3)

What is more, you should be global from the start:

> There probably is no business today that you can start that can afford not to be global. (Tim Koogle, CEO of Yahoo!)

This book is not going to repeat the evidence on the internationalizing world economy or defend globalization. In fact, in this book we will be using the terms 'internationalization' and 'globalization' interchangeably – despite the 'conceptual' difference between companies expanding their geographic coverage and trying to cover the whole world, what some call 'internationalizing', and others integrating their activities across borders, usually referred to as 'globalization' – because we consider this distinction unnecessary to most of the issues we are discussing in this book. Globalization is a fact of life. Consider it done. Just look around you:

- The economic traffic between countries around the world has never been more intense and trade and communication barriers are falling. We will spare you the graphs on the evolution of export, foreign direct investment, or cross-border transactions of bonds and equities over time. They all head north (Bryan et al., 1999, pp. 4, 21; Buelens, 1999, p. 147; Govindarajan and Gupta, 2000, p. 278).

- The clients' needs converge: clients desire and buy the same products – mostly for the same or a similar price – around the globe. Theodore Levitt argued, in his influential article 'The Globalization of Markets' (1983), that the world is one large market. There remain a few superficial regional and national differences, but they are not worth pandering to. One company that followed Levitt's advice (rather explicitly) was Saatchi & Saatchi, the UK advertising agency, which also invited Levitt to join its board. S&S's business model was based on the assumption that customers wanted to buy the same thing, the same way, everywhere. Companies could better use standardized advertising for these homogeneous products and would thus be happy to work with an advertising agency that could service them globally.

- The notion of the global corporation is becoming unassailable: 'The multi-national corporation [in the strict meaning of the word] is obsolete, the global corporation absolute' (Levitt, 1983, p. 93) and the national roots of multinational corporations are fading: 'We hardly know if a company is French, Japanese, Swedish, or American' (Marquardt, 1999, p. 2). Companies are stateless: it no longer matters where the company comes from, they all act in the same universal way. The globalizing economy has brought us generic Anglo-Saxon management styles, taught us how the Japanese reinforce quality across the business system, and introduced us to German engineering models so that we can no longer recognize a company's roots on this basis. The home country of the company is no longer dominant or, put even more strongly, it no longer matters. Countries and borders hardly exist any more, and if they do, we should ignore them – mainly for cost reasons.

However, there are always a few disbelievers. You may occasionally have come across an economist arguing that the world economy, despite its tendency to globalize, is not global yet; or have read about a manager who dares to thrive on the divergence of consumer preferences or prefer a small (foreign) acquisition over a large one so that the chance of learning and integrating improves (we still know some); and even encountered some courageous researchers pretending that global companies are more of an exception than a rule. You can call them fundamentalists, you can accuse them of having lost contact with the real world and being single minded. While that may be true for some of them, the increasing number of arguments against the current degree of globalization of the economy and companies make it harder to believe that all of them were completely off track.

While we do not want to embark on a political or technical debate if and how globalization is happening, fairness obliges us at least to draw your attention to a growing contrary view on the development of this global world. Without taking positions in this part of the debate, we start by looking at their arguments.

## The myth of globalization

Some 'globalization atheists' are convinced that the aforementioned conventions are not as unconditional as some people would have us believe.

### Global economies?

They question the real degree of globalization of the economic landscape, referring, among others, to some of the following facts and figures:

- The world we are living in is according to some about as integrated as the world of the 19th century (*Fortune*, 27 June 1994).

- If not about the actual degree of macroeconomic integration, questions are raised about the timing, and hence the speed, of the globalization of the economy. The current wave of globalization is only picking up where economic integration had left off before World War I.

  Most people regard globalization as a recent phenomenon, but in fact the process was well under way at the end of the 19th century. (David Hale, Zurich Financial Services, Chicago, in *Fortune*, 22 November 1999)

> We can say that the international economy was in many ways more open in the pre-1914 period than at any time since, including from the late 1970s onwards. The present position is by no means unprecedented. (Hirst and Thompson, 1999, p. 32)

▪ Almost 85% of the manufacturing output in the US still comes from domestic firms (OECD figures, reported in *The Economist*, 8 Jan 2000).

▪ While global integration may be going on, it is not happening more rapidly than it has been for years, and in fact, its pace may even be slowing (Foreign Policy – AT Kearny study, 2001).

David Hale, chief global economist for Zurich Financial Services, concluded:

> The processes bringing the world economy together seem all but irreversible. But it is not the first time people believed that.

Or, to summarize the argument differently:

> The best way to view globalization is, in effect, as an ongoing process that is not new, has not progressed far and is far from irreversible. (*Financial Times*, 25 January 2001)

## Global markets?

Others like to draw attention to the fact that, as yet, consumer preferences are far from homogeneous:

▪ It did not take long for Douglas and Wind (1987, p. 19) to react resolutely to Levitt's extreme vision of global markets. They manifested their disbelief by making reference to numerous barriers that prevent the world from becoming one market. There was at least as much evidence that consumer behaviour in certain countries was diverging. Jerry Wind recently repeated:

> The world is heterogeneous. You have local preferences and tastes. It makes a lot of sense … to acknowledge the regional or local differences and try to manage a portfolio of products that try to cater to different segments. (*International Herald Tribune*, 7 February 2000)

- Large-scale research by McKinsey (Bryan et al., 1999) and the United Nations acknowledges that most markets are far from being global or homogeneous.

The debate on whether there is cultural homogenization remains open. There are no surveys showing that people are becoming alike. (United Nations Human Development Report in *The Economist*, 11 September 1999)

Martin Sorell, who took a leading role in the Saatchi & Saatchi global-ization story and is now chairing a key competitor WPP which just managed to reach the world's top number one spot as global advertising agency, backs up this vision:

I am convinced that the differences are more important than the similarities. Not more than 15% of the activities of WPP are global (in the sense that we use the same marketing method all over the globe). (*De Morgen*, 1999)

- The timing of the market integration is subject to discussion as well: while it seems to go fast because of technological revolutions, in reality, it may not be new or recent at all (*The Economist*, 11 September 1999).

- Even if integration is happening, it does not preclude the fact that tastes are diverging at the same time.

Thus despite technological and economic forces for integration, or conver-gence, there are equal or perhaps greater forces for fragmentation, one of them being culture. (Schneider and Barsoux, 1997, p. 6)

Indeed, globalization can actually strengthen national differences, not erode them. (Kogut, 1999)

## Global companies?

Similarly, serious doubts have been raised about the belief in the global company ruling the world:

- Corporations are not stateless: board membership and stock ownership are still concentrated in the country of origin (Parker, 1998, p. 33; Ruig-rok and Van Tulder, 1995, p. 157). Head offices and top management teams remain firmly planted in their home country (Schneider and Barsoux, 1997, p. 223). The top management of French MNCs is 'very French, very male and very elite' (ibid., 1997, p. 224).

■ Evidence has indicated the significant effect of the company's home country on a wide array of activities and decisions: whether in corporate governance, financing structures, focus and style of innovations systems, R&D performance and funding, sector distribution of corporate R&D, or investment systems, there still are significant differences between Japanese, American and German MNCs (Doremus et al, 1998).

The global corporation adrift from its national political moorings and roaming an increasingly borderless world market is a myth. (Doremus et al., 1998, p. 3)

And some find this a desirable state of affairs:

However, it is ludicrous to seek some amorphous international culture. (Professor Hunt, London Business School, in *Financial Times*, 6 June 1999)

The UNCTAD's yearly *World Investment Report*, looking at the degree of globalization or transnationality of the leading world companies on the basis of its 'transnationality index',[1] reported in 1999:

■ Even the largest multinationals have on average only slightly more than half their assets, sales and employees originating outside the home country.

■ Some industries which are popularly quoted as 'global industries', such as automotive, electronics, telecom or even utilities, have a far lower average transnationality index than others, such as 'food and beverages', 'media' and 'construction'.

■ Several companies with a global reputation are at the bottom of the top 100 ranking or even completely absent, such as Coca-Cola, although Philips and ABB ended up in the top 10 transnational companies. General Electric (ranked 84th), General Motors (91st), Shell (44th), Toyota (94th) and IBM (55th) are in reality much less 'transnational' than they seem.

■ The overall transnationality of the 100 largest multinationals increased slightly between 1990 and 1997 (from 51 to 55%), but the growth of the average transnationality has actually been slowing down over the past few years.

These figures only give a snapshot on the transnationality of leading companies based on a few simple proxies, but they help to put the perceived degree of globalization into perspective.

While the impression has grown that the globalization of businesses and industry concentration were happening at an unprecedented pace, evidence seems to point the other way:

Empirical research indicates that global – or globalizing – industries have actually been marked by steady decreases in concentration in the post-World War II period. Executives, then, need to break free of the biases that lead them to pursue larger and larger cross-border deals. (Ghemawat and Ghadar, 2000, p. 66)

## Global strategies?

Global companies are supposed to sell standardized products, with a global brand, and a standardized advertising campaign at a uniform price. But most of these companies apparently are not treating the world as one single market. Corporations are clearly further away from globalization than their uniform brands seem to suggest at first sight:

> For a long time I believed in the emergence of the global company. I'm a little more sceptical now. (Professor Birkinshaw, London Business School, in *Financial Times*, 25 January 2001)

> The model of the fully globalized company has been realized by only a handful of giants. (Kanter, 1995, p. 71)

Despite the existence of global brands, quite a few of those still have a strong national identity.

Companies have come to realize that global products and strategies may not be as absolute as Levitt claimed. Douglas Daft, the new CEO of Coca-Cola – the symbol of globalization – announced:

> The changes [in strategy and organization] will allow Coke to 'think and act' locally. The responsibility for overall policy, strategy and control remains in Atlanta … but decisions will be made in the local market. (*Financial Times*, 9 February 2000)

And Coke is not the only multinational coming back from absolute globalization and standardization efforts towards more localization. AOL, the US media giant, is doing its best to show the world how local it is. A journalist reported, 'It is a delicate balancing act that AOL has turned into a new model of globalization' (*Financial Times*, 31 May 2001). McDonald's started to give in to local authorities and consumers and has redefined its international business model so that only certain core products are standard, according to its QSC standards, and any other menu items are decided locally. It is now referred to by its CEO as 'an amalgamation of local businesses, owned by local entrepreneurs' (*Foreign Policy*, May–June 2001). Matsushita and

Toyota are investing heavily to tailor their standard products to the European needs; and Ford, which was a pioneer with its global project 'Mondeo' (which was so global that it could not even be sold in the US under that name), is also refocusing on regional and local requirements (while keeping a few aspects global such as platforms and purchasing). Following the news that Wal-Mart's head of European operations had resigned because he wanted to adapt its strategy more to the European market, one observer commented 'When you go abroad, if you are going to be a good traveller, you have to fit in with the locals' (*Financial Times*, 8 September 2000).

Uniform pricing is not happening even at a regional scale: recent research has confirmed that even after the launch of a European single currency, price differences remain significant within the European market (Ahlberg et al., 1999). This will be discussed in Chapter 2.

As a result, there are many signs of companies abandoning their intention to build a global empire, and subsequently divest foreign activities altogether (maybe an overreaction or the wrong reaction in some cases). ING Group, the Dutch-based financial services group, seems to have given up its global ambitions in investment banking. As the *Financial Times* (31 January 2001) recently headlined, 'ING restructure signals the end of a global dream'. Kingfisher, the UK retail giant who aggresively internationalized mainly through acquisitions across Europe, is considering selling its German electrical business; Marks & Spencer, after years of failed internationalization attempts on the European continent, finally decided to pull the plug (and it appears that they did not even manage to do this without violating local labour laws); Allstate International Insurance is pulling out of India to focus on its US home market; Kinepolis and Spector, Belgian internationalization success stories in the theatre and film processing business respectively, are about to withdraw from the German cinema and photo business; Swissair Group announced the largest losses in Swiss business history after an aggressive international growth strategy in which it acquired a large stake in Belgium's Sabena Airlines; Lernout and Hauspie, the speech technology pioneer and Real Software, the Belgian ERP company, lost their shirts in their internationalization attempts in Asia and the US respectively. These are just a few examples, there will be many more throughout the book.

In the end, is globalizing what companies *say* they are doing, or is it what they *are* doing?

Don't believe in your own press releases. It's too easy to think that you're a global company because you keep saying you're a global company. Search for measurable indicators that your organization is behaving more globally than it was last year and the year before. Believe in behaviours not rhetoric. Celebrate your progress but never allow yourself to become fully satisfied that you have made it. Holding on to that nagging anxiety is what being globally minded is all about. (De Bettignies in Schneider and Barsoux, 1997, p. 223)

Globalization or the myth of globalization? Should the credo be globalization, localization or something in between? Think local/global, act global/local? International is the way to go? Even if there were a prevailing answer to this question – and there probably isn't – it may not really matter. What counts is what is good for *your* company and *your* business. This is the point at which this book comes into play.

## Beyond the myths

Where does that leave us? Is globalization happening or is it not? Is 'local' still the way to go? The above conflicting data has left many of us confused and frustrated. A survey from the Deloitte/World Economic Forum claimed:

Companies were confused about globalization. They were all expanding internationally, all – or nearly all – seeking to go global, but they were not sure what that meant. Worse, they did not know how to judge whether they were doing it right and, therefore, were nagged by fear they were doing it wrong.

Jacques Manardo, Deloitte's European Chairman added:

Globalization is a hollow word. There is no generally accepted understanding of what it means. (*Fortune*, 15 March 1999)

It is no surprise then that we find it hard to judge where to put most emphasis, and manage the different needs and speeds across our organizations. The reality is probably far more complex than a simplistic local–global dichotomy. Globalization is undoubtedly happening, but equally there are indications that we may have overestimated the *level* or *rate* of globalization (or both), and that we may have misjudged its distinct impact on different aspects of business life.

More nuanced and balanced, rather than fundamentalist or extreme, approaches are therefore required in running our businesses and companies. No matter how much we would like life to be simple – either the world is 'global' or it is not – most opportunities will arise not from simplistic slogans, but from careful attention to nuance and detail in a given specific context.

And, more importantly, whatever the generic conclusion may be, the key question remains: What is *your* conclusion for *your* company, in a given time frame? Who cares how transnational the top 100 largest companies are – unless you are managing one of these companies or holding their shares? What can you as a manager do with the idea that the world economy was as global in 1914 as it is in 2001? The really interesting debate is to understand what globalization/internationalization means for *you*, how *you* should go about it, and what it requires from *your* company. The objective of this book is to provide help in thinking through your own situation.

## The position of this book

Running a company on macroeconomic data and broad generalizations or even on industry statistics – no matter what direction they point to – seems as dangerous as ignoring the impending danger of an airplane crash on the basis of historical or statistical safety records of the aircraft, or advising an ill patient to move to another country on the basis of a higher average life expectancy in that country. Not only has empirical strategy research revealed the limited importance of industry, country or other 'external' factors in a company's performance (Hawawini et al., 2000), but also extensive in-depth case studies vividly illustrate that the real question you should be thinking about as a manager is, if internationalization is right for *you*, how do you deal with the pressures of the market, and how do *you* go about making it happen?

The objective of this book is to offer a moment and framework for reflection, regardless of the success rate or size or international experience of your company. The challenges are intrinsically identical for small or large, old or new companies. For those at the beginning of their internationalization journey, it should be helpful to know what successful companies did that others did not do. For those already engaged in the international market, it should be instrumental to look back and reflect on the progress made, and contemplate what to do next. In any event, the purpose should be to learn from the pitfalls and mistakes made, in order to avoid making the same mistakes again, and speed up the learning about your own and others' processes.

This book is not pleading for less or more globalization, and it does not want to take a position on the general degree of globalization. Nor do we want to discourage you in the face of internationalization challenges. Instead, we hope to clarify a number of management challenges in globalizing or internationalizing *your* business and *your* company, in light of the globalizing economies, disappearing country borders and homogenization of consumer preferences.

> For all the talk and action about globalization, what is missing is a way to think about it. (*Fortune*, 15 February 1999)

A way – one way – to make you think about it is exactly the mission of this book. We hope to deliver a road map for managers, shareholders and consultants to identify in specific cases where the problems and challenges are and how to deal with them. We will not *offer* an unambiguous answer to your questions nor will we elaborate on *all* questions in internationalizing. We want to trigger what we perceive to be key strategic questions, provide a framework to reflect on these and potentially offer (part of) *an* answer to your questions.


## The why, what and how of internationalization

If any generalization can be deduced from our research on conditions for successful internationalization – other than that we do not wish to make any simplistic generalizations – it would be the importance of coming back to the basics of understanding the *why*, *what* and *how* of internationalization in the specific setting of each business situation:

- *Why* are you internationalizing? What benefits should you get out of it, what value will you create and what type of strategy will allow you to capture most of these benefits?

- *What* type of *organization* will you need to get the maximum benefits out of your international presence: what organizational vehicle is needed to enter a specific market, direct investment or exporting for example, and what type of organizational blueprint is needed to achieve cross-border benefits?

- *How* should you *manage* the *process* of internationalization: how do you make sure that the strategy gets implemented and the organization functions? How do you support and manage internationalization as a process?

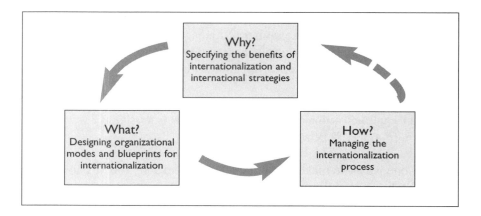

**Figure 0.1** The why–what–how loop of internationalization

More importantly, it is crucial to be aware of and carefully manage the interaction between these three key aspects. In order to identify what organization and strategy you would need, you ought to know what you are expecting to gain at the end of the day. Unless your organization and management process supports your strategy, you may miss out on opportunities for leveraging international presence. This is illustrated in Figure 0.1.

The logical approach – and therefore not often followed – is to move from the reasons for internationalization, over the organizational blueprint towards the question of how to implement this. This perspective is too rational and mechanical to be always useful, as it rarely matches the hectic reality of day-to-day business management.

Instead, we expect a cycle without a predefined start and end point: in fact, we count on the internationalization issues, problems and challenges to show up in any part of the loop, and ultimately to lead to questioning all three aspects. Mistakes in one area may lead to the right corrections if the other areas are properly managed and, above all, the full picture of the why–what–how is constantly revisited and re-evaluated. Conversely, getting it right in one of the aspects may encourage improvement in the others. We will elaborate on this perpetual motion aspect in Chapter 6.

■ We will discuss companies that had not specified clearly the benefits they hoped to gain from internationalization. Many of them got hit on their bottom line. Their expectations in terms of lower costs or additional revenues from international presence were not realized. This often led to a flawed international strategy and organization. As a senior executive privately observed: 'We did not know what we were after ... We had not really figured out what strategy we needed.'

■ Equally we came across examples of companies where the internationalization mode and organization were not adapted to the benefits of internationalization: 'We did it for the right reason but did not do it the right way.' The experience with organizational misfit led finally to rethinking the strategy, organization and implementation process on the basis of a clearer picture of the expected benefits.

■ Others had not really bothered too much about analysing their strategy or organization in any great detail. They just internationalized 'by doing': '*J'agis, puis je réfléchis*' (I act, then I think).[2] But their internationalization got stuck: 'We saw internationalization as a financial investment or portfolio decision like many others, we overlooked the management challenges of making it happen.' 'We had clearly in mind what the strategy and organization should look like, but never managed to make it work in our organization.'

  Or, during the process, they found that the internationalization benefits were much more limited – sometimes more compelling but different – than was expected, leading to a reconsideration of the strategy, organization and implementation process.

  Conversely, for some companies, the success of an international opportunity provided the basis for developing a more sustainable international strategy. A well-managed 'opportunistic strategy' allowed them to refine the missing rationale or internal conflicts in the course of internationalization steps.

In the daily life of internationalization discussions, it does not really matter where in this picture – strategy, organization or implementation – one would start questioning as long as the links between the different aspects are kept well in sight. A problem in one area – your organization is not working – may reveal an underlying problem in another – there may be no clear benefit from internationalizing or you have not identified it properly yet – and this process may take quite some time. Sometimes the lack of real benefit may even show up in the form of an organizational dispute within your client's organization, as we will illustrate in Chapter 6.

How the arrows will point in your situation, therefore, will depend on the specific circumstances. We believe that it is more important for you to figure out where you are in this flow chart and how you are managing it rather than imposing a simplistic 'logical' path. A successful internationalization could emerge from a thorough understanding of each of these different aspects and coming to grips with an integrated approach of the strategy, organization and management.

Beyond the holistic perspective, internationalization will require constant iterations through the why–what–how loop. Turning into a global master is a long route that will call for constantly rethinking the strategy and organization, in light of your changing ambitions, market evolutions, regulative progress, organizational development and so on. The strategy of the early international days may be less appropriate in the global consolidation phase of your organization; the ability to benefit from international presence will evolve; and the managerial challenge of setting up the first international office is quite different from managing the change from a multinational to a global strategy and organization. This process never stops.

## The structure of this book

The structure of this book (Figure 0.2) has been based on the above defined three key aspects of internationalization. In Section 1, we focus on the perceived and real benefits of internationalization and their impact on

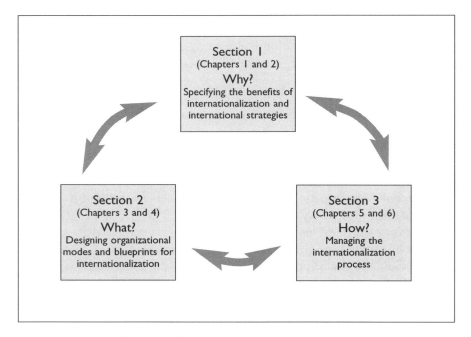

**Figure 0.2** The structure of this book

an adequate strategy. In Section 2, we shift the attention to the organizational aspects of internationalization and highlight how the specification of the benefits impact the appropriate entry mode and organizational blueprint. Their implementation raises a number of process and managerial aspects which could prevent a company from missing out on the benefits or getting stuck along the internationalization path, and these are discussed in Section 3.

However, this is not the kind of book that we expect most readers to read from cover to cover in one go, or even to read in a linear way. As reality never complies fully with the Cartesian logic of the why–what–how approach of any subject, although representing the basic structure of the book, we would be very happy if readers started somewhere in the middle or at the end, only to return to the beginning later. While we have tried to accommodate non-linear reading of this book, we realize that certain concepts and terminology introduced in earlier sections have, deliberately, been carried forward to later sections of the book. More specifically, we will occasionally allude to the cost, network or learning benefits of internationalization, in short the Conelearn benefits, referring to a specific approach for identifying the business benefits of internationalization which is introduced in Chapter 2. In addition, we will be using some of our examples throughout the sections, sometimes building on comments we made earlier on a particular case. For this reason, we have included an index of the companies discussed at the end of the book, allowing easy reference to earlier discussions of a particular case.

The checklist below is actually an invitation to start from where you expect most of the challenges to come from in your particular case. Nevertheless, wherever you start, at some point the question will be raised, '*Why* have you started doing any of this in the first place?', which will invite you back to Section 1.

### Self-diagnosing your globalization problems: frequently observed symptoms

Please check which of the statements or symptoms connects to your company's challenges:

■ Internationalization has not brought us much more than growth

■ We have more profits now as an international company, but we are less profitable

■ We still have the feeling we are losing out on a lot of cost synergies across markets

■ We are surprised to see that although we are international now, clients still do not want to contract with us across borders anymore than they did before

■ We believe we really have to become one global company, but in reality we work successfully with a portfolio of local business strategies.

If any of the above apply to you, you may want to specify your benefits better and zoom in on the 'why' of internationalization and globalization. You may want to turn to Section 1 of this book first.

■ Our organization seems too (de)centralized

■ Country managers complain that our people in headquarters do not understand how different the local markets are

■ The acquisition of a local partner has not brought us what we needed, other than quick access to that market

■ Our product organization has made us marginally more efficient, client focused or effective and we wonder if we should go for a functional organization now, or go back to a country organization

■ We are not sure how much formal coordination and control between the international subsidiaries and headquarters is needed.

If you sense some of the above issues in your organization, you may want to rethink your organizational set-up and check to what extent it is actually linked to the strategic objectives. Section 2 may provide some insights on how to do this.

■ We had decided on a clear international strategy and organization, yet, two years later, it is still not functioning

- We find our local managers resistant to central initiatives

- We thought that our international division was taking care of the international activities but find that this set-up is not working properly

- We internationalized by chance by taking on orders from abroad, and, all of a sudden, our whole business model and organizational set-up seems to be at stake

- We rigidly implemented the strategy and organization according to plan, and still it is not working.

If you observe any of the above, you should reconsider the implementation and management process, and ensure that it is adapted to the strategy and organization you need. We recommend you to move to Section 3 first.

# SECTION 1

# On the Benefits of Internationalization

In the current business climate, where companies are crossing borders almost by drifting down the winds, questioning the reasons for embarking on an internationalization journey seems to be reserved for social activists, lonely politicians or 'conservative' economists.[1] Companies that have not entered the international arena yet are the ones being challenged on why they are missing the boat. An atmosphere has been created in which a company does not need to explain why it is internationalizing, because 'we all know how important and beneficial it is to be international'. Following the deregulation and falling trade barriers between the previously secured European national markets, neither managers nor analysts tend to waste their scarce time on questioning the Europeanization of businesses as an inevitable trend or an objective in its own right.

Annual reports and press releases are not overloaded with arguments making the case for internationalization or international restructuring. They merely employ a variety of slogans, such as: 'There is no more growth in our home market, so we have to go abroad', 'Only a few large, international players will survive in our industry', 'Our clients are internationalizing, so we have to follow them', and so on. Defensive slogans indicating there was no choice; offensive slogans showing a hunger to make it in the global market; slogans referring to other parties in the market, such as clients or competitors, pulling the company to foreign markets; and slogans that blame the domestic market for pushing the company beyond its national 'limits'.

Even in times of slowing growth or decreasing profits, international-ization is probably not being questioned in its own right. There is more of a reflex to investigate and revisit *the way* the internationalization had been realized and implemented or the *speed* at which it occurred. In the middle of the Asian and South American crises, the economic recession was the first to be blamed for the slowdown in international operations. Altern-atively, the loyalty or quality of the local partner in the foreign market was reconsidered. Or did *we* in the end go about it too aggressively? Observers openly wondered if some high-tech companies' acquisitions came simply at a bad time in the economy, were they really as profitable as expected or had the *acquirer* simply paid too high a price for it – or a combination of the three?[2]

This chapter will try to look beyond the commonly accepted slogans about internationalization. What is, or should be, really driving companies to other national markets? What is, or should be, behind the frequently heard slogans? What is it *really* that companies are, or should be, looking for when internationalizing?

This is not an attempt to reinvent the wheel or kick open doors. The internationalization slogans are what they are: catch phrases used mainly in public speeches and conversations with journalists. The problem with slogans, however, is that, when overused, they risk losing contact with the underlying argument or reality and slowly become an argument in their own right. Slogans start to live their own life, drifting away from the PR talk or window-dressing they were created for. As one self-critical executive pointed out to us:

> It is time to take a step back and reconsider, when you start believing your own press releases and when the slogans start being the real strategy!

Conversely, one enlightened investment banker gratefully observed after a discussion along the lines laid out in this chapter:

> It helps to be asking these questions, sooner rather than later, because all too often when we have finalized a big M&A deal and have to write our press release, it is a sad moment: how to explain why we did this deal and why it made sense for our client's strategy.

By revisiting and critically evaluating the slogans in Chapter 1, we hope we can offer such a moment of reflection and bring the strategic debate forward in time. We will focus on identifying the real internationalization drivers and benefits and, in Chapter 2, further discuss them in the context of a simple but structured framework. We are not questioning the globalization of businesses as such, nor do we want to downplay the potential benefits of expanding businesses abroad. On the contrary, our objective is to help you to reflect on the identification of the *real* benefits for *your* specific case, with the help of an intuitive frame of reference.

## CHAPTER 1

# Internationalization: The Only Way to Go?

The power of one-liners can be enormous: they help with summarizing broader arguments, simplifying complex realities, lightening up and stimulating the debate and can generate a bigger impact on an audience than an elaborated and carefully argued contention. On the other hand, history has demonstrated – sometimes painfully – the risks and shortcomings of relying on one-liners in running a country, an organization or a company.

Therefore, in order to reach beyond the slogans, we started by inventorying the most frequently heard slogans we have come across in our research on internationalization. We will argue in more detail on their meaning and relevance.[1] We will also illustrate how different companies in a wide range of industries have been exploiting the slogans to their own advantage.[2] We then move on to countering the slogans through similarly generalized, unnuanced and equally deceptive counter-slogans. The only objective of this 'polite slanging match' is to bring the debate to what really matters: to focus on how internationalization really adds value to your company.[3] How will *you* benefit ultimately from being present in different countries? How can you avoid falling into the traps that many others have stepped into before?

In Figure 1.1 we present our view of the slogans in the internationalization scene. As you can see, there are quite a few and probably our list is not exhaustive. We also indicate how one slogan seems to lead to another. We acknowledge that the resulting picture is quite disorderly. By elaborating on each of them in more detail below and ordering them, we hope we can come to a more structured road map of the internationalization slogans, illustrate how superficial each slogan can be and how contradic-

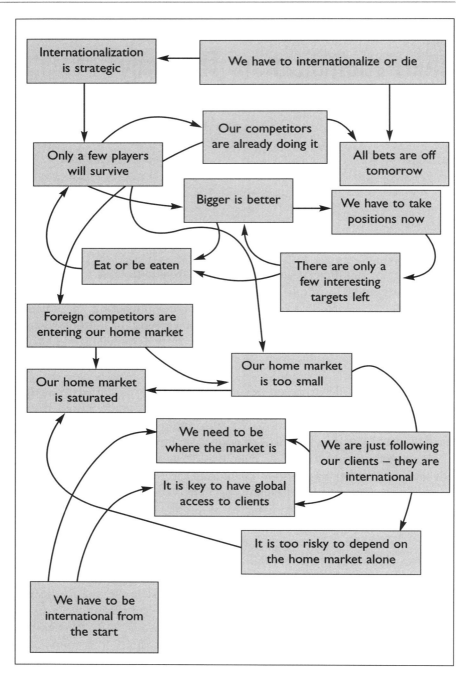

**Figure 1.1** A web of internationalization slogans

tory they are. We will summarize our criticism, and illustrate this picture at the end of the chapter by countering each of the clichés with 'an equally simplistic aphorism'. The discussion of each of the slogans is based on a similar approach. Therefore, you may decide not to read through all of them and select only those that apply to your case, without losing the general message of this part of the book.

## We have to internationalize or die

Several companies saw no alternative but to internationalize in order to stay in business.

> More and more companies, whether small or large, young or old, recognize that their choice is between becoming global or becoming extinct. (Marquardt, 1999, p. 3)

> Expand or expire. (*The Wall Street Journal*, 30 April 1998)

Chairman Lee Kun-Hee of Samsung was very clear:

> Globalization is Key to Survival in the 21st century. In this day and age, no country or company can survive without becoming globalized.

Managers desperately look beyond the borders of their domestic market to ensure survival. The ultimate rescue are foreign markets.

> More than 25% of *Fortune* 500 companies for a given year will not exist ten years later. Markets are rapidly changing and being competed for. Domestic markets, with their ever-tighter niches, will no longer be sufficient. (Marquardt, 1999, p. 8)

A commonality in several of the slogans is the unnuanced picture they are painting. If you believe this, staying a national player is no longer an option. However, we have observed, along with many other researchers, that the industries where only international players survive have been exceptions rather than the rule. Not all industries are like the airplane manufacturing business where only a few big players survive and the minimum scale goes beyond any national market.

Even in so-called 'global' industries, non-global companies will survive and may even outperform the global companies (Roth and Morrison, 1990, p. 541; see also Calori et al., 2000). A more recent study shows that while

most industries are globalizing, very few are really global: only one third of
the industries investigated were globally defined (Bryan et al., 1999, p. 45).
And even then, it is more often the nature of the competition than the
inherent structure of the industry that is global (Kobrin, 1991, p. 18).

In most industries therefore, you do have a choice. The central question
is not what type of player you *have* to be, but what type of player you *want*
to be in order to achieve your overall strategy. Indeed, the choice between
remaining a local player or becoming a multinational has a much broader
impact, beyond the decision on which geographies to cover. Positioning as
a local player implies that you define your business 'differently': you are
focusing on certain segments of the market, have a specific product and
service range, and/or different distribution channels. The discrepancy
between the local and international players is often that they approach the
market in a distinct way and compete on different dimensions – price,
quality, product scope, innovation – or take alternative positions on
these dimensions.

ISS is a well-known, successful international services group with Danish
roots, running significant operations in the cleaning services business
around the world. Does that make the cleaning business international?
Should that mean the end of the numerous local cleaning companies, some
of which are one-man organizations? Probably not. The amusement of these
local companies, as well as that of some of the local Jutland press in
Denmark, was great when ISS, while it was conquering the world (around
Europe and also the US), could not deliver and was struggling to escape its
local cleaning contract with the city of Aalborg, which it had obtained just
months before thanks to aggresive bidding. ISS's position as an international cleaning company has an impact on its overall strategy and
organization, far beyond its geographic scope, and implies that certain trade-
offs need to be made in terms of the segments to target, but at what price?

If such choices are not explicitly considered in line with your overall
strategy, the risk is that globalization implicitly marginalizes your position:
because you enter the global market with a standard product, you know you
are going to give up on parts of your market that would like to see your
product tailored to the local needs. When Gillette decided to sell a uniform
Mach3 around the globe, it knew that certain Vietnamese, Mexican or
Greek men would find the product too expensive or would appreciate a
razor blade tailored to Asian or Latin American skins and local shaving
habits. Gillette's global strategy may even be profitable in itself. But the
question remains: How much more profitable would it have been either to
stay close to home with a standardized product or to differentiate to
different segments and geographies? The point is: How much are you

leaving on the table, what opportunities are you giving up with a standard-ized, one-size-fits-all strategy?

The slogan becomes hazardous if it makes companies run in a certain – international – direction because they think they have no other option. In a way, the decision to expand into other markets sneaks in a very important strategic choice through the back door. Survival is about more than inter-nationalization alone: you need to realize how you will be competing in the international market. Being successful depends on much more than the number of different nations you supply or the size of your balance sheet, as the Hoogovens–British Steel merger, now Corus, painfully illustrates. Despite the pressure for international size in the steel industry, mainly for efficiency reasons, the merger between Hoogovens and British Steel was not sufficient for the merged company to regain its competitive edge. A much broader strategic repositioning, for example on its product scope and manufacturing strategy, was required, regardless of the size of the company. Similarly, Boeing's merger with McDonnell Douglas, while allowing it to reap economies of scale, did not in the short term solve the broader issue of its production and innovation strategy. When you ignore the other strategic, often *real* bases for success in your business, you risk the syndrome of 'internationalize *and* die'.

## Internationalization is strategic

Internationalization is a strategic goal in itself: 'our strategy is to intern-ationalize'. How successful you are will be measured by the degree of internationalization you achieved. The chairman of Samsung – the Korean conglomerate – added to his above-mentioned statement on the strategic importance of globalization: 'We must complete this process of globaliz-ation within three years to become a first-class company.'

The CEO of the Spanish media giant Grupo Prisa made it very clear: 'We want to be the number 1 media provider in the Spanish language' (*Business Week*, 10 July 2000). For that the international sales should account for 40% of the total in four years.

Electrolux, the home appliances company, aimed at doubling its sales in 'new' markets to 20% of total sales in three years (*Financial Times*, 29 September 1995). Pinault Printemps Redoute proudly announced in March 2001 that more than 50% of its turnover was now derived from its inter-national operations.

Internationalization *is* in many ways strategic: it is about the long term, it requires significant investments and commitments, it is hard to reverse and it has potentially a huge impact on the future success of a company. In light of that, it seems hard to overstate the strategic importance of internationalization: it is not something you do on the side, or delegate to staff members of an international division. It goes – sooner or later – to the heart of the company, its strategy, organization, resources and people.

That said, internationalization becomes subject to the same risks as other 'strategic' endeavours: it can be seen as *so* strategic that one is willing to take (short-term) losses for it, because it is believed to generate significant future profits. Immediate profitability is sacrificed for long-term earnings.

> I am perfectly willing to budget for a loss in my region, if it fits the global strategy. (John Ross, Executive Board Member, Deutsche Bank in the Americas, in *Financial Times*, 21 June 1999)

In that line of reasoning, the more money is invested, the more strategic it becomes, but this hides a danger: sometimes it becomes an excuse or a cover for bad investments. Strategic investments are fine, as long as they are not structurally unprofitable.

However, it is not always clear how we should interpret the notion that internationalization is 'strategic'. What does that exactly mean? What makes it strategic? What is the strategy in the first place? Internationalization can be a means to realize the strategy – and an important one – but it can hardly be an objective in itself. Internationalization, to do *what*?

It is as if the imperative is to simply plant flags in markets around the globe, but would it not be more important to see and know what to do with the world-wide presence or operations? Is the strategy to be everywhere you want to be?

> We are in all businesses we want to be – but not in all the businesses everywhere that we want to be. (Sandy Weill, Chairman and Chief Executive, Citigroup, in *Financial Times*, 8 September 2000)

What is so sacred about geographic coverage or omnipresence? Is it not crucial to have a well-defined strategy on how to turn this internationalization into value added that would otherwise be hard or more costly to achieve? How do you deal with the international network, clients and contracts, manage the operations in subsidiaries around the world, beyond just putting yourself on the map? We are happy to hear that internationalization is considered strategic and therefore our concern is to have it clear what exactly the strategy is that makes internationalization so essential and value creating. The remainder of this book is intended to help you realize how to do that. But it should not be an excuse for entering into or keeping up costly and questionable adventures. As one financier reminded us recently: 'I only know of two kinds of investments: profitable investments and strategic investments!'

## Bigger is better … only a few players will survive

It has been predicted in many industries, from car manufacturing,[4] electricity generation and distribution[5] to retailing, temporary work services, auditing and accounting services or more recently law firms,[6] that only a few big international players will survive. According to these predictions, there is room for a limited amount of players. Even in the e-business, it was expected that European companies needed to scale up in order to compete with giants such as AOL and Yahoo! that already operate around the world (*Fortune*, 12 June 2000). Size is frequently seen as the discriminating factor in deciding which companies will be able to stay in business.

Despite the forecasts that only two or three big players, in numerous industries, were to survive within five or ten years or the turn of the century, we failed to find any industry where these forecasts had materialized so far – to their full extent. On the contrary, several studies indicated that, notwithstanding a drive for consolidation or a perceived need to become bigger, industries which are publicly perceived as quickly consolidating are not always more concentrated today than they were years ago (Ghemawat and Ghadar, 2000, p. 65). The oil industry today is far less concentrated than it was 50 years ago and the automobile industry had, in the 1990s, only slightly increased its consolidation, which is still far below the concentration level in the 1960s.

> Across the economy as a whole, there is no general tendency for concentration to rise or to fall. Individual sectors go through phases of concentration and deconcentration. (Kay and Hannah, 2000)

Even if consolidation has gone pretty far in some industries and in some parts of the world and is still happening today, it is unusual to have only a few players left. Whatever has been claimed by experts and managers, reality still proves this point right: it will probably not go that fast – for good reasons (as confirmed by Ghemawat and Ghadar, 2000).

We become even more sceptical when we hear the scale argument brought up in service industries such as accounting, law firms or temporary work services. How can we expect scale to have such a dominating effect on a service business – typically not asset intensive – if we observe that the amount of players in scale-sensitive manufacturing industries such as the car industry, for example, are still far above the predicted level? Even if the expectation is that not only the production costs but also the marketing expenditures of a service business are subject to scale economies, it still remains to be proved how significant these cost savings are and what the required scale for them would be.

The even more interesting debate is to see if consolidation – if and when it actually happens – makes good economic sense, and adds value. The data here is not unidirectional either (Ghemawat and Ghadar, 2000): the risk of value destruction through consolidation is paramount, particularly consolidation realized by merger and acquisition – according to a Bain and Co. study, 72% of the M&As created no value for shareholders (*Newsletter*, Bain and Co., 1999). KPMG's recent conclusions were even more dramatic: they found that 83% of cross-border mergers did not deliver shareholder value (*Financial Times*, 29 November 1999; *Financieel Economische Tijd*, 29 March 2001). The pharmaceutical industry is only one of many sectors where the importance of size has been subject to much debate: on the one hand, we observe the difficulties of getting the merged entities to run smoothly – as in the case of Pharmacia & Upjohn – while at the same time Eli Lilly, Merck and a number of small biotech companies are hugely successful in coming up with the next idea or blockbuster:

> A few months after the big slogans about size in this sector, some of these bigger players seem to be aching for the benefits of smaller entrepreneurial organizations. (*Financial Times*, 2 April 2001)

But it is not the sector data that matters, it is to what extent size adds value for *you*. This clearly needs to be considered on a case-by-case basis. The only general statement that can be made on the subject is probably that the added value is not a given, and will definitely not turn up automatically.

Take one industry, truck manufacturing for example, where scale may matter a great deal, at least at a regional level. Production requires a significant scale in order to be efficient and competitive. Significant and growing R&D efforts and expenses are justified on an international scale only. It is no surprise that the number of truck manufacturers has been going down, and that almost every manufacturer is either allying with a competitor to do things together, or talking to another manufacturer to merge the whole or parts of the business.

Consequently, small and independent producers have had a hard time competing in the mainstream business of trucks and buses, as was the case for the Dutch company DAF Trucks, which eventually went bankrupt in 1993. It was restarted that same year with government support, to be finally taken over by Paccar from the US in 1996. DAF Trucks had for a long time focused on the Benelux market, and was one of the late comers in broadening its geographic scope in the European market. DAF Trucks had missed the European boat – or should we say truck – and was lagging behind in terms of production efficiency and an international distribution network to market its mainstream trucks. Even when DAF internationalized by, for example, buying Leyland from the UK, it failed to get most of the scale economies as Leyland was mainly in another segment and already had its own production capacities. So the problem was multiplied, not solved. Even the takeover by Paccar, a US player, years later may not have brought a solution to that problem, mainly it has offered the time and protection of the deeper pockets of their new parent.

However, a hundred kilometres away from the DAF manufacturing plants in Eindhoven, a Belgian bus producer, Van Hool, manages to remain reasonably successful as a family owned, independent company, focusing on delivering globally specialized products. According to some of its competitors, one of the benefits that larger companies have difficulty copying is Van Hool's flexible manufacturing. This corroborates the argument made earlier that scale can indeed matter and is an important competitive dimension, but it should not mean that smaller companies, by definition, are out of the competition. They may have a bright future in specific segments of the market.

There is a similar picture in the PC business: the survivors in this business were meant to be the mass producers. The lack of size was one of the reasons why European companies – too focused on their national markets to bother playing the volume game – had a hard time competing with Dell, Compaq and others. However, there is a new generation of European PC producers that are managing to stay relatively small and beautiful: Maxdata has a 6% market share in Germany, Tiny is giving the traditional players some tough competition in the UK (and recently in the US as well) and Cibox in France has conquered 4% of the local market by focusing on dealing with the hypermarkets that sell 80% of the PCs in France.

However, we should stress that not all industries or companies have equal pressures for (or against) size. Take, for example, the temporary work services industry where we have observed various large-scale mergers and acquisitions: the Swiss Adia and French Ecco merged into Adecco and recently bought Kelly of the US; Vedior International acquired BIS in France and Selection in the UK; and the internationalization of various European national champions to other European countries, for example the Dutch Randstad Group opening offices in Italy, and Creyf's Interim entering the German, Dutch and French market. This consolidation wave was justified by the prediction 'that only three companies would survive in the temp business'. Experience has indicated, and been substantiated by market studies, that while size matters in this business, the optimal scale may not even require a pan-European presence. One could even argue that targeting a big metropolitan area could be cost competitive. While size may matter, the question still remains: what should that size be: local, national, multinational, European, global? A senior manager in one of the rapidly internationalizing players in this industry recognized: 'As it turns out, many small agencies are more profitable than the bigger players, although the latter may have more profits in absolute terms.'

Is there indeed a trade-off between growth and profitability, as Roth and Morrison (1990) found in their empirical study in other industries? The chances are minimal that size alone will be the *main* judge to decide which companies can survive and which ones not. Even in the pharmaceutical business the real sources of competitive edge may lie somewhere other than in the size of the balance sheet:

> Scale does not bring the claimed advantages. We believe the only source of sustainable competitive advantage is to be able to discover breakthrough drugs. To get there is a question of insight, creativity and knowledge, not one of force. (Gilmartin, Chairman, Merck, *Financial Times*, 16 February 2000)

The truth is probably not that 'bigger is better', but only that 'better *can* lead to bigger'.

> The merger of several poorly performing companies served only to create poorly performing large companies. (Kay and Hannah, 2000)

Or as the title of a recent book indicates: '*It's not the Big that Eat the Small ... It's the Fast that Eat the Slow*' (Jennings and Haughton, 2001), especially if 'fast' refers to 'better', 'more competitive'. The merger between Dresdner Bank and Deutsche Bank was, before the idea was abandoned, criticized by outsiders for the same reason: 'Deutsche Bank becomes bigger, but not better' (*Financial Times*, 20 March 2000). Even in the telecom industry, size is not everything: 'But while Vodafone has become huge, it now faces the challenge of becoming great' (*Fortune*, 30 October 2000). We are not alone in questioning the importance of size in itself. Rosabeth Moss Kanter stated in her influential book *World Class: Thriving Locally in the Global Economy*:

> This helps explain why the argument rages about whether globalization favors large multinationals or small niche competitors. The answer: neither or both. (1995, p. 71)

The slogans above predict the often-cited economies of scale to hit the industry and decide which company has adequate size. The strive for scale economies has pushed more than one company beyond its domestic market. The trouble is that few of these really bothered to estimate the magnitude or significance of scale economies relative to the size of the domestic market, and in what part of their business chain. The rapid expansion of insurance companies, in Europe and globally, appeared to be an attempt to achieve economies of scale. The empirical tests, however, have indicated that, while scale does matter in the insurance industry, this only applied up to a certain point (Katrishen and Scordis, 1998). Large, truly international insurers do not experience scale economies, even worse, the insurers with the greatest international diversity suffer diseconomies of scale, and likewise in banking (Langohr, 1998; Dermine and Hillion, 1999; Walter, 1999).

If you expanded for scale reasons, you still have to ensure that the economies materialize to their full extent.[7] Even when the scale economies are theoretically significant, it may be that they are never fully realized. Seeing economies of scale is one thing, achieving them is another. C&A, the Dutch confection retailer, decided to coordinate its European purchasing in order to reap scale economies, but, in reality, could not fully capitalize on it because of the differences in tastes in the different European markets.

A company is not a black box where you put in capacity and get out scale economies. It is a living mechanism where a lot of things can happen, willingly or unwillingly, that prevent getting the maximum economies of scale. This is where management comes into the picture. A journalist beautifully paraphrased it as follows:

> Management, not mass, is what matters … It is critical men rather than critical mass that matters. (*Financial Times*, 28 March 1998)

Our cautionary notes on scale economies and consolidation do not exclude any other good reasons for internationalization, but mean that citing economies of scale as the value added of internationalization is just too easy.

The term 'scale economies' was typically adopted in the context of traditional industries, such as mining or steel production, and especially for production activities. However, we have noticed how in those industries the minimum efficient scale has fallen significantly due to new production processes, such as mini-mill steel production units or micro-breweries. Manufacturing scale economies are, according to research, less of a determinant of global company integration (Kobrin, 1991).

We should, however, look at other scale-sensitive activities, such as R&D, or purchasing, and evaluate what the effect of scale on the overall cost structure may be across the value chain. The massive R&D and clinical trial investments in the pharmaceutical industry have been a driving force behind the consolidation. More geographic scope means more sales, which means less R&D costs per 'unit' sold. You should therefore be very specific which activities are scale sensitive, to what extent, and what relevant market is needed to incorporate scale advantages.

### We have to take positions now, it is now or never ... all bets are off tomorrow!

Another common denominator in the slogans we have encountered is the sense of urgency they are trying to generate. This slogan is a good example of how time pressure is motivating companies to move, or should we say, to *bet*: you need to act today, tomorrow may be too late, hence the title of an article on Renault's internationalization: 'Renault's global gamble' (*Financial Times*, 30 May 2000). Similarly, these were the headlines concerning the expansions of Morgan Stanley, ABB and Motorola respectively: 'The Big Bet' (*Business Week*, 12 February 1996); 'ABB's Big Bet in Eastern Europe' (*Fortune*, 2 May 1994); and 'Motorola bets big on China' (*Fortune*, 27 February 1996).

Looking at international competition (Jeannet, 2000) as a chess game is a popular view and sometimes enlightening, but, as a general rule, we find it rather misleading. Doing good business is rarely a matter of *merely* taking positions. The business reality is not even close to a horse race where all bets are off before the race starts. Markets will not be closed or disappear tomorrow. And 'winners' rarely take it all (Galbraith, 1995). Successful companies are those that take the right positions at the right time, today, tomorrow and the days after that, *and* manage their operations accordingly.

> Business is one thing, chess is another. But when it comes to the endgame, companies are often confusing between the two. (*Financial Times* commentator)

The image of the endgame has frequently been used to dramatize developments in the European markets. We saw it around the turn of the previous decade, when the hype of 'Europe 1992' was building up: Europe would become a borderless market as of the magical 1 January 1993 date. The perception in the market grew that positions needed to be taken, and competition would decide which company was right and which was wrong soon after it. The expectations were huge, and they were rarely ever met.[8] Of course, Europe did not change overnight! The awakening or rather disenchantment of some business people was significant, as we will discuss later.

A similar climax had been swelling around the introduction of the euro in January 1999. The expectation was that Europe was going to change into an integrated market – finally! – because of a new accounting unit and currency. The first reflections on the post-euro era indicated that for many of the companies it still remained to a large extent business as usual.[9] We are afraid that it will take more than a White Paper and a new currency to turn Europe into the single market it is meant to be. And when it comes, it will definitely not happen overnight, as we will argue in Chapter 2.

Even in the financial sector, things were not as obvious as they seemed. Originally, many seemed to panic at the start of the euro launch. Urgent action was called for. It was hard to deny that the single currency would impact financial services and markets. Yet at the same time it was debatable whether financial services on 1 January 1999 would look completely different in all parts of the business and/or for all segments of the market. As early as 1997, studies had indicated that even in this business the likely effect of the euro was not as overwhelming as some would have liked us to believe (Praet and Wigny, 1997).

The examples of the 'Europe 1992' and 'Euro 1999' hype illustrate how potentially dangerous this type of endgame fallacy can be. The danger is that it distracts management's attention from the real question: what is the basis for success in your business and how can internationalization, and Europeanization, add value to your company? What is it that really matters in your business, and what will make the difference between the successful players and less or unsuccessful companies? How do you manage this change process? It is hard for us to imagine that the basis for success depends on big bets and strategic decisions or investments of today *only*.

In fact, bets have often led to significant disasters. The last thing you need when you are not sure what your ambition is, or where you want to go, is to make big bets and rigidly commit yourself. Keeping one's options open and embedding flexibility in business systems often seems a more fruitful strategy, especially in increasingly uncertain environments. Successful companies often keep options on as many future routes as possible, and create flexibility around which options to finally execute (Williamson, 1999).

Putting the debate in 'now or never' terms *can* help you to make 'the indispensable' happen and mobilize the necessary resources and attention around strategic projects. It may create the awareness that action is required to retain and build a competitive edge. The restructuring of the financial services industry in the European market was definitely a justified (r)evolution, with or without a euro. The euro, and any other concrete event, may help to raise the issues, for example around cost efficiency, but many banks and insurers needed to deal with these matters anyway. Building that comprehension, however, does not change the million dollar question: how can you add value through internationalizing?

## There are only a few interesting targets left

This slogan appears a natural extension of the previous one: we need to act now because there are only a few interesting targets left. Good deals are rare and nobody gets poor making a good deal. Unique business opportunities rarely present themselves more than once, grab them when you spot them. If you want to make it internationally, there is little reason to wait much longer. The best targets may already be taken, and therefore you better move soon. The target could either be a company to partner with or an acquisition to make in order to enter a market or 'secure' a market position.

It cannot be emphasized enough that, however unique the business opportunity may be and no matter how short the list of interesting targets may have become, the only thing that counts is the business logic for the project as such in light of your own strategy. Nothing justifies acquiring the wrong target or entering an uninteresting market. Ralph Larsen, Chairman of Johnson & Johnson put it this way:

> Would I prefer to be bigger? Yes. Would I do a dumb deal to get there? No!
> (*Financial Times*, 6 April 2000)

It is not because the number of interesting targets is shrinking fast that internationalization now or later will make more or less sense. The real name of the game is not to identify potential targets and get them, it is to do your business better than the competition. If your company can do so by entering certain markets or working with certain partners, it should identify the right target markets and partners, and try to grasp all the opportunities for getting these targets.

Vedior International, the Dutch temporary work agency, had entered the French market in the early 1990s with a greenfield operation. By the mid-1990s, the French operations were still relatively small. The management team considered some national French agencies for acquisition, and judged this to be a last chance to break into the French market. The number of interesting targets, however, was not impressive. The French acquisition dossier risked becoming an objective in its own right. Rumours in the market in September 2000 suggested that Vedior, which historically did realize its stated ambition of becoming one of the top three European players, by size, was willing to sell off its French subsidiary – so much for its entry into the French market.

Similar arguments have been heard in the beer brewing or financial services industry when talking about the Eastern European market, or internationalization and consolidation in the truck manufacturing industry, with Volvo, Scania and Volkswagen as protagonists. No matter how many targets are left in Eastern Europe or in the European truck industry, the key debate still remains as to how important internationalization through partnering with a target, or by entering the target market, is in the business. What will you be able to do better *with* the target?

This should not prevent you from being entrepreneurial or even opportunistic, nor should we underestimate 'first mover advantages' in entering certain markets. First mover advantages are important for certain players in specific deregulated industries, such as telecom companies or public utilities, where the limitations on internationalization were very abruptly discontinued, markets opened up quickly and companies had only limited opportunities for entering a market (Sarkar et al., 1999). However, in most industries, the economics of the business allow for several opportunities to enter a market and limitations on international investments shift much more gradually: hence being the first is less important. What we saw with the UMTS Third Generation Mobile Licences Auctions is a good example: the expectations, especially from the licenser, were that several companies would compete for a licence as it would be their only chance to gain access to the market. Nevertheless, the low response rate in most European countries shows that not all telecom companies see this as their one and only opportunity.

One can try to keep running away from the real strategic questions by acquiring new targets or entering new geographic markets every six months. More than ever, you would need to prove that you can do a better job than others. This may require you being international, or lead you to search for interesting partners in certain markets. But the rationale for making this happen should not be that only a few targets are left. The driving force should be to become better in what you are doing or want to be doing.

## Eat or be eaten

Why wait until some of the bigger competitors show an interest in our assets or execute their attraction to our activities by acquiring us? Better move yourself, by acquisition or merger, than being swallowed, rather eat lunch than be lunch; or as Gent, CEO of Vodafone, put it: 'Hunt or be hunted' (*Fortune*, 30 October 2000). Local champions often get roused to go international by the interest of others, mostly early or earlier movers on the international platform, in their domestic position. They may want to secure their independence, and one way to do that is through acquisition of or merger with a local champion in another national market.

As we are often reminded, fear rarely gives the best advice. Whether eating or not is the right thing for your company to do should not depend on a concrete or perceived threat from other companies to take over your company.

It seems increasingly acceptable to preserve the dynamics in the industry or defend your own position by 'eating'. This was painfully illustrated in 1999 with the bid from the Franco–Belgian oil company TotalFina on its French competitor Elf, which was immediately countered by a counter-bid from Elf on TotalFina. We had the impression that the technicalities of the bids – who was bidding, who was the target and at what price – overruled the business logic of bidding. The bidding itself turned into the core subject in the discussions, while the oil refinery, and petroleum business and industrial plan for these activities risked being reduced to a second order problem.

Something similar happened in the dossier of the big French bank: the bid of BNP on Societé Générale and Paribas, countering the bid of Societé Générale on Paribas, had been headline news for weeks. We only hoped that as much energy had been invested in developing and defending the business project itself as on the fights on who owned whom. The perception from the outside was that the latter dominated. The other observation in this debacle is that Societé Générale, after having lost Paribas to BNP, is ultimately looking for foreign partners to get out of the deadlock, and protect itself from being eaten by BNP. The risk of been eaten by 'the *small* big French bank' drove Societé Générale into the European banking market.

In the telecom industry, eating seems to be the name of the game as well:

> If Mr Colalinno [Telecom Italia] cannot find a way to match them [Vodafone, France Telecom, and others], one day he will have to sell. (*Financial Times*, 17 July 2000)

> Investors' confusion of who was doing what with or to whom reflects the states of play in today's telecom industry. (*Fortune*, 3 April 2000)

Yet, in this industry, the benefits of internationalization are not patently obvious across the board.

Even if and where a 'defence' may be in order, there are alternative scenarios: in the airline business, for example, a number of alliances have been playing on the need for international coverage. Similarly, four insurance companies from four different European countries set up an alliance called Eureko in 1992. Each of these small national insurers had initiated smaller or bigger internationalization projects, with mixed successes. Because they feared that their strong national position would make them attractive to some of the bigger insurance groups, and because each of them did not see how they could create value by taking the lead in M&A deals, they decided to join forces on the international scene in an alliance. Other partners have joined the alliance since, while each of the partners has been able to concentrate on consolidating their positions in their domestic markets. Even if it was considered a defensive move by some of the partners, it was worth it for them to consider alternatives to M&A, as billions of euros were not spent on questionable acquisitions.

## Our competitors are already doing it

Business is a game of action and reaction: one player makes a move and others are induced to follow or make a countermove. The *Financial Times* and *The Wall Street Journal*, for example, are closely following each other's global initiatives. That is what business games and the game theory approach of business and strategy prescribe (see, for example, Brandenburger and Nalebuff, 1996). Noticing a competitor's internationalization move may encourage you to internationalize too, but are you sure you should really follow suit?

At the very least, it should make you think: do they see or know things in your industry that you do not see or know? In other words, you should definitely evaluate what they may be after. But in the end, what matters to you is how you can add value through internationalizing in your industry and your company's strategy.

What counts is not what the competition is doing and how you can copy their actions, but why they are doing it and how they expect to benefit from it. When DAF Trucks saw the international expansion of its competitors, it should have made it think about how its competitors were expecting to benefit from expanding throughout Europe, and if it should consider doing the same. Unfortunately, it lagged behind in international scope.

However, even if your competitor sees good reasons for crossing the borders, it still does not mean that it makes automatic sound business sense for *you* to do the same. Your strategic objectives may, and probably should, be different since strategy is about being unique and finding company-specific sources for competitive edge. Is it because Arthur Andersen continues to build an international network that every accounting and auditing office should strive for the status of a big five? A local office with a focus on local clients and delivering specific accounting services to SMEs can be very successful in itself.

Internationalization can add more or less value for a competitor than it does for you, in light of the ambitions and mission of each. A business consultant rightfully observed:

> Think focus, not fashion. If your competitors are globalizing, do not let that bother you – they may be wrong. (*Newsletter*, Bain and Co., January–February 2000)

Also be careful that your competitor's specific internationalization driver – 'it only applies to his company' – is not a reason for the lack of immediate internationalization benefit. In that case it might actually be a good thing not to follow what your competitors are doing. We have even heard the opposite reasoning: since our competitors are occupied with their foreign adventures, it might be good for us to stay home and fight them there, with much more muscle. In many so-called mature markets there may be a lot of life left at home.

Colruyt, a very focused local discount retailer in Belgium, decided to focus on growth in the domestic market first, while many of its competitors were into internationalization or global plays, with the added benefit of enabling it to face new foreign competitors coming in, such as Carrefour's acquisition of a major Belgian competitor, GB.

### Foreign competitors are entering our home market

This, in a sense, is a special case of the previous situation. And it makes things even worse: our competitor is not only internationalizing, he or she is also threatening our position in our domestic market. And that is why you start hitting back and attacking the competitors' home turf, so the argument goes.

Having your home position attacked by a competitor, whether local or global, is a serious thing and should make you think about your own position. But it should not automatically mean that you ought to fight back by entering his domestic or any other market for that matter. It might be exactly the wrong reaction, as it distracts your attention from where the real problem and threat is: the home market.

Assuming that your competitor is able to take market share in your home market still does not guarantee that you will be able to do the same in his home market. Instead, does it not indicate that you have an issue to deal with in your own back yard, rather than pushing to go international too? Our biggest concern is that it may actually keep you from dealing with the real challenge: to be competitive in the domestic market. Moreover, by having entered your home market, your competitor *may* already have improved his position in his home market due to the internationalization benefits he has gained.

On the other hand, when your competitor has difficulties in his home market, and runs away from them by giving you a hard time in your market, and you have the competencies to build a sustainable competitive advantage in this market, internationalizing can make sense. As has been indicated in research conducted in the context of the game theory view of strategy making, the argument for a competitive counterattack in order to block the competition from gaining advantage, rather than to build up your own advantage, can be beneficial, but only in specific cases of competitive interaction (see, for example, Brandenburger and Nalebuff, 1996; Graham, 1998).

Faced with the competitive threat from Fuji in its home market, Kodak entered the Japanese market but with little success. It was shut out of most of the distribution channels in Japan, as relationship-sensitive distributors preferred to stay with well-tried Fuji. Kodak took its case to the WTO complaining about unfair trade practices on the part of the Japanese government and Fuji, but lost its case.

The European telecom business has gone through an unparalleled wave of consolidation and internationalization in the past few years, in face of deregulation. It was remarkable to see the traditional national telecom operators enter other European and often each other's markets as a reaction to the rapidly changing regulative environment. Belgacom, the Belgian telecom operator, decided to bid, with its partners, for a Dutch mobile network licence; KPN, the Dutch telecom company, had entered the Belgian market a few months earlier with its newly created subsidiary Orange. Vodafone has had a special interest in the US market, where it acquired Airtouch, and the German market, where it successfully bid for Mannesmann, in search for volume. Not surprisingly, Deutsche Telekom, perceived to be one of Vodafone's competitors for European or even global leadership in the telecom industry, has made bold moves in the UK with One2One and in the US with VoiceStream Wireless Corp.

Without wanting to claim that these companies had no good reasons to invest in other markets – only an in-depth analysis of the benefits of internationalization for each of those companies could tell – we continue to raise the questions mentioned above, if only to know better what each is trying to achieve. Otherwise it could simply be a case of 'an eye for an eye' ... .

Jolibee, a Philippines-based fast-food chain, found a different way out from the threat of a foreign competitor, McDonald's, on their home market (Bartlett and Ghoshal, 2000). It used the competition from a leading competitor to strengthen its operating systems and challenge its customer service at home. After it managed to out-compete McDonald's in its expansion in the local market, it entered other Asian markets successfully by adapting its concept with local meals, finally breaking into the US market, where it is on the verge of rapid expansion.

The key issues in these kinds of discussion is to realize where exactly the problems (and the opportunities) are and what is the best strategy to deal with them. This leads us to another often cited incentive.

## Our home market is saturated ... our home market is too small

The typical growth path of a national champion moves from expansion of activities in the national market, to entering foreign markets to find additional growth potential. Looking for opportunities across the border is a natural next step. In some instances, the home market is simply too small for the ambitious growth of the company.

Sonera, the Finnish telecom operator, has sought growth in the US and Turkey, because the 'customer base in Finland is not inexhaustible'. eBay, a leading US online auctioneer, very actively started looking for expansion in Europe for similar reasons:

> With an estimated 85% of the US online auction market, eBay has little room to grow at home. (*Business Week*, 16 October 2000)

SAir Group, parent of Swissair, recently acquired a 49.9% stake in LTU, the third largest German charter airline and third biggest tour operator, to secure a foothold in the biggest market in Europe worth DM50 billion a year. Another motive for the cross-border acquisition is to expand the network of alliances within the Swissair group. Hannes Goetz, SAir Group Chairman, clarifies the motive with the following words: 'We Swiss cannot grow much more within our home market.' And so it acquired a 51% stake in the Belgian airline Sabena, itself limited by the size of its home base.

This has been the history of internationalization in many companies from smaller countries, such as Switzerland, the Netherlands and Belgium, across a range of industries.

> Several of the Swiss companies that internationalized because their domestic market was too small, like Swissair, Vontobel in private banking and Sulzer in engineering, seem to have run into trouble recently. (*Financial Times*, 19 March 2001)

However, before you conclude that the market is too small or saturated, and in some instances that may be the case, we invite you to ask a few additional questions. Is it because *your* growth in the domestic market has slowed over the past two years that the *market* has reached saturation? Does market saturation mean that you accept your current position and do not feel like looking for ways to grow at home? Make sure that it is not an excuse for not becoming more competitive or innovative at home, or getting a larger slice of the market. If you cannot increase your position in a market you know and where you are already an established player, how will that guarantee you a better position in a new and foreign market? Entering another market will probably not make your home market bigger or less saturated.

Wal-Mart, the US retailer, came up with several different retailing formulas in its home market (successfully moving from medium-sized discount stores in 'off the beaten path' locations in rural America to superstores in very competitive areas and into Sam's Wholesales Clubs) before it decided to go international. You could say that it has probably managed to exploit the opportunities to create a new market in the US every time it felt that saturation in an existing segment was near. But even with its impressive track record, it was struggling in Argentina and blundered in Asia. And the jury is still out on its recent investments in the UK and Germany.[10]

K-Mart, a major competitor of Wal-Mart in the US, followed a different strategy: they expanded into the South-East Asian market much earlier, when the home retail market was saturated. It had a disastrous experience in Singapore, where it could not compete with entrenched local players. K-Mart could not bring anything special to the market and could not produce any significant benefits from its Asian business compared to the costs involved. As a consequence, the company destroyed value by venturing outside its domestic market, and increasingly had problems with consolidating its home position.

Interbrew, the Belgian brewer that recently strengthened its position as the number two beer company in the world through the acquisition of

Whitbread and the disrupted attempt to buy Bass in the UK, committed significant resources to Eastern Europe, Asia and America, when it felt its growth slowing in Western Europe, and the home market more particularly. Not only was there not much room for growth in Belgium, but Interbrew seemed to have lost market share in a declining home market, even though it had more than a 50% market share. While this market situation put up the pressure for internationalization, it also raised the question of how to solve the problem at home. Initiatives for regaining its market position in the domestic market through new products, innovative packaging and alternative distribution channels have been reported lately (*Financieel Economische Tijd*, 5 April 2001).

Growth and internationalization for the sake of it is dangerous and risky. Growth is not a driver as such, but the result of doing something right. The trigger lies in identifying what it is you can do right or better by entering foreign markets. It can identify sources for value creation that are the sound *basis* for profit and growth. Growth and entering a foreign market might look attractive at first sight. But the 'attractive' markets are exactly the places where many other players will be betting on and hence quickly become much more competitive.

The argument of a small home market goes often hand in hand with the need for scale: the domestic client base is too narrow and does not deliver the minimum required scale. In that respect, it is not the market that is too small in itself – while Luxembourg is big enough for temping or accounting services, it is too small for the car industry – it is the size of the market relative to the scale requirements that may force you to cross borders and internationalize.

## We are just following our clients – they are international

Then there is the most pressing and convincing argument for internationalization: our customers want it! In the current business environment, it would not be surprising if you came to the conclusion that a bigger share of your clients are operating internationally. What choice do you have but to follow the client to foreign markets if he chooses to do so? There is also a shared belief, which has probably affected your clients as well, that one should minimize the number of suppliers – call it key *supplier* management – and create long-term relationships with them. Yet another reason to follow the client, because we do not like to lose him.

As with the other slogans, there is some truth in this reasoning. Look at all the companies that got involved in international operations by an accidental order from a client in the domestic market requiring the same products in one of its international subsidiaries. Think of the global account management programmes that are set up between suppliers and international clients. Indications are that the demand for such global offerings will only increase in the future (Montgomery et al., 1999). In the telecom industry, for example, global communications companies are desperately trying to control the lucrative accounts of multinational corporations. Caterpillar's early internationalization was helped by the demand for repair and spare parts following the US Army's activities in Europe during World War II where Caterpillar's equipment was used.

The trap, however, lies in blindly following the client. The example of BIS Banking Systems, a UK company that developed and sold specialized banking software, is worth mentioning in this context. A lot of its key clients, big banks, expanded to different geographies in the 1980s, closely followed by BIS Banking Systems. It opened offices around the world to deliver the banks MIDAS, their flagship software. By the late 1980s, however, banks started restructuring their international operations and heavily centralized decision-making back to the headquarters, mainly for cost reasons. The BIS Banking Systems' managers, who had been operating quite independently on a country-by-country basis, had a tough decision to make: should they overhaul their international network as the banks were doing?

The company decided to do so and subsequently started streamlining its international network. The lesson it learned was that it had over-internationalized by setting up offices in every single city where banks had opened branches and mismanaged the level of independence of the foreign offices. The restructuring of its network resulted in the installation of regional offices that could service its clients on a flexible basis, in every single branch if necessary but mainly in the headquarters of the bank in the first place. By the time it got its act together, however, many of its clients had started wondering whether centralizing IT management to such an extent was desirable or even feasible, and some of them were moving back to decentralization. The result for BIS was a constant lagging behind the moves of its customers, with all the attendant confusion, costs and frustration. So before you start following your client, it may be worthwhile asking yourself why your clients are doing it and what are their reasons.

The slogan implicitly assumes that the client has very good reasons for internationalizing, which may not always be the case. Therefore, the first thing to do is to understand your customer's business and strategy: what is he after? The client may be driven by economies of scale in his value chain, but how does that affect you? If the client gets no particular added value from his international expansion or cross-border integration, he will find out soon enough and probably decide to restructure or shift the centralization–decentralization balance again. It is better to anticipate that, convince the client that it does not make sense in the first place and not fall into the trap of promising non-existent advantages.

A rightfully internationalizing client may nevertheless see little incentive to buy from you in other markets. Why would the client stick to the same supplier in different markets, if the scale in his own operations was what he wanted in the first place? The question is what the value of working with the same supplier would be.

The cross-border contract between a multinational and a temp agency is a good illustration of this point. Shortly after the official signing of the international contract, the client realized that the *real* benefits of cross-border temping were limited and the contract was hard to manage. The deal was quickly undone, because the national subsidiaries of the client were in net terms worse off with the cross-border contract than with their contracts with the best local agency. The subsidiaries had a valid reason for not buying locally from the centrally contracted agency: there was no benefit to them at all.

If you are the local potato supplier to the McDonald's restaurant, should you internationalize just because McDonald's is global? While McDonald's has its own reasons to internationalize – leveraging an international concept – the potato supplier is in an intrinsically different business. McDonald's may be interested in buying certain products internationally, but they know they are better off with local potato companies. If an international potato supplier stands up, he would still have to prove to McDonald's he can do a better job than the competitors in the local market, who have been in that market for years, know the local requirements, and have established the conditions for serving the local restaurants.

There is a term for the inherent handicap of foreign rivals over local companies: 'the liability of foreignness' (Rangan, 2000, p. 119). HSBC, the British financial service provider, has always ruled out big acquisitions in Germany, arguing:

> If the Germans cannot make any money out of German banking, how can we?
> (*Business Week*, 1 May 2000)

This has not prevented it from paying big money to enter the French market through its acquisition of CCF. Still, multinationals increasingly see a benefit in working with their key suppliers on an international basis. Contrary to conventional wisdom, uniform pricing does not necessarily seem to be their key concern. The key motivation and advantage of global account programmes lies in the consistency and standardization of the offering and a single point of contact with the supplier (Montgomery et al., 1999). The client likes to work with you in other markets, because he knows your products and services, and has high supplier switching costs, real or imagined.

It is good to know the client benefits from it, but ultimately, you would want to gain from working with international clients as well. What is in it for you? Will you receive any benefit from following the client, or will you only bear the cost? Temporary work agencies claimed that they needed to internationalize because the clients were asking them to. While this statement was debatable in itself – only 5% of all temping contracts between agencies and clients were truly cross-border, and this was expected to grow to only 15% by 2010 – industry data showed that the cross-border segment was the least profitable one. So would following the client be a good idea for a temp agency? An adviser to Vodafone had the following warning about its focus on global accounts:

> It risks alienation of a very profitable consumer base for the sake of achieving, on a visual basis, global scale. (*Fortune*, 30 October 2000)

And once you know that there is a benefit for the client and you may be able to get part of that, you will still have to be able to deliver the benefit to the client. Saatchi & Saatchi hoped that its clients would contract advertising services across the world, which they did not for various reasons. But even if they had, it could never have delivered a global advertising contract because it ran its operations in a very decentralized and independent fashion.

## We need to be where the market is

Not only do you want to *be* where the clients *go*, you also may want to *go* where the clients *are*. Who would not be interested in a large, untapped market, with lots of potential and actual clients and demand? A board member of ING, the Dutch financial services provider that decided to withdraw from the global investment banking scene but has mapped out a different internationalization strategy in the US since, commented: 'Is there a role for ING in the UK? If it is a big market, there is a potential role!' (*Financial Times*, 22 May 2001). The temporary work agencies are all rushing towards Italy at the moment. The Italian government has recently opened the market for labour services, the unemployment rate is significant enough to leave plenty of opportunities for flexible workforce solutions. While this is a serious consideration to be guiding your international presence requirements, it is worthwhile realizing the exact meaning and therefore limitations of this rationale.

What will you get out of being in Italy? Is your mere presence there sufficient to be successful? Probably not. Going to Italy is attractive for a temporary work services agency because of the market's growth potential. The assumption is that it should be easier to grow in Italy than in the home market. This might not necessarily be as easy as it looks at first sight: significant investments may be required in order to enter the market and build up a minimum presence, there is no brand or reputation established, and just because the market is open does not mean that it will grow as fast as expected. So there are plenty of reasons why one should not rush blindly to Italy but first understand what is required to become a successful player there.

This notion of being where the market is resembles a portfolio approach to business. You go to all geographies where you think there is a market for your services or products. The question is still how it adds value for you to be in these different markets. Being there could be nice, but is it crucial? What does it bring extra?

EMI, a UK medical, electronics and leisure company, entered the US market in the CT scanner business in the late 1970s. While contemplating whether or not to enter this business, EMI management realized that an entry decision would automatically require them to internationalize this business to the US market. Because of its size and market potential, the US medical market clearly represented a major opportunity for a new device such as the CT scanner. However, maybe the biggest advantage was the know-how, sophistication and technology that was most prevalent in the US market.

This slogan can also have a second and quite different meaning, beyond the presence of customers, referring to a broader set of conditions that influence the development of a certain type of business in a particular location. The place to be in the IT business is Silicon Valley, or Wall Street and the City of London if you are in the financial services industry. Can you afford not to be in Antwerp if you are in diamonds, in Milan if you are in fashion, or in the US in the CT scanning business, as in EMI's case? You need to go where the 'action' is. Not only are the customers there, and probably also the most sophisticated ones, but also the suppliers, infrastructure, competitors, resources and relevant technology are centralized in the 'valley' (see also Porter, 1990). In fact, if the world were perfectly borderless and global, location would not really matter, but it seems that the whole argument behind the development of valleys is quite the contrary. And it still seems to hold (*Washington Post*, 6 October 1999).

By moving into the 'valley', companies expose themselves to a highly demanding and competitive environment. They leave their safe home market and position, and enter a dynamic market in order to force themselves to think beyond the obvious and remain at the cutting edge of the industry. It challenges you and ultimately makes you stronger and more competitive. The *Washington Post* reported on the creation of a new software company by three IT experts, who immediately moved to Silicon Valley, and admitted: 'This was the right place. We could never, ever, ever have gotten this reaction in Singapore!' (*Washington Post*, 6 October 1999). Who said that location has become irrelevant?

Especially for industries that seem intrinsically local by nature, typically service businesses, this might exactly be the added value of international presence. Through internationalization, you learn to compete and become more competitive 'the hard way'. You put yourself up for competition against many other players, and force yourself to become stronger and more competitive, rather than trying to escape from competition. Bear in mind, however, that this effect will by no means come automatically and will require a completely different set of mechanisms and instruments. If you put yourself up to the most demanding customers and best competitors, the stakes are high.

Another benefit you may get from being in the right place is the access to input factors, such as cheap or skilled labour, primary products or know-how. Because the company is competing on this market, it gets the feedback from the market on its products, it is in the middle of all the industry know-how and technology developments, and is forced to be in tune with it.

This is how the idea of industry clusters has gained influence, mostly with the support of governments. If these clusters develop as the world centre for a particular industry, it can be crucial to have a foothold there: it secures access to important input factors, such as know-how, and allows companies to meet competitors and clients. Nevertheless, it still means that the company should aim to build a unique and sustainable competitive advantage, and that will not be gained from simply having an office in Silicon Valley, or any other valley.

Both connotations of this slogan have very different implications as to what you should do and how you should proceed. The corresponding strategy, resources and management processes differ substantially between both cases. While you may want to build a full-scale sales network in untapped markets, you only need a small office or 'antenna' in order to tune in on leading market developments. Either way, presence in the relevant market is no guarantee of success.

## It is key to have global access to clients

This other form of the previous slogans has become popular, particularly in those industries where interconnectivity is key, such as the telecom or airline sector. The perception goes that you need global access to customers. This is more than just being where the client or the market is, access to the whole world is what it is about. And the players are willing to go far in that search: look at the M&A wave in the telephone, fixed and mobile, business (Deutsche Telekom, Vodafone, KPN, Telefonica and so on), internet service providers (T-Online and so on) and media business (Time Warner and AOL).

> Long term, Deutsche Telekom will need to be in all the big markets. (*Financial Times*, 11 August 2000)

> Economies of scale and business synergies are no longer as important as access to customers. (Villonga, Chairman Telefonica, *Financial Times*, 3 May 2000)

How often are telecom companies compared to each other on the basis of their number of fixed phone connections, mobile customers and/or internet subscribers (*Business Week*, 4 December 2000)? The success of portals and their pricing to client–advertisers are based on their span of clients.

Is the real issue whether clients want global access to your products or services, or is it the supplier's global access to clients that matters? The difference between both arguments may rest in the detail, but it raises a broader strategic issue: is this a market or a supply driven phenomenon? And how big is that segment of the market that wants you to be global? And at what cost are you willing to ensure global access?

Even if the market understands that you are global, mere access to clients will not guarantee you or the clients anything: it does not ensure that clients will buy from you globally and will not guarantee clients a good value proposition. The trick is probably to deliver the best local service, which is more than just an issue of presence, as we argued before. Some portals, such as MSN or Yahoo! in Europe, admit: 'We're focused on providing a localized service'; 'Yahoo! is blending universal attributes with local content, language and cultural nuance' (*Fortune*, 12 June 2000).

## We have to be international from the start

In the high-tech or so-called 'new' economy, a lot of start-up companies do not follow the traditional path of the classical national champions. They do not start as a small company that typically grows to be a considerable player in a national market first, before facing the challenge of how to proceed next and often internationalize. The internet businesses and specialized technology companies hardly think about the national versus international dilemma. Acting conservatively in start-up businesses, internationalizing slowly, is risky: others will leverage your hard work and quickly take market share that you feel rightly is yours. You should be international from the minute you start – at least that is what a lot of them claim.[11]

> There probably is no business today that you can start that can afford not to be global. (Tim Koogle, CEO of Yahoo!)

For some of them, this is quite an obvious decision. The national markets for their products and services are mostly too small – 'my home market is too small' – to justify the investments in the business. Lernout and Hauspie Speech Products (LHSP), a world leader in speech technology and recognition based in Belgium, has never been a real 'Belgian' national champion. It was on the world market for speech applications from the beginning, so much so that its hunger to grow led to mismanagement and presumed fraud in the books of the company. The demand in Belgium for its applications and services could never generate the cash for the huge investments in product development that the company required. For companies such as this, there are significant arguments for entering the international playing field directly, as in reality they have no choice.

Other companies choose to compete in their industry in a very specific way, and this competitive position is based on international presence. The business concept of Bezos, founder and CEO of Amazon.com, started from the global book market, accessed through the global distribution channel of the internet. If Bezos had chosen the classical bookstore outlets, he would probably not have internationalized that fast or on that scale. The business proposition was international, because he chose to compete that way.

You could say that this reasoning applies to all internet businesses: their distribution channel is by definition borderless:

> The Internet was created from its inception without borders. (Choi et al., 1997, p. 501)

> Place a store on the Internet anywhere and it is, in effect, everywhere. (*The Economist*, 14 September 1997)

But apparently, it is more complicated than that: internationalizing often requires significant investments for them in foreign offices, employees in different countries, marketing campaigns and even translated, national websites, as Amazon can testify, not forgetting the often expensive logistical solutions for the distribution of physical goods, sold virtually. And as dotcom companies mostly need all the cash that they are offered to get their business up and running, immediate international coverage may be one bridge too far.

> Geography and physical space are not rendered irrelevant in electronic commerce. Much web-based commercial activity is regionally focused. (Steinfield and Klein, 1999, p. 1)

Boo.com, recorded in the history books as the first big internet business to go bankrupt, covered more than seven countries from its start-up. Dressmart.com, a Swedish textile retailer, managed to save the company by withdrawing in time to the home market, a venture capitalist noting that: 'They over-internationalized, without first building up their business concept in the home market.'

OneSwoop, a Dutch internet company that sells cars in the UK, decided to postpone the set-up of activities on the Continent. Recipeweb, a culinary website, decided to licence its recipes in Spain first instead of setting up their own website and office.

This indicates how alike the rules are for the old and new economy. Regardless of the distribution channel, there is little reason why internationalization for an internet company might be easier. Reaching clients globally does not mean you can *serve* them globally. While country borders do not immediately show up on the distribution side, they may be as clear when it comes down to actually doing business in foreign markets: how do we get people to buy our goods, who is going to service clients locally, how do we get the goods or services to the end consumer, will our offer catch on in different markets with different habits?

> A first principle: a startup should never look abroad until it has achieved some progress at home in revenues, customers or profitability. (*Fortune*, 26 June 2000)

Maybe the urge for internationalization says more about the ambition of the dotcommers than anything else.

In truth, for most companies, there is a choice to be made, there are alternatives to be considered. International is rarely your destiny, unless you make it yours. The stock market wanted us to believe that the future is bright for all internet-related businesses. Chances are pretty high, however, that the winners will be those companies that understand what it takes to be successful in their business, adapt their strategy and organization to it and manage their activities accordingly – locally or internationally. And we believe we are starting to see some of that realism – in the dotcom companies, their venture capitalists and the financial markets (see also Rangan, 2000).

## It is too risky to depend on the home market alone

The argument of geographic diversification aspires to reduce the vulnerability of the company to economic cycles in a particular market. The underlying rationale is straightforward: through geographic diversification, companies can switch their fixed costs from one country to another when times are bad or good. By doing so, the company can reduce uncertainty, either on the demand side – security of demand – or on the supply side – security of inputs to production.

There are considerations to make around geographic diversification. It is unclear to what extent the hedging for economic conjunctures should happen internally – in the company – or externally. If the objective is to reduce the financial risk of the shareholders, we may want to leave that to external mechanisms, such as financial markets. A finance director of a bank told us: 'A company should never diversify for its investors.'

If the aim is to limit the operational risk, we may have to reflect on various issues around diversification as well. In order to hedge, the economic cycles in different countries should not be fully linked to each other. There may be reservations about this condition, especially in light of the economic integration and regionalization that is taking place all over the world – Europe, Asia, Latin America. Hedging also assumes that the fixed costs can be swapped – all or partly – from one region or country to another. This might apply to industries such as home appliance manufacturing where produced machines can be shipped from one place to another – to the extent that the output in one country can be sold in another – but this is not the case for most service companies where the fixed costs are often primarily personnel and where local 'inputs' should 'produce' locally.

The economic crisis in many emerging markets in Asia and Latin America led to a series of profit warnings from major Western and

Japanese companies. While these companies may in the long term be able to diversify their systematic risk over different markets – the purely South American or Asian companies had more trouble surviving the crisis – their internationalization into these markets increased their short-term risk profile. Research similarly confirmed that internationalization and geographic diversification in the first place *increases* the systematic risk of a company (Reeb et al., 1998).

### Summary: where is the beef?

In Figure 1.2 we summarize our journey through slogan-land and cluster the slogans according to their reference to the competition, clients or markets. We also indicate how the slogans relate, almost like a reinforcing loop.

Our conclusion from this overview of the slogans is that internationalization deserves a more in-depth discussion on what you are aiming at, and should not be managed through one-liners or generalizations only. These do not have the nuance and depth needed to make a strategic decision on internationalization. What is right in one industry does not necessarily apply to another, and one company's internationalization should certainly not make all companies in that sector embark on international projects.

A good way to show how partial the view of the slogans is on the challenges in the business was to counter each of the slogans, and raise doubts about the slogan-like arguments. The most problematic situation is where the slogans prevent companies from looking at the real issues and challenges. The counter-slogans launched above are meant to go beyond the superficial talk and enter into the real debate. Although they cannot claim the status of absolute truth, they should force us to think beyond the 'obvious'. Therefore we overlay the road map of the slogans with a chart of similarly 'simplistic mottos', as indicated in Figure 1.3.

The purpose of this is to separate the sense from the nonsense in the internationalization debate. While stimulating the reflection on internationalization, neither the slogans nor the counter-slogans tell us exactly what internationalization should bring. They do not guide us in making up our mind on why and how to internationalize.They illustrate that it is not growth, or competitors or clients, that we should necessarily seek in general terms. We therefore need to go into the detail of what specific benefit(s) we are trying to achieve. In Chapter 2 we propose a simple framework to help us to make such an analysis. Before we can make it happen, we have to know much better what it is we should go after.

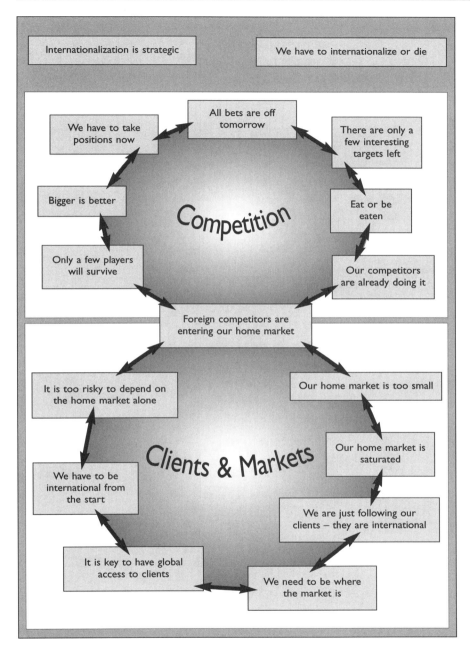

**Figure 1.2** Road map of internationalization slogans

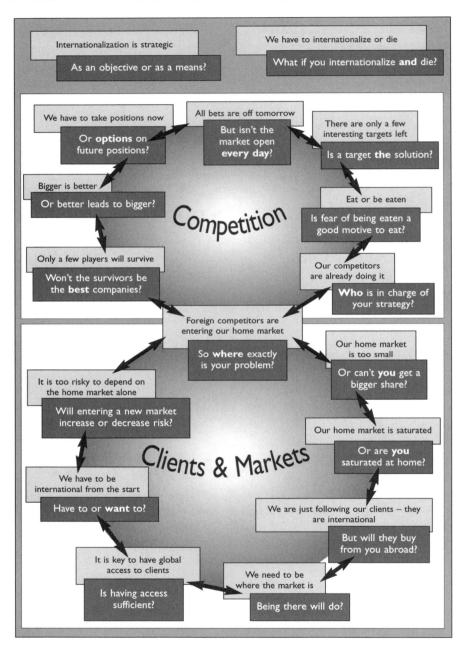

**Figure 1.3** Countering the internationalization slogans

## CHAPTER 2

# The Conelearn Framework

Notwithstanding the many questions and remarks raised in Chapter 1 on the popular internationalization motives and impulses, there *are* several good reasons to internationalize, and various ways you can take advantage of it. We do not aim to promote undue scepticism about internationalization, or to scare you with examples of unqualified failures or internationalization horror stories. The vast majority of the companies we ran into in our research did manage to profit from their internationalization one way or the other, although often not to the extent or in the way expected. The aim of this chapter is to understand in what way(s) one can expect to realize real benefits.

If one assumes that the fundamental question on globalization is not *if*, but *when*, *where*, *how much* and *how* to internationalize, then why bother about specifying the reasons and benefits of international market coverage? Why is it important to pin down specific fruits if you know you can harvest them in any case? We see three principal reasons for detailing the underlying reasons and benefits of internationalization: to better understand what *type of benefit* to go after, to assess the *importance* of the advantage and to get an idea of the *urgency* or *priority*.

■ First, despite the fact that each company can benefit from internationalization, not all companies profit in the same way. In some instances you hope to improve your relative cost position, such as in the truck manufacturing industry. In other cases, you expect to do more business with your clients and increase turnover by working with them on a crossborder level, as in certain segments of the auditing business. Or you may want to learn from your international exposure how to improve the value proposition to the client. And it is not that hard to imagine that the underlying strategy and organization for achieving these different types of benefit should look quite different.

- Second, we do not expect all companies in all industries *equally* to take advantage of international presence. We strongly recommend that you specify and assess the importance of the benefits in *your* business and company. Clients who are setting up international offices may want to work with their supplier base across borders, so you must ask yourself how important that is for your business with these clients. Look at the temporary work services business: we keep hearing about the growing demand for cross-border contracts between temp agencies and client companies as a basis for the rapid internationalization and consolidation of the temporary work services industry in Europe and even globally. Looking beyond the surface, however, shows us that the 'old' style local contracts still count for 95% of the turnover in this business and will remain so for a long time to come, and questions the importance of following the clients to international markets. As a temp agency, would it not be powerful to know *to what extent* internationalization on the basis of clients' international initiatives actually makes sense?

- The previous example also indicates the importance of timing: the fruit may be low hanging for some, but high up in the tree for others. How urgent is internationalization, really? There is a vast difference between a strong strategic imperative to be international now, as in the aircraft manufacturing business, or an ambition to grow to a European or global competitor and eventually reach for some of that fruit – as in certain segments of the insurance or catering services industry. While numerous companies want us to believe that they *have* to be international today, some of them may *want* to be cosmopolitan more than they have to. Not that being ambitious is a dishonour or a bad thing or that paving the way for long-term benefits is foolish. But management should be aware that their growth ambition is driving the internationalization efforts in the first place and the real dividends of it will show up only after a significant time span. And they should not fool their shareholders, clients, employees and ultimately themselves by spreading the news that they had no choice but to go abroad today.

Once you have specified exactly *where* the benefit is, how *important* it is, and what *time horizon* it will take to cash in on it, you also will have learned what could be a good way to enter a country, and what international strategy and organization to draw on. The *why* part of internationalization helps to fill in key parameters on the *what* part – what markets to focus on,

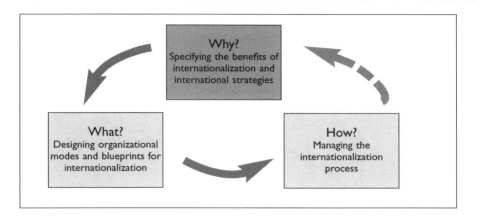

**Figure 2.1** The why of internationalization

what entry mode, strategy and organization to use and eventually the optimal path to take, the *process* or *how* part, which we will discuss in Chapter 5 (see Figure 2.1).

In this chapter, we present a simple framework to help you to understand how internationalization can add value to your company. However, do not expect ready-for-implementation answers to all your questions. We consider the contribution of our framework as an incentive to look beneath the surface and beyond what one can read and hear every day in newspapers and public announcements; as an aid to structuring a profound strategic debate about internationalization; and as an indicator to the real underlying strategic questions and dimensions when internationalizing.

Based on our examination of many different situations, we have found it useful to distinguish between the three main types of potential benefits from internationalizing: *cost advantages (co)*, *network benefits (ne)* and *learning opportunities (learn)*, simply called the *Conelearn* framework. It can be visualized as in Figure 2.2.

We will first discuss the horizontal and vertical axes, cost advantages and network benefits, and indicate how they steer international strategies and the need for cross-border integration. Later we will add the third axis, learning opportunities, and indicate the intrinsically different nature of this internationalization benefit. We will apply the framework in a more detailed way to the European context, and elaborate on the role of the regional perspective relevant in managing multinationals in the global context.

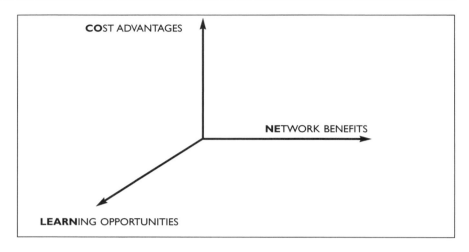

**Figure 2.2** The Conelearn framework

## Cost advantages

Let us first have a look at cost advantages. These refer to the efficiency aspects of the business: how can you build a superior cost position from being an international company? What are the positive effects of international operations on your cost base? The importance of the potential cost drivers, which you could not exploit by staying local, are depicted on the vertical axis of the framework.

More specifically, the cost advantages of internationalization can come from:

- Economies of scale

- Better use of capacity

- Better access to inputs

- Moving down on learning (cost) curve

- Applying existing concepts and formulas in foreign markets.

### Economies of scale

By far the most frequently heard cost advantage is *economies of scale*. This classical business concept refers to the assumption that companies may be able to lower their costs, more specifically the cost per unit produced or delivered, by working on a larger scale. Traditionally, scale economies were particularly subsumed in a production environment. As long as the marginal cost of an extra unit produced decreased, it made economic sense for the company to increase production. However, scale economies are manifest in other functions as well: especially in technology intensive businesses that require considerable investments in fixed assets, writing off the fixed cost base over more output units is availing. In the pharmaceutical industry, R&D is subject to scale benefits, and in service businesses, the marketing scale can be sensitive to economies.

Scale economies could represent an imperative for developing international coverage, when the domestic market is too small to reap the advantages. The important criterion for internationalization is therefore not only the minimum efficient scale (MES) in itself, but the required size compared to the relevant market. Some bigger national markets may suffice to produce or develop efficiently, while smaller geographic areas will not. Take the example of car production: the current technology in the car industry does not allow a company to produce efficiently state-of-the-art cars for most local or national markets only. Far greater amounts need to be produced than most markets can absorb in order to reap optimal scale economies. In some industries, however, the developments in technology have led to smaller scale operating units, for example micro-brewing installations in beer or mini-mills in steel production, that could compete in smaller geographic markets.

However, we should point out that important limitations seem to impede reaping scale economies to their full extent. Differences in customer tastes, and regulations, to name only two, might force you to adapt products or services to the local requirements. Imagine how many scale economies a mass consumer goods company such as Procter & Gamble or Unilever could achieve from producing the same packaging and formula of laundry detergents in every country around the globe. Unfortunately, the scale economies for their packaging and detergent production are restricted by the local prerequisites in the market. One way out of this dilemma is to standardize certain parts of a product, to allow use of the same part in different models or segments. That is what happened in PC production and assembly: they created standard platforms and built on plug compatible modules.

Given the market limitations, it should be clear that scale economies could most easily be achieved in the domestic market. For example, Fortis, the financial services group active in Benelux, has focused on gaining critical mass in its home market first. Its recent acquisition of 'Stad

Rotterdam Verzekeringen' in the insurance business gives the group a better platform for its insurance business in the Netherlands, and probably gives better chances for realizing synergies than acquiring an insurance player abroad. In fact, Fortis has also started to divest some of its businesses in the US. In general, the many domestic banking mergers in the US and even within small European countries (in the wake of Europe 1992 and the euro introduction), such as Belgium, Denmark, Sweden and Spain, may allow scale economies to be realized first closer to home, rather than with cross-border constructions. At first sight, these strategies seem to make sense, to the extent that substantial scale economies exist, which is a questionable general proposition in itself.

However, scale will need to be managed effectively. Bigger scale is not automatically equal to lower unit cost: good management will ensure the translation of size to a better overall cost position. We will elaborate on the limitations in the market below and the need for managing the benefits in Chapters 3, 4 and 5.

## Capacity utilization

Another cost advantage of internationalization can be found in superior *capacity utilization*. While this may at first sight look similar to scale economies, it is a conceptually different cost advantage. Capacity utilization refers to the degree to which the capacity is used. It stipulates to what extent the fixed costs of the capacity have been exploited. For example, a unit can produce 5,000 bottles of glass a day, but today it only produces 3,000. This means that the capacity is not fully used, regardless of its optimal size. In that scenario, the fixed costs of the 2,000 bottles need to be paid, whether they are produced or not. The conveyor belts and the packaging machine may not be working today, but you still pay a price, if only through the initial investment costs. By conquering international markets, you may find a market for the remaining 2,000 bottles and hence improve the overall cost position.

Let us examine the 'capacity trap': on the one hand it is beneficial to fill up the capacity through internationalizing, on the other hand there is a need to question why you started with unused capacity in the first place. This is not just a 'chicken and egg' problem. Was the capacity there first and should we therefore internationalize, or was there simply an overcapacity problem from the start that we are trying to hide or shift out of the way? Buying Leyland in the UK was not a solution for DAF's production capacity problem, neither was Paccar's (US) purchase of DAF later. It just added the capacity in two different geographic markets.

Especially in a cyclical business, companies may want to internationalize in order to optimize their use of capacity. The conditions are that the market and demand cycles in different national markets should not be perfectly correlated, and the capacity or its output can be shifted to the foreign markets. European steel companies often use export as a buffer for produced but unsold steel or unused production capacity. The foreign markets ensure that when orders from the regular clients slow down, they can still keep producing at almost full speed, and ship the produced steel at a, hopefully, acceptable price abroad.

Here too, external limitations can make it hard to fill up capacity with production for foreign markets, as the product requirements in non-domestic markets could be different.

## Access to input factors

An argument which at first sight seems to be of changing relevance in the developing global economy is the necessity to ensure *access to key input factors*. In the early days of industrialization, companies set up international operations because they needed better or cheaper access to key production factors. The location of traditional steel factories was to a large extent driven by the geographical distance from iron ore sources or easy transportation of coal to the particular location by water or railway systems.

The importance of this benefit has diminished in its traditional meaning. State-of-the-art distribution modes of tangible goods, falling trade barriers and lower transportation costs have in many sectors made it less pressing to be close to your suppliers or input sources. Only in oil and gas exploration do you need to be close to the oil fields, which explains the rush of some major and smaller Western oil companies, including Norway's Statoil, to look for deals in Russia and other oil-rich former Soviet republics.

Recently, access to cheap labour has become a major driver in the internationalization of many companies across a variety of (presumably labour-intensive) sectors. Labour is not perfectly mobile and hence still a reason for internationalization: Western companies ship their fish, such as shrimps, to be cleaned in Asia and transport the cleaned fish back to Western markets. Textile production is spread all over the world, from Eastern Europe, Asia to Latin America. A labour-intensive job can be performed more cheaply in those countries, which makes up for the transportation costs, therefore some of those fish or textile companies set up foreign subsidiaries in Asia. Cheap, skilled manpower has driven many software companies to work with Indian engineers, and even to establish a local subsidiary there.

A decision on relocation should be made on a broader set of relevant cost factors and over a longer time frame. Easy access to cheap labour is only one part of the overall cost picture. Cheap labour may have much lower productivity, making it more efficient in the long run to produce in Western countries. Or the cost base of labour is outweighed either by the transportation costs of the input factors and finished goods from and to their marketplace, or by increasing costs in other parts of the business system.

Also, many sources of cheap labour dry up as a result of the competition and increasing level of development in those countries. In fact, casual observations offer many examples of the temporary nature of these advantages, such as the sharp increase in wages and location costs in Ireland, especially Dublin, where many companies recently moved part of their operations.

Or take the example shown recently in a fascinating BBC documentary of a major Canadian textile manufacturer, bringing together different pieces from all over the world, based on the relative labour costs and availability of raw material, from shearing the wool in New Zealand and Australia, spinning it in India, and manufacturing the basic parts in China. The button was the only part still made in Canada! The company subsequently shipped the components to Hamburg, for assembly first in Eastern Germany, then Romania, then Russia, and when Moscow became too expensive and corrupt, it had to move even further east, only to be closely followed by its competitors who have about a six-months time lag in catching up with this company in finding the cheapest country. One wonders what will happen in six months time – while continuing to move east, will the company end up manufacturing back in Canada? Of course not, but this case illustrates vividly the limits of short-term labour costs related to internationalization. In addition, it also made abundantly clear how this kind of advantage, beyond its temporary nature, cannot be a source of sustainable advantage as these lower costs are equally available to competitors in the same business.

More academic studies have also been trying to take a more strategic long-term view on this question. Some of these studies have evaluated, for example, the relocation of the US car industry across the border into Mexico, and other places (US Congress, 1992, 1993). They showed that the net benefits of relocation are questionable, when taking into account all costs and barriers, such as start-up costs, the cost of managing a new faraway plant and the local quality, the lack of knowledge and skills that needs to be compensated for or built up over time, the cost of logistics and the dynamic effect of rising costs in the location.

In the new economy, however, a new type of strategic production factor has come to the fore. The input factors that certain companies want to ensure better access to are increasingly of a more intangible nature, such as information or expertise. It is exactly because the market for know-how and expertise is imperfect, incomplete or opaque, due to the intrinsic characteristics of the market, regulative restrictions and other barriers, that this cost driver still has certain validity. Reliable information is acquired more readily and more reliably locally than from afar (Rangan, 2000).

The 'valley' syndrome, representing a cluster of related companies that are located next to each other, such as Silicon Valley, is based on the hypothesis that it is meaningful to be 'where the action or expertise is'. Even in a 'global economy' with few barriers to the free flow of goods and services, and decreasing transportation costs, location may still count. 'At this point geography matters' wrote Fred Hiatt in a *Washington Post* article (6 October 1999), thereby exploring the paradox that, even for increasingly intangible sources of competitive advantage, location does seem to matter. This brings us to the next major source of advantage: the learning curve cost advantage.

## Learning curve

Microeconomists have also emphasized extensively the *learning curve* phenomenon. This cost advantage incorporates the decline in costs as a company gets more accumulated units produced or delivered. The learning curve visualizes the cost advantages of a company that masters its technology and systems, improves the technology, and makes it more cost efficient.[1] Internationalization can, and hopefully will, increase your output, and as a consequence make you move faster on the learning curve (Figure 2.3).

The importance of accumulating output in order to ride down the curve first has been translated into the need to have the highest market share. Going for volume through international sales can help you to bypass the limitations of the home market in building up learning curve effects and hence move from the domestic to the global game. Although finding a pure example of the learning curve effects driving internationalization is not obvious – except maybe for the Japanese companies entering the US motor-cycling business – we do believe that in some production environments, where scale and capacity utilization were the main drivers for internationalization, such as the truck manufacturing industry, it may have been a beneficial side effect of internationalizing.

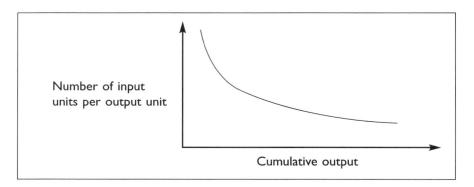

**Figure 2.3** Generic learning curve

Note that the learning curve effect, which is *cost* related, is intrinsically different from what we will define under the third axis in our Conelearn framework as learning. The question there is how internationalization can help you to speed up your learning process in a different, more general way.

## Applying concepts across borders

Another cost driver refers to the ability to copy or leverage an existing concept, formula or system to other markets. It allows a company to recoup some of the investments in a concept, formula or system – many of which are sunk any way – by copying it to other markets and writing the expenses off over a bigger total market.

Although there are limits to the ability to copy systems (as illustrated below) it seems that, particularly in service businesses, this has been a key bonus of internationalization. The assets and resources leveraged across country borders are mostly tangible one way or another, for example in the form of patents or franchise systems. How can a retail chain of hamburgers, beauty products, shoes or even a shoe repair shop take advantage of their international network? McDonald's is not just a hamburger restaurant and The Body Shop, Brantano, Mr. Minit and Kinepolis are not just retail chains. McDonald's is a concept that has been built around fast delivery of a hamburger menu within a certain environment, atmosphere and pricing. The factors that distinguish McDonald's from other restaurants are not the hamburger itself but the characteristics that you find in every single McDonald's around the world, despite their attempts to localize their product offers to local tastes. They have found the formula to successfully leverage their business model across the world, without any major adaptations. Even at the other end of the food market, top chefs such as Ducasse have successfully managed to leverage a proven top-class restaurant concept across borders.

The Body Shop, as a distribution concept of environmentally friendly health and beauty products, has done a similar thing. Brantano, the Belgian shoe retail company, is in the process of copying its marketing concept in the UK and Denmark. The concept of selling fashionable shoes, of good quality for a competitive price, in large shops outside the city centres, seems to catch on in different countries. Mr. Minit, the instant repair shop of shoes and other services, started by an American visitor in Belgium, whose wife was ruining her shoes on the Brussels cobblestones, ended up leveraging its store concept successfully across many countries, expanding into lock services, number plates, business cards and so on. Kinepolis, the Belgian cinema company that according to some reinvented the movie experience (Kim and Mauborgne, 1997), is similarly turning its investments in the cinema concept to work across Europe, although it has recently run into some problems, precisely because it went outside the logic of its original business formula (*Financieel Economische Tijd*, 31 August 1999).

These businesses presume that there is a market for these standardized concepts and formulas. The marketing literature seems to confirm that the days of the 'horizontal world' are coming (Kinnear, 2000): the winners in global business will be those who focus on market segments defined by consumer needs and not geographic criteria. The size of these segments may in some countries simply not be sufficient to address them profitably, but the global segment could justify the required investments and focus, as in the case of Ferrari and Porsche.

The existence of these horizontal segments may provide exactly the opportunities for the above-mentioned companies to copy their systems and concepts across borders, using global brands even in the local market. The management of the concept and particularly of the brand that goes with it should, nevertheless, be handled with care. It has been suggested that even for these companies it may not be optimal to work with a uniform concept or one single brand identity across markets (Aaker and Joachimsthaler, 2000). One reason for that is the market differences across nations.

Companies such as these should be aware of the limitations of duplicating concepts, formulas and systems. There are ample reasons, ranging from legal, social, cultural, legislative to language differences, why a concept may not be completely copied to another market, and why horizontal segments are not the rule – yet – but probably more of an exception (see the discussion on limitations below).

## Network benefits

Network benefits, the horizontal axis in the Conelearn framework, cover the advantages to clients of having an international supplier. How important is it for your clients to know that they will be able to draw from your service and product range around the globe? The benefit for you, as the international supplier, is derived from the value to the client of having global access to your offer. Network benefits refer to the importance for your business to 'be where the client is'. Financial services provider HSBC advertises: 'Wherever you are in the world, wherever you are in your life, HSBC will be there for you.'

Network benefits are situated more on the income side than on the cost side. Network benefits are *pulling* you towards the foreign markets, while cost advantages are *pushing* towards internationalization. While you will more frequently find network benefits in a business-to-business environment – that is where clients are 'international' themselves – we do find a number of examples in a business-to-consumer context, particularly for those businesses that focus on the market segment of the 'global travellers'.

Being international is for some – mostly service – businesses the essence of the value proposition to the client. Take for example American Express: one of the key success factors in the credit card business lies in the international network and acceptance of the card across different nations. Each of us, as an individual card holder, has an interest in the international network of Amex. It is because we value the credit card company to be omnipresent that Amex needs to build, and benefit from, its network.

You find other examples of network benefits in the parcel delivery service business and telecom industry – linking the international activities of AT&T and BT in Concert, or Deutsche Telekom's ambition to

> make sure the German business woman can go on a trip to New York via London and have her mobile phone working in all these places. (*Business Week*, 4 December 2000)

Portals consider it key to have international coverage as well:

> Suppose an e-commerce company that sells French wine wants the best distribution possible. The wine seller could do separate deals with different portal

firms in each country, but that would be time consuming and inefficient. (*Fortune*, 12 June 2000)

International hotel chains are after network benefits as well. Business men, which may be one of the horizontal market segments that cut through nations, love to find a Novotel or Hilton in their various business destinations. The customer's search cost for a hotel bed in the various destinations decreases as he or she can find the hotel close to the airport or highway, and already knows what service, for example the room's outlook and luxury level, restaurant facilities, price range, to expect from a Novotel or Hilton.

In the TV broadcasting business, CNN is a good example of a company that leverages its network internationally. The target market of CNN is mainly the international business traveller and the horizontal segment of the market that is interested in world news around the clock: CNN International should therefore be available around the world, and ensure a global network of journalists. Does this mean that all TV channels should be internationally available? Probably not, unless their strategy is to focus on that particular segment of the total world market and address this audience with a certain type of programme. Only then, international presence becomes a substantial part of the positioning, as for CNN or the BBC World Service. Even CNN has now supplemented its 'global' or 'international' offering with regional and local-language programming in Europe. And many local TV channels have been launched as a reaction to the CNN approach, serving different needs and/or reaching a different segment of the market.

Network benefits mostly entail a standardized product or service across the different countries. It helps Hilton to have worldwide presence, but only if they fall back on the same system and standard package of services, prices and food range. Looking at it that way, network benefits on the client side often go hand in hand with a cost benefit for the supplier. But this relationship does not work the other way around: it is not because you standardize your product offering across countries that you reap network benefits. McDonald's is not reaping network benefits, as most customers are buying burgers in one city, region or country anyway and only a small segment of travellers appreciate their international network. The change of brand name in the Belgian market from 'Smith's' to 'Lay's' chips by Frito Lay (part of Pepsico Group) was defended by the fact that 'customers could from now on also find the same chips with the same brand name in Germany' (*De Standaard*, 9 January 2001). As if there are major network benefits in the chips business.

On closer inspection, network benefits should not be taken for granted, not even in the businesses mentioned above. John Kay argued that the model of network externalities, in which the company that is first to create the largest network denies access to competitors and establishes an unassailable monopoly, is in most cases only a theoretical possibility, except maybe for Microsoft. The only cases of it happening, according to him, seem to be those in which governments have imposed it (*Financial Times*, 23 August 2000). American Express may not need to cover the whole world itself, but could work with partners globally to ensure interconnectivity. Deutsche Telekom should not necessarily buy a US and UK company to service the German travelling business woman. What if she changes her mind at the last minute, and decides to fly to Paris, rather than London: should DT then buy a French mobile phone operator? This interconnectivity argument is, however, more about *how* to ensure that you offer clients more than just a local network, than about the existence of network benefits in itself.

Lately, we have noticed the development of unconventional international organizations aiming explicitly for the networking benefits without necessarily fully internalizing the network. Nexia is an alliance of local auditing and accounting companies, and Eureko is an alliance of European insurers. A number of European newspapers, some of them with a focused section on job advertising and HR news, joined forces in August 1999 to build a European database of vacancies and job applications, available on a website. The strength of these organizations' proposition towards clients is in the broadness of the network in combination with strong local brands and presence (we will elaborate on these and other ways to internationalize and capture network benefits in Chapter 3).

Even in the credit card business, it is not a given that you should have access to an international network. When applying for a credit card in France, you have the choice of a French or an international one. Not all hotels base their value proposition to their membership in an international chain, nor do all newspapers have a global reach, like the *Financial Times* or *The Wall Street Journal*. Offering a global network should be an integrated part of your overall strategic positioning and targeted at specific portions of the market. Network benefits may not be attractive to all segments of the market, at all times, and the global segment, although growing, may not be that big.

It is certainly not enough to have international clients to call for network benefits as an incentive for becoming international yourself. A precondition for network benefits to materialize is that clients appropriate value to an international offering from suppliers. In the financial services industry, banks seem to have a strong desire to follow their clients across borders, like HSBC. But the average retail customer of ABN AMRO, heavily advertised as the 'global network bank' for a while, does not or should not care about offices in Hong Kong or Brazil. Furthermore, would they be willing to pay a premium for this global network that will not deliver them any specific value? This is of course not the case for investment banks or large corporations to which their advertising apparently was aimed. Other financial services providers, such as the Dutch–Belgian Fortis, have tailored their investments in an international network to the needs of their corporate or private banking clients close to home.

The mere existence of a network will obviously not do the job. Will your offer to the client be more attractive, better or cheaper because of your international network? How do you make the client pay for the network that you have built up? While a lot of attention, energy and resources have been deployed on expansion, one should be very clear about what clients are expecting and what they are really getting from it. This should be carefully tested and built upon.

And last but not least, can you actually deliver a network benefit to the client? Saatchi & Saatchi, for example, built their empire in the 1980s on the real or perceived demand of clients to have an international advertising agency that could develop advertising in multiple countries, while keeping local adaptations to the concrete advertising themes. Of course, *delivering* this benefit to the client requires organizational mechanisms and capabilities, which not all networking organizations and particularly not Saatchi & Saatchi in those days seemed to be able to produce. We will return later to this organizational and managerial challenge in Sections 2 and 3.

## Cone and international strategies

The unique feature of the cost advantages and network benefits (Cone) is that their presence and relative level should allow you to evaluate the added value of international presence, and provide guidance on the appropriate international strategy and level of coordination and integration between the international activities.

We are acquainted with the success stories of one-size-fits-all products and brands: Coca-Cola has for many years been the ultimate example of a 'global product', although even this image has shown its limits as we will discuss below. The same Gillette razor blades, such as the new 'Mach3', are sold in Thailand and Argentina, and advertised similarly in Frankfurt and Washington.

Others tried out a similar approach: Ford built the Mondeo, literally a world car, but quickly experienced problems and shortcomings in their international strategy. You surely know other stories about advertising campaigns and product launches that failed because they were not adapted to the local culture and habits of consumers in different countries and parts of the world. Entire books have been published on these and other international marketing 'blunders' (Ricks, 1999; Mitchell, 2001). Even globally successful companies such as Marlboro failed in South America with their cowboy campaign because it was 'too American'. The Japanese design of cars was not well received by the European public, being considered 'too Asian and too little European'.

Others tailor their offering very specifically to the local market requirements: the laundry detergents of Procter & Gamble were marketed in France in bigger package sizes than in the Netherlands, due to the different consumer buying habits. Unilever could only sell its shampoos in India in simple mini-size, which was designed as travel size for the Western market. Amazom.com has a German website with German as well as international content.

These examples illustrate the subtlety of the localization–globalization balance in the product offers, advertising and ultimately the overall strategy of a company. You can decide to have one single standardized or *global* strategy in all the countries you operate in: you produce homogeneous products, use the same advertising, the packaging is uniform, the price is equivalent. Ikea uses a uniform retail concept and product range all over the world: 'One furniture store fits all' (*Financial Times*, 8 February 2001).

Alternatively, you focus on your local market and tailor your offering specifically to the local requirements: you go for a *local* strategy. In the European beer industry, several local British, German and Belgian brewers successfully sell their beers only to the local population, in their own city, county or province. Their craft has survived the industrialization, competition and acquisition hunger of some of the larger brewers.

Others have a more international coverage, but still adapt their product to the local preferences; the advertising theme and marketing mix change from one country to another; the packaging contains four products here and ten in another country, is red here and orange there; and the price is 20% higher in Northern Europe than in Southern Europe. This other extreme is the so-called *multi-local* or *multinational* strategy (Figure 2.4).

These stereotypes simplify the total spectrum of available international strategies. A strategy where every single activity, task, or process is standardized across the different geographies is often not realistic. Even Coca-Cola changes its product composition slightly from one part of the world to the other – more cherry here, less sweet there – and has differentiated pricing policies. All the more reason to understand what aspects of the

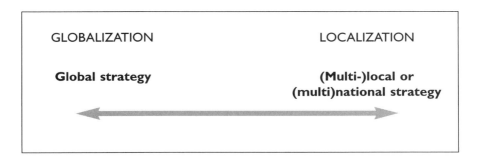

**Figure 2.4** International strategy prototypes

company's strategy and activities *can* or *should* be standardized and what *needs* to be adapted to the local peculiarities.

On the other hand, a collection of purely local strategies cannot obtain any of the Cone advantages outlined above. 3M Europe realized that its multi-local strategy was inefficient in producing and developing new products and left its clients' demand for cross-border delivery unanswered.

In between the two extremes on the global–local continuum, you offset different degrees of standardization in some activities with varying proportions of local shades. The daily reality of markets and companies with their global *and* local traits prompts more elaborate and nuanced typologies of international strategies[2] (Calori et al., 2000). The art is to balance at the right time the right extent of global–local in the right place in the organization. A thorough understanding of the market and analysis of the various pressures for cost and network benefits across the business system, and the dynamics and rate of change in the Cone force field, will certainly contribute to finding the appropriate equilibrium.

However, do not expect the 'correct' international strategy to be defined by the analysis itself. The analysis does not deliver unidimensional conclusions. There is no simple 'right or wrong' answer to the question of how global your strategy should be: you need to constantly weigh the various tensions at hand with incomplete information; define your position in the market based on your market vision; aim at understanding the critical success factors for that position; and manage the balance and trade-off. However, assessing cost and network pressures in what we will call the international playing field and their changing nature should help us in the process.

In addition, many external and internal barriers may prevent us from reaping and delivering the benefits to the market. To the internal organizational barriers, we will return later, especially in Chapter 5. We discuss below, in more detail, the external barriers or constraints on the globalization potential in our business. This is what defining the *international playing field* is all about.

## The international playing field

The balancing act heeds on the one hand the pressures for more standardization and coordination in different geographies, the so-called *globalization potential*, and on the other hand the many *limitations* on globalization, such as different national cultures, diverse regulations and languages, and other localization pressures inviting a more multi-local approach. The optimal degree of globalization harvests the maximum globalization potential, taking into account the globalization limits and localization pressures.

The globalization potential is the opportunity space defined by the amount of cost advantages and network benefits as identified in the Cone framework (Figure 2.5). The more cost advantages and network benefits available from international operations, the higher the pressure and potential to globalize the strategy.

Imagine international *learning curve* cost advantages, or chances to improve the utilization of your production *capacity* or the existence of *economies of scale* through internationalization, in whatever part of your business; each of these cost drivers will constitute a conclusive urge to standardize the operations in the respective part of your value chain. Without this standardization, the cost advantages risk getting lost. One can hardly move quickly on the learning curve, or use its capacity better if the products need to be adapted or changed for every geography. PC

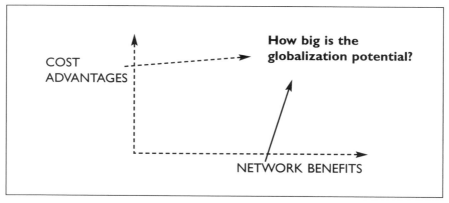

**Figure 2.5** The globalization potential in the Cone(learn) framework

companies can clearly reap economies of scale in production and purchasing, and use their production capacity more effectively in an international environment. The cost benefits further stimulate these companies to produce PCs that are as standardized or modularized as possible, with as few changes for the different geographies as one can manage. Hence there is considerable *globalization potential* for a PC producer. A similar rationale applies to the ability to recoup sunk costs by *copying systems and concepts* across borders. The more you feel you can leverage the investments made in systems and concepts across borders, the more stimulus there is to just 'copy', with little alterations.

The more customers value a supplier's international presence – *network benefits* – the bigger the potential to standardize the customer offering. Why would customers want your company to deliver internationally and prefer your product to a local competitor's product? Because they value buying the same or at least a similar product or service from you around the world. Clients know what to expect in Novotel, no matter where they check in: rooms look similar, the services are meant to be universal, positioning and prices will be comparable and so will the restaurants and types of food offered. The more the customer motivates you to be everywhere he is, the more it increases the potential to standardize all or part of your strategy in the international scene.

In other words: the more you see opportunities for adding value by internationalization, through cost advantages and/or network benefits, the more you will feel a need to standardize the strategy. A standardized approach to the market will maximize the cost advantages and network benefits (see Figure 2.6).

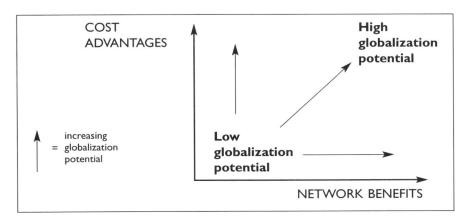

**Figure 2.6** The globalization potential

However, opportunities for complete standardization of the (functional) strategy(ies) are rare in real life. Various *globalization limits* often limit the benefits from harmonizing the company's strategy. The obligation to localize may find its roots in the specific and different customer behaviour and preferences across markets, or in the various external limits to globalization. The legal and regulative environment might be intrinsically distinct, what type of advertising is allowed, what norms are applicable to our products and services, what permits are required to do business in the market. Language differences impact the ability to standardize packaging or advertising. Cultural differences and varying social habits can influence the image and role of your product and service across nations. Adapting to these idiosyncrasies in national markets, however subtle they may actually be, is crucial in order to penetrate or develop a market.

The potential for globalization can intrinsically be tremendous because of the significant cost advantages and network benefits from standardization but simply unrealizable because of the differences in regulations, customer needs, language and so on. A recent study by AT Kearny confirmed the significance of market limitations in capturing the cross-border cost benefits, in very specific areas of the business, in the European insurance industry. While companies seem to understand the benefits, which according to the study account for as much as 5 billion euros per year in non-life insurance only, they have made little progress in achieving pan-European integration:

> Contrary to the widely held belief that roadblocks to integration are primarily related to legal and legacy systems, the insurance giants ranked language, cultural barriers and social constraints as the main factors keeping them from maximizing their efficiency. (AT Kearny, 2001)

While some of these limitations may have an internal company component as well (we will return to this in Chapter 5), clearly the language and cultural differences across European markets limit the insurance companies in their ability to capitalize on international scale.

How Ford would love to sell a uniform car around the world, as they tried with the Mondeo. Besides the regulatory differences, consumers seem to have different expectations from a car in different parts of the world and attribute different value to various aspects such as engine power, design, reliability, durability, safety and so on.

Globalization limits will obstruct the maximum degree of globalization: transverse lines on the Cone axes indicate the constraints on the cost and network advantages and hence show the maximum realizable globalization potential (Figure 2.7).

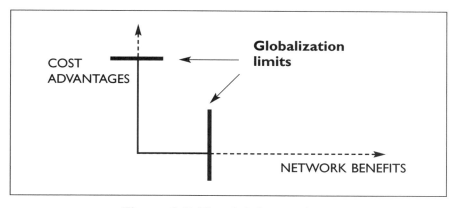

**Figure 2.7** The globalization limits

When integrating the globalization potential and limits on the Cone dimensions, the boundaries of the playing field within which the company can define its international strategy emerge. The maximum degree of globalization one can realistically achieve within the context of the market limits is indicated by the upper right corner of the *international playing field* (Figure 2.8).

Inside the international playing field you leave potential cost or network benefits on the table. Of course, you could decide to deliberately ignore part of the cost advantages, network benefits or both, as in positions A, B or

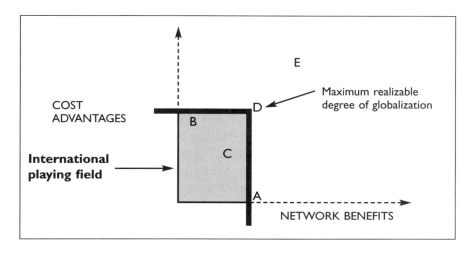

**Figure 2.8** International playing field

C respectively. The other extreme, depicted by position E, is not optimal either: you overestimate the network and cost benefits, and will hence over-standardize your strategy and products. If we assume that companies want to maximize the globalization potential, while remaining within the limits in the market, the optimal international strategy is indicated on the edge of the international playing field by position D. There you combine cost and network benefits according to their existence and importance, and the relevant limitations, and you benefit from the maximum realizable degree of globalization.[3] While the resulting graph presents a useful composite picture to visualize the analytical discussion of the internationalization benefits, we now want to go into more detail.

## Analysis to a fine level of detail

Nobody has ever disputed that some industries have and should have more international and global presence than others. While the car industry has very few pure national players, the catering services business has a very different balance of smaller, local players and bigger multinational service providers. The Cone benefits and the size of the international playing field in both businesses explain why: cost advantages in the car industry such as economies of scale and capacity utilization force companies to operate internationally, while the cost and network benefits in the catering services business are much less persuasive.

Cone analysis at industry level should reveal to what extent the cost and network pressures are an industry-wide phenomenon. If they are, you could expect most, if not all, companies in that particular industry to be forced to internationalize and globalize sooner or later. Truly industry-wide benefits are typically found on the cost axis: in airplane production, for example, the only way to survive and be able to compete is through global strategies, mainly due to cost reasons. It *is* a matter of 'internationalizing or dying' in this business.

However, there is no reason why all companies in an industry should have the same learning curve, minimum efficiency scale, capacity to be filled, or clients that value as much international delivery. The economics of the business permitting, in many industries there are different segments of clients to be defined on the basis of the international network advantages to be achieved (network axis). This means that in many industries there is a lot of room left for strategic choice and different positioning. Why would we assume our competitor's internationalization initiatives to be right for us as well?[4] Indeed it is not hard to find examples of competent local or regional niche players outcompeting global giants in most industries, even in industries once considered prime targets for global consolidation (Kanter, 1995).

The PC market is dominated by large-scale producers such as Compaq, IBM, Dell, Hewlett-Packard and Packard Bell. Still, a number of smaller producers have managed to build up a considerable position in national markets, and yield decent profits. Cibox in France, Maxdata in Germany, Tiny and Viglen in the UK compete successfully in a market dominated by price competition and the resultant thin margins. The CEO of Viglen, a company that receives one third of its income from sales of PCs to schools and universities, paraphrased its strategy: 'The watchword for a company like us is: Get niche or get out' (*Fortune*, 6 March 2000).

Large-scale academic research by Roth and Morrison (1990) has found that in what were considered global industries, industries where the pressures for global coordination of activities are paramount, companies with a (multi-)local strategy exist and can be successful. According to the data, the multi-local companies were even outperforming other companies in the sample in terms of profitability. Local strategies succeeded despite the globalization pressures because their business system and organization were tailored to the needs of local companies. According to the researchers, the local companies had selected profitability over growth. Maybe there is no such thing as global industries. You may only find global and local *companies* in industries that have typically slightly more or less globalization potential.

The accounting and auditing services are a good example of how the Cone drivers differ by player and strategy. The big five auditing companies are globally present and expect multinational clients to appreciate the network benefits of working with the same auditing and accounting office around the globe, and of coordinating the accounting practices of the different corporations in the client group. But what about the local accountant who ensures the accuracy of the books of local dentists, doctors, bakeries and newspaper shops?

Why did we recently see a number of industrial bakeries internationalize, while the bakery industry is seen as traditionally artisan and local, not internationalized, and definitely not globalized? Despite some minor cost advantages – some economies of scale in purchasing and production – and network benefits – international supermarket chains know the bakery's brand and like to contain the relationship across borders – the globalization limits in this business are perceived to be much stronger as the tastes for bread may differ from one city to another. The industrial bakeries are, however, in a 'different business' from the local artisan baker: they concentrate on a specific segment in the bakery business where standardized products will be accepted and tastes differ much less between neighbouring countries. Those industrial bakeries will supply these retail and supermarket chains which can and will complement their product range with local specialties and pastries, and adopt and exploit the configuration and operationalization of their value chain accordingly.

Potential cost drivers and network benefits may differ by functions and activities within the value chain, representing the different value adding activities that a company performs. Looking at the domestic appliances manufacturing chain in detail reveals considerable cost advantages in R&D, sourcing and production. The R&D budgets 'ought' to be written off over as many output units as possible and leveraged worldwide. The economies of scale in production are paramount, while the final products should differ substantially from one market to another, for example front versus top loading washing machines or large versus small refrigerators. The compromise often lies in modularizing the machines, such as Whirlpool did: this allows for a certain level of standardization and foresees opportunities to tailor products to the consumer preferences 'at the end of the chain'. In marketing and sales, local presence and responsiveness is key. Nevertheless, some of the bigger distribution chains started to buy cross border from the appliance producers, delivering network benefits down the value chain. However, in the after-sales services, strong local presence and maintenance still make a big difference.

This explains why Kingfisher, the UK retailing group that recently went through a dramatic internationalization phase, kept the local brand name and store that they acquired. It also raises the question as to where exactly the benefits of their internationalization strategy, initially perceived as very successful,[5] were to be found, especially given the rather local management approach, exploiting locality and diversity.

Figure 2.9 gives a more elaborate illustration of how the key cost and network pressures across Ford's value chain may have looked.[6] Clearly there is significant pressure for cost, particularly for capacity utilization and scale, in design and production, whereas the network benefits seem to be present more in sales and service.

This also perfectly illustrates how the cost advantages are typically more important in the upstream activities – such as R&D and production, while network benefits are more prevalent in the downstream activities. This explains why companies typically standardize 'what the customer cannot see', purchasing, production, R&D, rather than the other activities in the value chain, typically marketing, sales and servicing.

In the pharmaceutical industry, for example, the scale economies that justified many of the recent global M&As in the sector are mainly on the R&D and maybe the production side, and much less prevalent in distri-

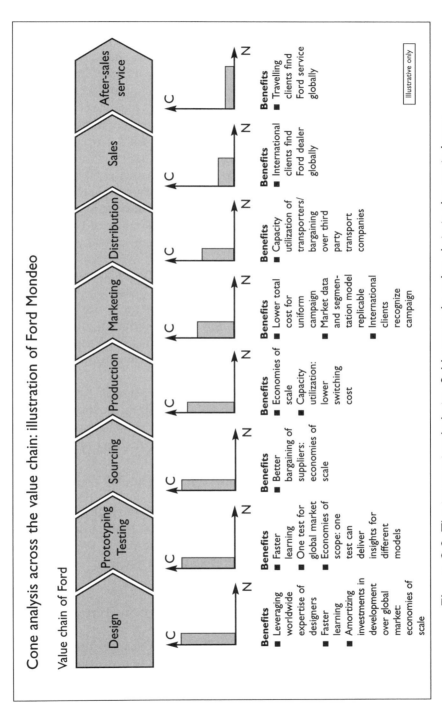

**Cone analysis across the value chain: illustration of Ford Mondeo**

Value chain of Ford

| Design | Prototyping Testing | Sourcing | Production | Marketing | Distribution | Sales | After-sales service |

**Design**

**Benefits**
- Leveraging worldwide expertise of designers
- Faster learning
- Amortizing investments in development over global market: economies of scale

**Prototyping Testing**

**Benefits**
- Faster learning
- One test for global market
- Economies of scope: one test can deliver insights for different models

**Sourcing**

**Benefits**
- Better bargaining of suppliers: economies of scale

**Production**

**Benefits**
- Economies of scale
- Capacity utilization: lower switching cost

**Marketing**

**Benefits**
- Lower total cost for uniform campaign
- Market data and segmentation model replicable
- International clients recognize campaign

**Distribution**

**Benefits**
- Capacity utilization of transporters/ bargaining over third party transport companies

**Sales**

**Benefits**
- International clients find Ford dealer globally

**After-sales service**

**Benefits**
- Travelling clients find Ford service globally

Illustrative only

**Figure 2.9** The international playing field across the value chain in the car industry

bution. The more the considerable research investment and early discovery can be written off over a bigger output, the better in terms of efficiency. Experience seems to indicate, however, that even in the middle phase of drug development – going from hits and leads to drugs with a proof of concept – scale delivers very few benefits. On the contrary, what matters in that phase is agility, focus and speed, characteristics that one typically finds in smaller autonomous units. However, drug distribution remained largely a local matter and required a more local than global focus, although this may be changing now. This challenges the need for mega-mergers in all aspects of the business, and raises the question whether alternative organizational models, aside from M&As, could not deliver as much of the cost benefits in the upstream activities, and avoid the post-merger integration problems that we have seen, for example, with Pharmacia & Upjohn, or as the *Financial Times* caption ran: 'Big pharma sees the beauty of thinking small' (2 April 2001).

These examples show how a detailed Cone analysis at activity level can be much more powerful than the simple general conclusion that there are cost and network benefits in the domestic appliances business or car industry. A more detailed analysis allows one to think in more concrete terms about what coordination mechanisms will fit in order to cash in on the identified benefits and how to adapt the internationalization approach accordingly.

One should even go even further and perform this analysis at the level of individual tasks, activities and processes within each function. Malnight (1995) concluded from his in-depth research on globalization that even *within* functions important differences were highlighted in the timing, sequence and objectives of the globalization (see also Calori et al., 2000). Within marketing, it can make sense to standardize the market research and the packaging size because of cost advantages; while localizing the advertising because the limits to standardization are too high.

Thus the challenge is to differentiate to the finest level of detail in your international approach both internally and externally. We may have opportunities in the market to be discriminating on a regional level.

## Regional strategies: a third or a middle way for multinationals?

The risk of any globalization debate is the lack of nuance. The Conelearn framework wants to support you in thinking beyond the pure trade-off between genuine globalization of the complete value chain and country-by-country strategy making. What we increasingly see is that companies balance the advantages of globalization (efficiency) and localization (responsiveness) through *regional* strategies and organizations (we see regions[7] in terms of the trading blocs such as Europe, NAFTA, Asia) (for more detail on this topic, see De Koning et al., 2000).

Procter & Gamble transformed their loose European subsidiaries into a coordinated and integrated European network, with headquarters in Brussels. 3M balanced its strong US organization with a European counterpart, led by a European management team, coordinating the European product line strategies. Matsushita saw no other option than to set up regional headquarters in Europe, aiming at translating the global strategy for the European market. Toyota transformed its Brussels organization from a distribution centre to a fully fledged headquarters responsible for the whole of the European market.

What could explain this increased attention to regional approaches?

- Economies of scale that drive numerous companies towards an international coordination of activities can be partly or even wholly captured with a regional approach and do not necessarily require full blown globalization, or cross-border supplier–client relationships are happening at a regional level anyway (globalization potential limited).

- Market convergence seems to be taking place at a more regional level – Latin America, Europe, Asia Pacific – in the first place, following the macroeconomic evolutions in the EU, NAFTA, Mercosur and so on (relevant international playing field on a regional level due to market and other external barriers).

- Global strategies and organizations may be hard to manage and not worth the cost (for example because of internal barriers, see Chapter 5).

In short: the Cone benefits may be realizable at the regional level. Some companies realized that the potential for further integration, beyond regionalization towards a global level, is very limited. At the same time, regional strategies allow for a more flexible attitude towards local requirements in the market.

This should not lead us to the false impression that choosing the regional approach is an easy way out of the difficult balancing act between local responsiveness and global efficiency. Building the regional strategy and organization is hard enough in itself. It entails all the complications of coordinating and integrating the limitations into the strategy and organization. In many respects, the key challenges remain the same as for a global organization: how to overcome the national interest and align the strategies across countries? In which part of the chain should we coordinate actions and how much? What are the potential benefits and which barriers do we see?

While we observed several companies embarking on regional strategies, we had the impression they had different reasons for operating regionally:

- Some of the global pioneers, such as ABB or Coca-Cola, moved towards regionalization because they realized that their original global strategies were potentially 'a bridge too far'. They overglobalized and had to take a step back, and allow for more regional approaches, to take into account regional differences in consumer demand and other market limitations. Matsushita, Toyota, and several other Japanese companies felt the need to adapt more to the European market and regionalized their global strategy and organization.

  We also saw quite a few car producers, such as Ford, moving in that direction. Recent research suggests that, in the automotive industry, regionalization comes after globalization, rather than the other way around. Having gained efficiency through global approaches in those areas where it pays off, such as purchasing, car producers regionalized in some other parts of the value chain. And these regional approaches seem to be even more complex to manage and hence only work for those companies that had already succeeded in globalization (Schlie and Yip, 2000).

  Global strategies in those companies become 'multi-regional': the role of the global strategy is to coordinate and integrate across regions those activities that require genuine globalization, which in fact may be the case for far fewer of their activities than they initially thought.

- Other companies were on their way to globalization, and initially used the regionalization as a stepping stone, a *transitory* stage. We have seen managers put the regional agenda forward because it is a more realistic target, and a more tangible step, on the way to becoming a fully fledged global company. Within 3M, the objective of the European integration of their dispersed activities was to align the European and US parts of the organization, and ensure coordination between the two. This step approach gives them the opportunity to catch their breath, reflect on the lessons learned from their regional integration and use it as an experience in the process of building the global corporation. Regionalization is their call-option for future globalization.

  But several of these companies ended up getting stuck at the regional level, and never really moved to the global scene. Either because the market *did* not allow them or because their company *could* not globalize, the regionalization became the *end point* of the cross-border integration and coordination.

No matter where the regionalization comes from, the key challenge remains to understand how much coordination is required, where, and when. Regionalization is not the 'deus ex machina' for all globalization pressures and limitations: it may be an answer, and hopefully also a more feasible answer, to the global–local pressures, nonetheless it requires a thorough understanding of the pressure on the company and the speed of change in the market. To what extent regionalization can or should be a permanent state will depend on the dynamics in the industry, market and your company.

## The dynamics in the international playing field

A purely static application of the Cone framework and a snapshot of the resulting playing field at a given moment in time is worth investing in but will tell only part of the truth, and maybe not the most interesting part. Changes in the regulatory environment, evolutions in technology, developments in the market and shifts in consumer behaviour can alter the cost–network benefit balance significantly. Any one of the developments mentioned above has been extremely pertinent in the European context over the last decade. More detail on the European scene will be provided later in this section.

Falling globalization limits are typically driving for an enlarging international playing field. Either the globalization limitations are falling – regulations are changing, transportation costs are decreasing, new technology is eliminating the barriers between national markets – or the localization pressures start waning – consumer habits are converging, the international mobility of people is increasing.

Another reason for the playing field to expand is the increasing benefits of an international network for a growing number of clients, who are either looking for a seamless delivery of goods and services, and/or trying to cut down on costs by working with fewer suppliers for larger volumes. Cross-border contracts to deliver catering services around Europe or the world are initiated; car producers want their suppliers to be present and deliver to all manufacturing plants; transportation companies expect uniform maintenance and repair services for their trucks in Europe; some people expect their mobile phone to function globally.

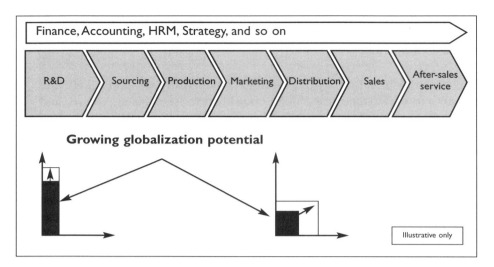

**Figure 2.10** Dynamic analysis of the international playing field across functions

We can graphically outline the changes in the shape of the international playing field in the Cone framework, and do this at the level of functions for example, as illustrated in Figure 2.10.

Beyond the external developments in the market, you may reshape your Cone balance and playing field, by repositioning and reconfiguring the value chain. Over the past decade, many companies have evolved from a traditional manufacturing company towards a service company perspective. ICL, the UK IT company, traditionally produced hardware, but transformed itself completely into an IT systems and services company. Obviously the pressures for globalization along its value chain evolved drastically with its new focus and strategy. The shift from mostly cost aspects in production towards network-oriented benefits is beautifully illustrated by its joint advertising with its global partners, Fujitsu and Amdahl, using the slogan: 'Global IT solutions delivered locally (and vice versa).'

No matter what the exact source of the changing international playing field is, it would be dangerous to expect the global–local balance to remain unchanged for a long period. In rapidly changing markets, timely reaction and even anticipation of the evolving landscape is of utmost importance for successful strategies. It is therefore crucial to follow up on changes in the playing field and tune in on the rate of change in the market.

## Over- and underglobalization: the critical role of timing

This is exactly where we observed many accidents happen. An in-depth analysis and judgment of the current and future internationalization pressures can prevent the two timing mistakes we have come across in our research: either *too much internationalization, too soon* or *too little internationalization, too late*. The first leads to *overglobalization*: you globalize while the market remains of an intrinsically local, or at least less global, nature and the benefits of internationalization are hence more limited than anticipated. The latter leads to *underglobalization* when you have a hard time competing with international companies which for various reasons perform better.

Saatchi & Saatchi, the UK advertising company that heavily internationalized in the 1980s, put its faith in the economies of scale in media purchasing and the network benefits to justify international growth. The market, however, did not seem to be ready for this: most international clients did not buy its advertising campaigns on an international level as its strategy and organization was mostly still multi-domestic and anyway it preferred to account for national sensitivities in its advertising. Having an international network was not a criterion for choosing the advertising agency, what really mattered was creativity. It was not because some of the globalization limits fell or were believed to fall – globalizing advertising channels such as global TV channels, international newspapers and falling regulative differences – that all of a sudden the advertising business was global.

In addition, Saatchi & Saatchi was not ready to take and deliver the benefits of its international coverage. After a while, its size and network became more of a liability than an asset. In many respects, Saatchi & Saatchi was 'too international, too soon'. Why then was it so successful for a long period of time? Because its strategy was financially driven and on the operational level, it was not really implementing the global strategy that it claimed it was following. It was pretty competitive on a (multi-)local basis: had very creative people, location by location, and was even using competing local agency networks. Luckily for Saatchi & Saatchi, the two negatives of not implementing the 'overstretched' strategy gave a positive (at least, for a while).

DAF Trucks could not be blamed for overglobalizing, on the contrary, they probably became international too little, too late. The internationalization benefits in this business were paramount and DAF underperformed the competition because it lacked the cost advantages that the competition had already incorporated through internationalization.

The timing issue remains an extremely difficult dilemma: the balance between anticipating the changes, with the risk of overdoing it such as Saatchi & Saatchi, and reacting to the changes, with the risk of under-globalizing and coming too late such as DAF, is a delicate one.

## Analysis and vision

We observe that some companies dare to go beyond the international strategy playing field and overglobalize *on purpose*. They seem to ignore the localization pressures and/or exaggerate the globalization potential. Yet, they eventually avoid the 'too much, too soon' mistake because they realize that anticipating market evolutions or overdoing globalization may prepare them for further developments in the market. We will return to this point in Chapter 6.

Nevertheless, this kind of strategic vision goes hand in hand with careful analysis. The best vision in our opinion is deeply rooted in a thorough understanding of the industry dynamics and therefore requires an even better understanding of the globalization potential and the pressures for cost and network advantages. Sometimes, the belief that markets are standardizing acts as a self-fulfilling prophecy: when all believe that the business is going to be global in five years time and act accordingly, the industry might in fact become much more global. But in the end, such globalization still needs to prove its added value over local or national strategies that sooner or later may start to challenge the 'common beliefs'.

Other companies simply do not count on the playing field to enlarge: they are willing to take the consequences of ignoring local differences, and adapt their strategy, organization and management to it. This is what Gillette seems to be doing with the launch of the Mach3 shaver. They have completely standardized the product and its advertising campaign, deliber-ately ignoring the differences in culture, customer needs, competitive offer, price sensitivity, and other globalization limits. Hence they managed to cash in on significant cost advantages from global R&D and unified advertising. There remain, however, considerable limitations to the standardization of razor blades: differences in shaving habits (wet versus dry), different price sensitivity, different environmental regulations for the recycling of used razor blades, and so on. For most players in the industry, the international playing field in fact looks relatively small, because the cost drivers are not as significant, and the limits still substantial.

Another way to look at it is that, if you have invested $700 million in the development of a new razor blade, the estimated cost of the Mach3 project, the only way to get your money back is to sell the same product around the globe! In a sense, the Gillette strategy is a virtuous circle. And when other players start following this example, then a self-fulfilling prophecy may appear. This still, however, leaves these players vulnerable to nimble and keen local competitors that come in with a very different approach, as indeed many international companies are repeatedly experiencing, such as Unilever in the soap and detergent market in India.

Moreover, the gap between the optimal international strategy and the actual strategy implies that the management is overinvesting in the globalization of the strategy, and leaving the localization potential on the table. The Cone diagram shows that a strategy that balances the global and local characteristics more subtly could potentially be more effective (Figure 2.11). The question is how much is given up and what is gained by overstandardizing the strategy. In other words, to what extent are you narrowing your target audience by standardizing? Is Gillette marginalizing its strategy by marketing a uniform product in a homogeneous way?

This is similar to the explicit choice that companies such as McDonald's, The Body Shop, Kinepolis and Brantano are making by standardizing their strategy and copying their concept in different geographies. As long as this strategic option is based on real barriers and benefits, and you are realizing the management and organizational implications of this option, this may be a viable strategy.

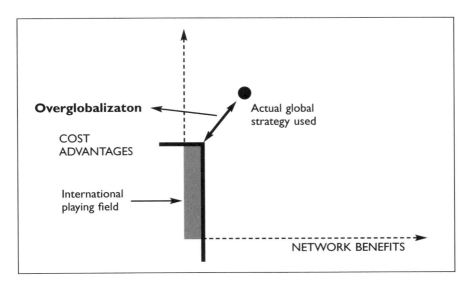

**Figure 2.11** International playing field: example of Gillette Mach3

## Cone in the European landscape

The question of market convergence and the pressure for globalization, or should we say 'pan-Europeanization', has been very much in the forefront within the European market over the past two decades.

Europe was for a long time characterized by significant competitive, customer and especially regulatory distinctions from one geography to another. A Belgian customer could not, until recently, legally buy his insurance policy in the Netherlands; importing a car from Germany to Denmark meant weighty import taxes; trucks could not just transport whatever product from one EU country to another EU country; tax-deductibility of many financial services products was limited to those purchased at home or related to products such as cars and houses which were registered or domiciled in the home country.

As a consequence Europe was an amalgam of national markets, each of them requiring their own logic and tailored approach. Seinosuke Kuraku, head of Matsushita's European operations, noted: 'It took three years to study the differences between the European countries in which our company operates.'

Subsequently companies were also organized, structured and managed with that in mind. Many multinational companies set up relatively independent subsidiaries around Europe, with little, if any, coordination between them. Multinationals were still *multi-nationals* in the strictest meaning of the word: they competed mainly on a local, that is national, basis.

But those were the old days, judging from the movement in the European markets. Two particular events, the 'Europe 1992 programme' and the euro introduction, have come to pass within the European context, with a perceived revolutionary impact on business that provoked widespread company restructuring and deal or alliance making.

## Europe is no longer Europe

The European market is in many industries no longer comparable to the fragmented market it was 20 years ago. Long is the list of industries where deregulation, elimination of country borders and free traffic of people and goods have changed the name of the game. Extremely fragmented service industries (such as the temporary work services, banking, insurance or retailing), nationalized and regulated industries (such as telecom and electricity) and manufacturing industries (such as car and truck production, pharmaceutical and consumer goods) have all changed their outlook considerably.

The Conelearn balance has undergone rapid change. The European single market programme has eliminated significant barriers and limitations all over the EU, although not all and certainly not all at the same time. While it may be dangerous to generalize, it seems fair to say that for most companies the *international playing field* has extended, on both axes, since 1992 and in many cases significantly.

Just look at the insurance industry. While this sector is still perceived to be one of the slowest moving industries (so far), one can barely recognize the outlook and structure of this sector compared to ten years ago. In less than a decade, the industry changed from a mainly nationally oriented industry ruled by a few national champions and many smaller players, all making good and stable profits, to an industry with a few European giants, Royal and Sun Alliance, Allianz, Generali, Axa to name only a few, amid a larger group of medium-sized and niche players such as Skandia and First Direct, all heavily repositioning to secure profit levels, and some newcomers such as Virgin and MLP.

The danger of this type of anecdotal perception is that one starts believing that countries no longer matter. Envisioning Europe as one single integrated market risks ignoring what seems to be the more relevant factor in this game, namely the significant barriers that exist across Europe, even after 1992.

## Europe is not Europe yet

Having observed for some years several companies and industries operating in Europe, we have noted many *disappointments* within companies with respect to the results obtained from their corporate restructuring and strategy/organization integration projects, following 1992. A key reason for this disappointment in our view is that the European market was not really as uniform as anticipated, and only limited Cone benefits could actually be gained from integration (as confirmed by studies of the Commission of European Communities, 1996). A Eurostat business survey confirmed that only 47% of the companies surveyed saw an effect of the 1992 internal market programme on their business.

The impression we got is that 1992 was not only overestimated in terms of its total effect, but also in terms of the timing. Philippe Bodson, CEO of Tractebel, admitted that 1992 had had only a *symbolic* value in the electricity industry:

> The question is when Europe 1992 will come. In some industries, Europe 1992 already happened in the mid 1980s, in some other it will only happen in the next century. As such Europe 1992 has only a symbolic value.

This could also be the case for the insurance industry where the big surprise (beyond the moves in M&As) to some has been that changes in the business and market are taking much more time to realize.

If Europe 1992 did not turn Europe into an integrated market overnight, how can we expect the euro to do so? Even though we know that one currency has a significant effect (for example on trade, see Rose, 2000), national borders still seem to matter a lot, even in highly open and integrated trading areas (McCallum 1995; Chen, 2000).

There are high hopes that the euro introduction would quickly converge markets in Europe. But the cost and network benefits generally do not significantly boom because of a new currency only, while the most important barriers are not influenced by it either. The size of the international playing field in most industries has not been considerably altered (for a more detailed discussion on the strategic implication of the euro introduction, see Verdin and Van Heck, 1999b).

Market convergence will not end with the Europe 1992 programme or the euro. Europe is not one market yet. A lot of limitations, some of them more important than currency or import duties, remain. Karel Van Miert, former European Commissioner, observed recently:

> Forty years after the signing of the Treaty of Rome and the European Community for Coal and Steel, we are on the verge of a real integrated European Market – for coal and steel.

Some managers fear that the integration may never come and certainly not in the way it was expected.

> On the one hand you have all the big dreams of the industry and on the other hand you have the dreams of the European authorities – and in reality you have the local situation. (Eric Van Keerbergen, Coditel)

What is key is that companies realize that the tendency towards homogenization is an ongoing process that they should carefully monitor and adapt their approaches to. The Cone balance is changing fast: more than ever, maintaining the status quo is a risky option. However, the real market convergence and rate of change remains the result of a complex and difficult interaction between various elements, stretched out over a long time scale.

This is all the more reason to be aware of the 'too much, too soon' trap in the European context. Attracted by the high expectations of 'Europe 1992' in the early 1990s, Federal Express was an early mover in the European parcel delivery business, providing excellent services at competitive prices, only to realize that the parcel delivery business in Europe was mainly focused on intranational delivery services. This context was not sufficient to maintain the service level and infrastructure of FedEx, and after a couple of years of significant losses, FedEx decided in early 1993 to retract and focus its European operations on transatlantic services only. It had hoped for 'too much, too soon' in the European cross-border market. Others, such as DHL and UPS, then came in aggressively after them, but FedEx returned recently via a different channel, that of alliances with some national, express postal services.

Another typical example of 'too much, too soon' is the euro-pricing debate: companies need one single price all over Europe, especially after the euro introduction. While there has undeniably been a downwards pressure on prices in the European market, and there are reasons to assume that this will continue because of the increased competition, price transparency, new distribution channels, and changing customer preferences, we are still far from a single euro price (see also Verdin and Van Heck, 1999b). Recent research confirmed that major price differences exist across countries in Europe, even for so-called standardized products, such as CDs, credit cards or cars, and in industrial products and consumer durables (Ahlberg et al., 1999).

And rightly so: the purchasing habits of Euroland consumers have obviously not changed because of a new currency. A major effect on prices was expected to come from increased transparency, but, apart from the question of how much the introduction of a new unfamiliar accounting unit will contribute to transparency, we should realize that transparency is only one element responsible for existing price differences, and probably not the most important one. The main reasons are the different costs and market structures and these will not significantly change just like that. We would like to draw the parallel with the US market where, despite the use of a single currency for years, price differentials still hold, and also across NAFTA where, despite falling trade barriers, 'geography still counts'.

We would therefore like to question the initiatives of certain companies that rush into price homogenization and warn them about over-Europeanization. Such companies might price sub-optimally, lose opportunities for price discrimination and jeopardize their own profitability. Or as the McKinsey study noted: 'Too rapid harmonization [and excessive large price differences] destroys value' (Ahlberg et al., 1999).

The smartest way to deal with European convergence and dissimilarities is to see it as an opportunity for value creation. The market integration across borders (even when and if it really becomes a reality) should not eliminate discrimination or segmentation. On the contrary, it might unleash opportunities for *more* segmentation or discrimination rather than less, but on the basis of 'economically' relevant criteria, rather than (artificial?) geographic ones.

However, we do not expect that, even if new ways for creating value in a uniform European market do show up, it will happen overnight. This type of convergence in one direction and divergence in another will take a long time to become operational and effective. And therefore we must be wary of the same kind of 'managing by slogans' in Euroland as we observed on the globalization debate. Any 'big events' such as Europe 1992 and the euro can contribute to this development and help to foster the debate on how much Europeanization is really needed. It may make us aware of more rather than less chances for customer responsiveness and differentiation. And this is where the third axis of our framework comes in.

## Learning opportunities

So far, our focus has been on cost and network benefits as motivations for realizing the benefits of internationalization and globalization. The resulting model for international business and management is one of harmonization, standardization, and one-size-fits-all approaches, as one tries to exploit the international playing field to its maximum and take into account market limitations. What is missing in our frame of reference so far is a more dynamic, interactive perspective on managing international activities. There is more to gain than simply standardizing output, copying concepts to new markets and pleasing clients with similar offerings in other geographies.

We believe that the power of internationalization is increasingly shifting towards a very different type of benefit: the power of diversity, the ability to learn and upgrade the know-how and knowledge from operating in many different places and environments, and ultimately to become a more competitive company at home and elsewhere.

Sir Martin Sorell, former CFO of an early mover in globalization (Saatchi & Saatchi) and now CEO of what recently became the world's largest advertising agency (WPP), who acknowledged that today the global segment of this business represents only 15% at best, noted that:

Globalization is leveraging an economy where everything is about knowledge and co-ordination: the creation, refining, management and implementation of sharp ideas; rather than leveraging an economy built on economies of scale, whereby one sells the same product the same way everywhere. (*De Morgen*, 1999)

Internationalization is a two-way street, where you get the opportunity to learn from the diversity of clients, competitors, markets and regulations that you are exposed to. The underlying assumption is that you benefit, become better, more competitive and stronger through internationalization. You can learn a lot about doing your business that you could never have learned as quickly in the domestic market alone. You are forced to stand up against more diverse companies in more diverse countries and types of business environment as legal, socioeconomic, geographic, demographic and cultural aspects differ. You are confronted with enormous opportunities to develop, learn and capture the experience, to actively manage knowledge and intellectual capital, beyond the mere transfer of it. This actually turns you into a stronger, more competitive company. The implication is that you manage diversity rather than avoid it and use the learning to improve, upgrade and even fundamentally change your business concept.

The Belgian energy holding Tractebel is a good illustration of a company that used its international experience and the necessity of managing the international diversity in regulation, market development, and competition and turned it into a key potential benefit of its internationalization. After many failed attempts at internationalization and diversification in the 1970s and 80s according to the 'old' logic, applying the logic of a financial holding strategy without reaping the benefits of international cost or network advantages, Tractebel was deliberately one of the early movers in Europe.

Tractebel was exploiting the learning dimension before any substantial cost or network advantages in electricity generation and distribution could be reaped. It got involved in the US and Scandinavia where electricity deregulation was way ahead of its home market. It put itself up for electricity contracts against some of the industry champions around the world. Its internationalization to far-flung markets such as Chile, the US and Kazakhstan, while initially rather opportunistic and unintended, allowed it to build up experience and know-how to compete in deregulated and less-developed electricity markets and to leverage this know-how in the domestic market.

These early movements will give Tractebel a head start when the European electricity market significantly opens up for competition in the

21st century and when real cost or network advantages may show up. In other formerly regulated industries, such as telecom and postal services, several of the traditional monopolists are currently internationalizing, and are facing huge opportunities to take advantage of their foreign experiences to turn themselves into highly competitive, dynamic corporations.

Other players, such as Telefonica of Spain, despite aggressive moves especially to South and Central America, have not moved into this stage yet. Telefonica has merely acquired and captured dominant market positions in less developed markets with the same language and a similar culture, where it could afford to buy big stakes. In the meantime, it was struggling at home with the legacy of a well-protected, regulated monopolist. Carrefour, the French retailer, internationalized to South America early on with a high degree of attention to the local environment. This gave the organization pole position in the internationalization race that we saw in the sector in the 1990s, especially against its arch rival Wal-Mart, which has been driven by the sheer scale and size of its extremely successful US operations.

The Eureko Alliance, grouping eight national insurance companies in Europe from as many countries, including BCP of Portugal and Achmea of the Netherlands, explicitly did not concentrate in the first place on cost or network advantages. It realized that the international playing field in European insurance would remain small for many years to come and, from its inception, it focused its attention and raison d'être on developing, sharing, and managing the knowledge of the different partners. The aim was for each partner to become more successful in the local market, through the support of the alliance partners (notice they went for an alliance and not a merger; see Chapter 3). International knowledge creation and management, and innovation between the partners would strengthen the domestic position of the insurers. In the meantime, some of the traditional integrated players in this business, such as Zurich Financial Services and Axa, have come to realize the importance of knowledge management and learning:

> A local player with capital is as well off with an alliance [as with an acquisition] because it provides him with access to local knowledge. Blending 'local' with 'global' knowledge gives a strong formula. (*Financieel Economische Tijd*, 13 July 1999)

Ranbaxy, an Indian pharmaceutical company, had, between 1975 and 1993, limited its international exposure to exporting generic drugs to Russia and China (Bartlett and Ghoshal, 2000b). In 1993, however, its approach changed dramatically and it entered the US and European markets, where the company needed to meet much more stringent regulatory requirements. By doing so, the company forced itself to develop competencies in brand image and management, alternative distribution channels, and leverage its R&D expertise, in which it had a comparative cost advantage over European and US competitors. This company developed a culture of continual cross-border learning which became its source of competitive edge and would never have developed in its safe, protected home market.

This third dimension in our Conelearn framework, the learning axis, is conceptually quite different from the benefit of merely copying systems and formulas, which we discussed earlier as part of the cost benefits. The question here is not how we can recoup some of the investments or sunk costs in concepts and formulas (duplication of what we have) but how to leverage and build more know-how and expertise for the future, and upgrade the company resources by being exposed to international markets (building new and innovative ideas and resources).

It is not hard to imagine that the mindset and organizational vehicles for this kind of learning to happen will not necessarily correspond with those for realizing cost and network benefits. The cost axis is clearly about efficiency and *bottom line* management; the network axis refers to an improved proposition to the client, and has got to do with *top line* management. The learning axis goes beyond *linear* '1 + 1 = 2' management: it is about opportunities to innovate, learning from experience in different markets, and using this knowledge to surpass the competition and delight customers. The purpose is seeking and facing up to competition and diversity rather than avoiding it.

What makes this learning aspect difficult is the problem of quantification and operationalization, not to mention the challenge of managing the learning opportunities and the resulting benefits. Not only do you need to see the learning, but the learning has to be built up, applied and used across locations.

The learning opportunities are special because they differ from the two other dimensions of cost and network. While the cost and network benefits refer more to the 'need to be international' in order to exploit cost savings or value to the customer in the short or medium term, the learning benefits create longer term '*opportunities* for international companies' which are less defined in advance and probably only materialize along the way.

More importantly, unlike cost or network advantages, these opportunities are a priori not so limited or defined by the specific industry or company economics (see also analysis of value chain above). Here, all companies should gain from international presence in one way or another. Especially in local businesses, with hardly any cost or network benefits, internationalization benefits still may exist along the third axis. Nestlé, the food and consumer goods conglomerate, has always approached markets with mainly local brands and products, but capitalizes on its international network by ensuring that the learning from its international markets is integrated into its global activities. Competence centres, such as Nestec, are its organizational vehicles for capturing these learning opportunities (Boutellier et al., 2000).

In this sense, all companies should internationalize, if only to learn, whatever the size of their international playing field. But it is important to realize that you are after learning and deal with the consequences of that. Learning will not happen automatically. It will require a much longer term perspective than cost benefits. It will require intrinsically different organizations and management practices, as we will discuss later. All of this, however, is not a good excuse to be missing out on potentially critical cost and network advantages. It is not enough to say that you are in it for the long-term learning benefits, because you missed the cost or network benefits and are underperforming!

## The Conelearn framework: beyond the internationalization slogans

We now have completed our introduction of the Conelearn framework. Internationalization adds value through cost advantages, network benefits and/or learning opportunities (Figure 2.12). The first two axes shape the globalization potential and indicate opportunities to *leverage* assets beyond the home market. They define the relevant international playing field, and in combination with the existing external limitations, prescribe the desired level and speed of standardization in managing the international operations. The third axis indicates an alternative route to successful internationalization: to create opportunities for learning and *build* on the diversity in international cultures and markets, even in local businesses where neither cost nor network benefits seem to justify foreign adventures.

This instrument is by no means absolute in its own right: we would not claim it to be the only frame of reference in the field of international business and management. Rather it should be used to complement other useful frameworks and tools in the domain. Therefore we are grateful to other

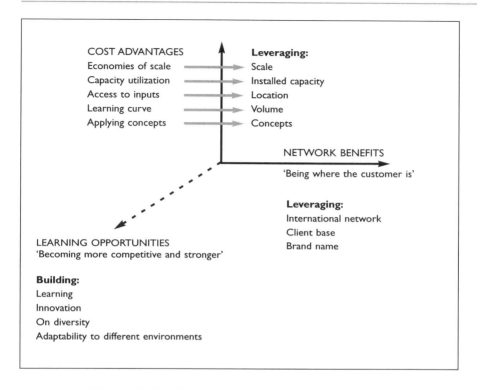

**Figure 2.12** Conelearn framework: what are the benefits of internationalization?

scholars in the field as their insights and interpretation of the issues served as an inspiration and pushed our thinking. We believe, however, that our framework is innovative and adds value to the field in the following ways:

- Our framework seeks to the link a number of the core issues in managing international businesses. Not only does it give guidance on what international strategy or organization to use,[8] it precedes this question by forcing companies to think about the *why* of international presence in its own right,[9] and connects this aspect with entry decisions, target markets, and strategic and organizational positioning[10] (see subsequent sections). In that context, we would see it as both an intuitive and more integrative frame of reference on internationalization and globalization.

- Previous models risk presenting the strategic issues as upfront choices for one or another extreme stereotype or model,[11] which are mostly overstatements of real-life examples and tend to focus on the *industry* as the appropriate level of analysis.[12] How often do we think about international management as a trade-off between centralization or decentralization, or global or multi-local strategies or organizations, and talk about it in terms of 'global or local industries'? We would hope to avoid jumping too fast to these archetypes, and are confident that seeing globalization decisions in a continuum of strategies and organizations, at the level of the company and functions, with all the nuances required, is ultimately more relevant and useful. Our framework should be seen as an invitation to push down to as much of the *detail* as possible. Out of the analysis and discussion you should develop your own idea about which form or shape happens to be most appropriate for your situation at a given point in time.

▪ Limiting the decision criteria for setting up and managing international operations to simple, operational criteria risks underestimating the importance of strategic reflections.[13] Hence our repeated plea for a *strategic* approach of internationalization. We see a clear and explicit debate on the drivers and opportunities for a given company in a given strategic context as a precondition for answering organizational and management questions.

The Conelearn instrument is pragmatic, straightforward, qualitative and visual. The first objective of the instrument is to launch and focus the debate on internationalization in a clear and intuitive way. It does not reduce the discussion to calculating the outcome of a simple equation or applying a magic formula. Internationalization, as any other strategic decision, is not just a matter of 1 plus 1 makes 2. It is a matter of understanding the complex reality, the various decision variables, and of making a judgement on what to do and when and how to manage it, in the specific strategic context of the organization. It is a top management task, not only that of an analyst.

Our mission is to put the internationalization debate in the right perspective; to make you think about aspects of internationalization that you may otherwise overlook or not give the attention they require in an integrative context; and to help to structure the debate and integrate the various strategic decisions that have to be made when turning into an international company. It is an intuitive instrument for people needing a frame of reference in order to understand the challenges of managing internationalization and international companies. As perceptions are crucially important throughout the organization, visualizing the problem, as we have tried to do, usually helps to focus the mind and develop a shared view.

The Conelearn framework should help to *prioritize* the benefits. It is possible, although not necessary, that several types of benefit are available, but it is most probably going to be tough to achieve all of them at the same time and adapt your organization and capabilities for all three types of benefit to materialize fully at the same time. Quantifying and hence prioritizing and selecting the benefits might prevent you from missing all or getting only part of them. Estimating the order of magnitude and prioritizing can and should be done even if no exact numbers or figures can be put on the different drivers or axes.

The Conelearn framework allows us to revisit the internationalization slogans and give guidance as to when and where the slogans do or do not apply. As a general rule, our advice to internationalizing companies remains simple but powerful: the only way to benefit from internationalization is through an improved cost position; a network that allows delivery of products and services to international clients who value and benefit from it, and the learning that can be created and captured and which stimulates a company to become a more competitive player.

In industries with significant cost advantages, there might be good reasons to have a fear of *dying without internationalization*. Those might also be the industries where only a *few big players will survive* and where *bigger* companies have a fair chance of performing *better*. The domestic market could be *too small* to benefit from the cost advantages. When the *clients are heavily internationalizing*, you may be able to gain network benefits from following them in their international expansion. It may help *to be where the market is*, if this allows you to learn and become a more competitive player overall.

The perception that the *competition* is ahead of you and has managed to cash in Conelearn advantages, earlier and/or more than you have, should be a trigger for you to investigate the importance of internationalization and globalization if you had not already done so before (you should!). The question is then how to bridge the gap and catch up with the competitors in terms of cost, network and/or learning benefits.

External pressure from the competition, competitors interested in taking over your activities, or threatening your home turf, or any other wake-up calls that make you look at the dynamics in the Conelearn framework are welcome at any time. The slogans may raise the questions that should have been discussed in any case, but were simply not at the top of the agenda, without a certain catalyst bringing them up. Slogans invite or force a look at the underlying economics of internationalization and this is exactly where the slogans prove their value. No matter what the impulse is for your company to act, you should be able to specify clearly what cost advantages, network benefits and learning opportunities you are after. We have attempted to help you to look beyond the slogans into the real added value of internationalization in your specific situation. Now you need to know what organizational vehicle will be most appropriate or what management approach should be followed. These aspects will be discussed in the next chapters.

# SECTION 2

# On Organizing for Internationalization

Imagine that you have a local electronics shop, and are suffering from the tough price competition of the big international chains. They can sell at a lower price, while you are attracting clients for the level of service you can offer, reflected in the price premium. Even if you would want to match the prices of your competitors, you would probably not be able to do so, as their purchasing prices were much lower to start with. Their centralized purchasing resulted in better negotiation power with producers and lower prices for bigger volumes. And you find out that a lot of your colleagues, small shop owners, in different countries have the same frustration or have given up and closed or sold out.

While you and your colleagues know that size would deliver cost advantages on the purchasing side, it is not clear if and how you should capture these. Do you wait until one of you starts buying the others? Dress up your business and try to get the attention of the big chains to acquire you? Or could it make sense for you to join forces on the buying side with your colleagues, other independent shop owners?

The latter option is what has driven Carrefour, Sears and other retailers, although most of them were already international companies of significant size, to join forces in GlobalnetXchange, an electronic marketplace. This joint venture allows these retailers to optimize their purchasing policies and efficiency, by creating a virtual meeting and negotiating space for retailers, suppliers and wholesalers.

Let's return to the story of Saatchi & Saatchi. The advertising agency was thriving enthusiastically on its conviction that cost and network benefits were there to be captured in the global advertising business. While there may have been some truth in this assumption, we were not very optimistic about Saatchi & Saatchi's chances to cash in on them. Its organization was managed in a very decentralized manner and any cost or network benefits, if there were any, were bound to fall between the cracks of the independent subsidiaries.

The underlying message of the above examples is not so different as it may look at first sight: the trick is to find ways in the organizational set-up to ensure that the benefits of internationalization are turned into reality. The common interest of Saatchi & Saatchi, the local electronics shop and many others besides, lies in translating the analytical insights emphasized above into the appropriate organizational vehicles and mechanisms. It is of little help to see what is there to be won if you are not preparing to participate in the race.

The organizational side of internationalizing and globalizing has two aspects: it is about finding a suitable organizational *mode* for *developing* foreign activities – do you enter markets on your own, find local partners, and, if so, how do you link up with partners? – and about *establishing* the *mechanisms* for the coordination and cooperation of these foreign activities. Chapter 3 will elaborate on the choice of entry modes into foreign markets, as a way to secure the cost, network or learning benefits, and link it with the

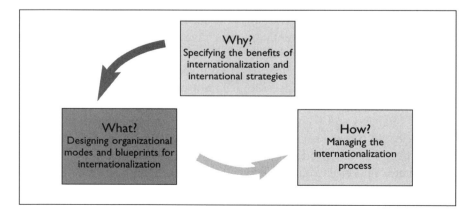

**Figure S2.1** The what aspects of internationalization

decision on which type of markets to enter. Chapter 4 will then discuss issues of organizational blueprints and mechanisms for international companies, and their influence on the actual benefits of internationalization (see Figure S2.1).

As you will see, we have classified all of these issues under the 'what' question, and have deliberately kept the management issues for the next section on the how question. We have unbundled the two aspects in this way to signal clearly that the choice of entry mode or organization chart is in the first instance an analytical question, as distinct from the more behavioural or process questions involved in the implementation. At various stages of Chapters 3 and 4 we will point to the process issues to be elaborated in Chapters 5 and 6.

## CHAPTER 3

# On Entry Modes into Foreign Markets

So you want to enter foreign markets. How do you do this? You set up a sales office, build a plant, look for a local partner to franchise your concept to, or you look for a local player to buy, or a combination of any of the above. Relander, CEO of Sonera, was clearly thinking in terms of entry modes when he said:

> Sonera's internationalization involved seeking partners, corporate acquisitions, establishing joint-ventures, making agreements and creating global service business activities.

We will refer to this statement again at the end of this chapter.

Obviously, the appropriate entry mode should also be influenced by the characteristics of the local market. But on what grounds should you select which markets to focus on in the beginning? Should you really go to neighboring countries first? Or should we all go to Eastern Europe, Asia or South America, because of the market potential?

We now elaborate on these two aspects of selecting markets and entry modes.

## Target markets

Many books discuss the selection of foreign markets in the internationalization process (see, for example, Porter, 1990; Usunier, 1993; Segal-Horn, 1994; Daniels and Radebaugh, 1995; Parker, 1998; Piggott and Cook,

1999; Rugman and Hodgetts, 2000). According to these authors, a broad range of issues affect the selection of countries to enter:

- the distance from the home market: you start preferably in neighbouring countries

- the resemblance of the market characteristics with the home market: you go to similar markets first

- the degree of openness of the market: you prefer to invest in markets where the customers and government welcome your local investments and products

- the size and growth rate of the market: you prefer to go to big markets with a big potential for your product, preferably unsaturated and growing rapidly

- the strength of local competition: better invest in those markets where you face less strong competitors.

This list may not be complete. It is only intended to illustrate where the emphasis traditionally is in selecting target markets: the objective seems initially to leverage size or replicate existing concepts and formulas. The underlying assumptions tend towards cost advantages, either in scale, capacity filling or applying existing concepts, as the driver for internationalizing. Where do network advantages come in? Is learning subsumed in any of the above criteria? It is important to see how a broader, more strategic perspective that includes cost, network and learning advantages may, in the long run, affect your choice of market.

Whether you are on the international scene for cost, network or learning reasons affects the type of market you may want to look into first. It is not very helpful to build a network internationally, focusing on Mexico and Thailand first, when none of your clients actually has operations in those countries and are European in the first place. Why would you enter adjacent markets that in many respects are comparable to the domestic market, if learning was what you hoped to bring back home with you?

Economies of scale and learning curve cost advantages will mostly stimulate companies to find markets that are *big* enough or growing rapidly, allowing them to reap cost benefits faster, and are *close* enough so that cost gains on the one side are not nullified by the increasing transportation costs. The latter will be of importance for capacity utilization motives as well. When cheaper or secured access to input factors is your driving force, you will find it crucial to enter a *more developed* market in the context of the relevant input factor. If you hope to copy your concept, formula and systems to the target market, it is better take a market with *similar* characteristics and consumer behaviour.

DAF's acquisition of Leyland in the UK did not bring the advantages DAF had hoped for. Shipping trucks over the Channel to the Continent, or the other way around, was not a very efficient solution. It certainly did not solve DAF's main problem of the sub-optimal scale or capacity utilization of existing plants on the Continent. And the acquisition of DAF by Paccar in the US years later does not seem to bring much of a solution to this either. Interbrew's acquisitions in Russia and Korea would hardly allow it to optimize brewing capacity in Leuven, its home base in Belgium, and of course that is not the reason why these markets were bought into.

When networking advantage is your goal, what matters is to reflect which markets *your client would like you to be in*, probably because the client has his own interest in this market one way or the other. Nexia and Eureko, two alliance organizations that wanted to provide an international network to their corporate clients in accounting/auditing and insurance/financial services respectively, were focusing on completing their coverage in the relevant European markets first, rather than jumping to Asia, Africa or even the US where, for their existing clients, it was probably less important to be.

How do you best challenge and improve your own business system and competitiveness? One way to do it is by entering *lead markets* in your business, such as Honda when it entered the US motorcycle market, even if it means failing several times before succeeding. You focus on markets where clients are demanding, competitors are pushing for customer value creation and fighting fiercely to stay ahead of each other, and governments give you as much stimulus to innovate as they can. Alternatively, you go to markets which in no way resemble the ones in which you have been building up your business so far. If *diversity* is what you want, diverse markets are going to deliver that.

Why did EMI go from the UK to the US with its CT scanner business, and not to the European continent or Asia? Because the US was the lead market in the medical equipment business in those days: competition was there and hospitals were ahead of the rest of the world in terms of investments and equipment requirements as well as in terms of technological innovation. One of the problems of EMI's aborted strategy was that they had no clear view as to what was driving their entry strategy into the US and their short-term success selling (exported) machines in the booming US market blinded them from the real underlying strategic question of how they would face up to growing competition which was bound to emerge sooner or later. They ended up losing on both counts: they lost market share in the lead market, and did not manage to benefit from the advantages of being near the most competitive centre of the market. They failed to transmit the responses from the US market, their customers and competitors back to the UK home front where major decisions on strategy and investments were made. Their final attempt to duplicate the UK organization entirely into the US as a fully integrated business represented the final blow: they did not manage to capture obvious economies of scale in R&D and production and were not able to capitalize on joint learning in the UK or the US (see Figure 3.1).

The electricity generation and distribution business theoretically allows for the reaping of substantial cost advantages. Most of these would, however, require entry into neighbouring countries since the generated electricity cannot be stored and transmission over a long distance is very costly. However, in the early 1990s, the globalization limitations, mainly of regulations, restrained the ability to actually benefit from the efficiency gains across borders. Realizing this, Tractebel went for rather opportunistic international investments in deregulated electricity markets, such as the US, UK and Scandinavia, and capitalized on the need for restructuring in very different 'exotic' markets such as Northern Ireland, Thailand, Chile, Hungary, Oman and Khazakstan. In most of these markets, the potential for learning was tremendous and it ultimately made Tractebel a well-respected energy company in the world.

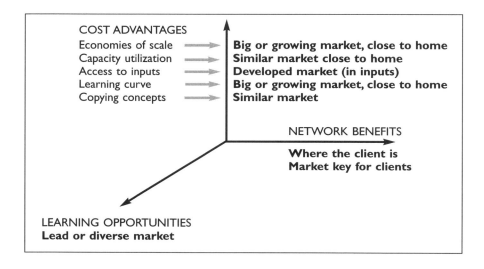

**Figure 3.1** The Conelearn framework and selection of target markets: which markets to enter first?

Only recently, as some of the adjacent European markets started opening up, the potential cost and network benefits have become more of a driver for Tractebel. It invested, in cooperation with Dutch and French competitors, on the exchange of excess capacity (cost) and on joint projects with clients such as Solvay Chemicals in Italy (networking). The shift towards the horizontal and vertical axis of our Conelearn framework even led to the divestment of some of the early learning projects, as in Northern Ireland.

Our main point is that the choice of target markets will very much depend on the specific objectives and benefits that you are after in your internationalization strategy and should therefore be put in a strategic context.

## Entry modes

Once you decide to enter a certain market, the question remains as to which entry mode to use. Different market entry modes have typically diverse advantages and disadvantages. The pluses and minuses of foreign direct investment (FDI), export, franchising, licensing, joint ventures and alliances, or mergers and acquisitions have been highlighted by several authors on the basis of a broad range of criteria: market, legal, social, financial or other. In Table 3.1 we have summarized a selection of commonly mentioned advantages and disadvantages on each of the entry modes, as discussed in the literature (Hirsch, 1976; Gomes-Casseres, 1989; Bleeke et al., 1990; Jeannet and Hennessey, 1992; Root, 1994).

Looking at this table and relating it to our observations in companies, we see that:

■ The discussion around entry modes often starts from a rather traditional view of business as 'running operations and production'. Selecting the entry mode is centred around the decision on where to manufacture your products (home country – export, or foreign country – FDI). The importance of other parts of the value chain, such as R&D, marketing, or distribution, let alone intangibles such as knowledge management or creation, are often overlooked in favour of the production aspects.

■ Frequently, there is a 'home country' bias, suggesting that the foreign market is less developed than the home market. The tendency is to think of companies coming from more developed markets investing in less developed markets.

■ The debate on entry modes is focused generally on operational aspects such as transportation costs, political environment, risk management,

**Table 3.1** Some commonly accepted advantages and disadvantages of different entry modes

| Mode (including definition) | Advantages | Disadvantages |
|---|---|---|
| *Export:* to supply foreign demand from home production | ▪ Little or no investments required<br>▪ International learning experience at low cost | ▪ Cost of transportation<br>▪ Possible trade barriers |
| *Licensing/franchising:* to grant an independent foreign firm the use of an intangible property, a trademark or other asset, for an agreed-on compensation | ▪ Licensee/franchisee takes the political and economical risk<br>▪ Requires little time, resources and knowledge about market | ▪ Dependence on licensee/franchisee<br>▪ Risk of creating a competitor |
| *FDI (greenfield):* to establish from scratch an operation that you own entirely, in a foreign country | ▪ Signal to customer and other stakeholders<br>▪ Cost savings in transportation or production | ▪ Investment cost<br>▪ Requires more time, resources and knowledge about market<br>▪ Management control of foreign operations<br>▪ Possible unfavourable government policy |
| *Cross-border M&A:* to establish a wholly owned affiliate by acquiring (or merging with) an existing firm in a foreign market | ▪ Quick access to the market | ▪ Difficult to find right target<br>▪ Possible unfavourable government policy<br>▪ Management challenge – potential conflicts |
| *Joint ventures/alliances:* to invite a foreign company to share stock ownership in your company or a separate unit | ▪ Knowledge of local market is available<br>▪ Reduced risk | ▪ Loss of control<br>▪ Potential conflicts of interest between partners, particularly over time |

control issues, and is only indirectly integrated into an overall strategic reflection on what you are trying to achieve and what could be gained or defended in terms of long-term sustainable advantage.

When choosing an entry mode into a specific market, you should in our view equally take into account the type of benefits that you are pursuing. Different entry modes offer different potential with regard to the relevant benefits.

For instance, the chances of export delivering cost advantage through economies of scale, capacity utilization or learning curve advantages in the short to medium term are probably higher than for greenfield operations in foreign countries. Korean steel companies prefer to export to Europe rather than set up local plants, and European steel producers similarly use the international markets as their buffer for excess production, through export.

On the other hand, if network benefits are the key motivation for internationalization, exporting may not be the most appropriate way to deliver to and service foreign clients. Instead, FDI and mergers and acquisitions seem more suitable at first sight to ensure local presence in different countries. Several banks have opened branches or bought local banks to ensure a representative office in off-shore or other important locations, such as Hong Kong, Singapore, Eastern Europe or America because their corporate clients appreciated that.

If there are significant advantages in accessing less expensive input factors, such as labour, raw material supply, energy, FDI and M&As may come first. Textile companies have invested significantly in setting up production units in Asia in order to profit from lower labour costs. Philip Morris similarly preferred a local plant over export into Russia, driven by cost motives.

If you want to take advantage of learning opportunities, joint ventures and alliances could be the most apt vehicle. Toyota Production System is a network of Toyota and its suppliers that has been widely admired for its ability to create and manage knowledge. Its capacity for inter-organizational learning is considered superior to any intra-organizational learning due to the intrinsic diversity of knowledge that resides with a network of different companies (Dyer and Nobeoka, 2000).

Licensing and franchising is more frequently adopted in order to leverage concepts, especially if the company is reluctant to invest directly in foreign countries. Mr. Minit and McDonald's are two examples of business concepts that are internationally leveraged throughout a franchise network.

Although franchising and alliances may at first sight look attractive in order to build the required international network, it may in the long term not be the optimal route to network benefits in all businesses. Building the network requires a significant degree of coordination among countries, and a high level of consistency from one place to another. This may in some cases be hard to build and control through a franchise or alliance model, and may require direct investment through greenfield sites or acquisitions in certain countries.

As the benefits may shift over time, it may force you to adjust the entry mode. Exporting could reveal the potential for networking with clients, and could lead to FDI. The original objective of learning from a local partner may evolve towards opportunities to leverage existing concepts and processes, and turn the alliance into an acquisition.

Figure 3.2 attempts to illustrate possible links between the different entry modes and axes in the Conelearn framework.

Obviously there is not an exclusive, one-to-one relationship between the target market description, or entry mode and the benefits it gives access to. Nevertheless, we distinguish certain hierarchies within the entry modes depending on the desired international benefits: if the clash of different ideas and diversity of markets is what you would like to capture, it may not seem right to think about export first. Joint ventures and alliances in unknown markets seem more obvious entry modes for learning (Gomes-Casseres, 1989).

There may be good reasons why you end up using a sub-optimal entry mode for capturing certain benefits, such as you lack the resources to acquire, or you do not find suitable partners to join with. Going for the sub-optimal entry mode may then be justified. However, make sure that you do not jump to entry modes that prevent you from creating the desired added value out of your international presence.

A company in the consumer goods business ended up regularly using alliances with local partners, often because acquisition of the local parties was, for various reasons, not feasible. An alliance was a back-up solution for them. The difficulty was that the alliances were managed on their side as if they were acquisitions while the partners were expecting them to be

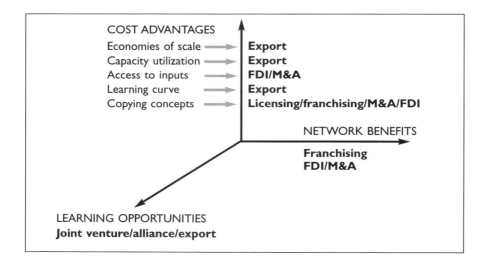

**Figure 3.2** The Conelearn framework and entry modes: which entry mode to use

true alliances. This led, on various occasions, to tensions and different visions on the alliance strategy between the two parties and ultimately to failures in the cooperation. We even developed a new term for this: *a cynical alliance*.

In an alliance, the selection of a partner should be carefully considered. What type of partners do you want: strong or weak, big or small? Again, it depends on what you are trying to achieve: strong partners may expose you to different ways of doing business and allow for learning, while weak partners may eventually suffice to build the required size or provide access to input factors.

The question of what the different parties bring to the alliance or joint venture, in the short and the long term, is also critical for the success of the formula. If a partner brings added value in the short term only, you may not expect the alliance to last very long. Daewoo was at some point a contracted manufacturer for GM in Asia, until it had built up enough knowledge and expertise in car manufacturing to go it alone. The benefits of an alliance must be balanced among partners, over time, unless all parties agreed that the alliance perspective was mainly a short term one.

Selecting the 'right' entry mode is recommended but definitely not sufficient to capture the benefits that you are after. The management of the chosen vehicle will contribute as much to its success as the selection itself. And vice versa, it is not because a vehicle is seemingly not delivering the required benefits that the vehicle itself was wrong.

The wave of strategic alliances in the car and truck industry, with DaimlerChrysler–Mitsubishi, VW–Scania and Renault–Nissan to name but a few, seems like a significant change of course in the industry. Up till then, mergers and acquisitions had been the leading method for consolidation. But the frustration of difficult integration in the post-M&A phase, as shown in the DaimlerChrysler debacle, seems to have pushed for less committed partnerships in the form of alliances. The justification is that alliances create less integration headaches while allowing for the synergies and technology sharing. An analyst observed: 'This may show that you can get 80% of the synergies by acquiring a fairly small equity stake' (*Financial Times*, 28 March 2000).

But where did it go wrong with the previous M&As: was the organizational instrument not adapted to the intended benefits or was it simply mismanaged? Turning to alliances to ensure the cost synergies seems odd if they did not materialize in outright M&As. According to research, M&As are much better suited for realizing cost savings than alliances (Bleeke et al., 1990). Are alliances preferred now because previous M&As may have been mismanaged? If management is the real problem, shifting to another mode will not solve that: one could expect similar issues to come up in the context of alliances. We will elaborate on these management challenges in Chapter 5.

## A strategic reflection on entering a foreign market

We are not suggesting that all other criteria on entry mode and market selection are thrown overboard. Many of the parameters that we found in the literature are very relevant, and should be included in the reflection. The problem is that limiting the discussion to these criteria risks neglecting the broader strategic agenda and the required focus on the internationalization benefits.

While there is nothing wrong with reducing your risk through an alliance, or gaining quick access to a market close to home by an acquisition, it does not automatically give you a *strategic* perspective on internationalization. Internationalization is about more than buying market share or limiting foreign investments through licensing: (overcoming) the disadvantages of an entry mode or target market may be exactly the reason why you choose that option! If you want to build a long-term sustainable advantage, you may want to take the 'hard route'. Your competitors can capture the advantages of an acquisition or a big market tomorrow as well, by entering the same market through the same mode. Strategically, you may want to think beyond the 'low hanging fruit' and look for ways to build a sustainable competitive edge.

In any event, you should realize that there are options. Any purely mechanical approach to market (entry) selection is dangerous. There is no need to rush into concrete decisions on which market to enter and how, without contemplating the potential alternatives and their impact. It may seem a natural next step to set up your own sales office after having exported for two years to a particular market. It should be no surprise when you start internationalizing to neighbouring markets first. You may have serious doubts about going with local partners because you had bad experiences with disloyal partners before and want full control of foreign activities this time. You quickly buy companies locally, because you cannot wait to build up a local network through organic growth. Sooner rather than later, however, you should think about how important speed is, how you would manage and control foreign activities, and whether a sales office actually makes sense or not. What other routes are there, and what could they bring to the company?

Once again, there is no general answer to each of these questions: there is no single best way to select and enter markets. What is important to understand is how a particular market would allow you to reap some benefits more than others, and will suggest a different way to enter it. The cost, network and learning dimensions will in this context provide as much guidance as some of the other criteria or reflections. You may be able to supplement some of the above criteria with our approach, and complement their primary operational orientation. It should persuade you not to jump to quick conclusions or decisions on practical aspects only, but to take a broader strategic perspective.

Alliances or mergers and acquisitions are not strategies, they can and should be just the instrument through which strategies are realized. Therefore, the quote by Relander at the beginning of this chapter indeed points to the available options but does not give much guidance as to what Sonera's strategy really is and hence which of these vehicles are the preferred ones. In any case the pros and cons of the different entry modes should be considered in terms of the specific benefits that you are after in your particular situation. And those may, and will, be different from those of your counterparts in other sectors or countries, and even different from those of your competitors in the same industry, even in the same place.

## CHAPTER 4

# On Organizational Structures and Blueprints

When your activities are spread widely around the globe, it is all the more important to organize them properly. Who manages which part? Who should report to whom and what are their exact responsibilities? How are units related to the company headquarters and the other units? What is the relationship of staff to line managers? Are responsibilities based on a geographic region, a product line, or a function? Does this responsibility count for the whole of the organization, the European part or just the home country? This is what organization charts are supposed to handle: they 'draw the lines' within and across the organization.

The organizational structure should allow the company to manage and control its people, products and other assets as effectively and efficiently as possible, wherever they are located. Division of labour and responsibilities will no longer be an option but a requirement for international companies. Headquarters and top management can no longer take care of worldwide activities on their own. Ever more diffuse portfolios of international activities, more complex product and service ranges, more diverse markets and competitive arenas will call for more complicated organizational set-ups and communication and reporting lines.

While the right organization structure by itself will not be sufficient to turn your company into a global master, the wrong structure will certainly hinder your aspirations. It can constrain or slow down the appropriate strategic and management decisions, or lock out the possible cost, network or learning benefits. This explains the omnipresent and ongoing struggle to do away with the strong geographically based structures in most multi-nationals operating in Europe, for example, as the focus now is on the expected and perceived benefits from cross-border integration. In other words, the operating structure often adds additional *internal* barriers, preventing you from creating and capturing the full benefit of the international playing field (see Chapter 5).

For many years, even decades, companies such as Philips in Europe had been trying to 'tilt the matrix', moving away from the dominant geographic dimension in their matrix organization, to release the synergies and cost benefits across the country organizations. ABB's recent restructuring from technologies towards client industries should unleash what they called the 'brain power', the potential for sharing and creating expertise and knowledge about the client. Matsushita's decision to set up a regional headquarters in Europe aimed to incorporate the market limitations in the European markets, while trying as far as possible to retain the efficiency of its formerly uniformly global organization.

We will argue in this chapter how international strategy and organization go hand in hand, and how the organization should or can bolster the implementation of the international strategy. A detailed discussion on the organizational modes of international companies and all the aspects that go with it is beyond our scope. We only want to draw your attention to some key considerations around organizational structure (organizational dimensions, coordination mechanisms and role of subsidiaries) that we have found to be critical in most companies and their link to the strategic imperatives that we have identified at this stage of strategic reflection.

In several of the cases we looked at, it became apparent that other elements, apart from structures, coordination mechanisms and systems, were important in making a new organization work, including the critical role of effective process management to change over from operating the existing structure, based on past strategies and experiences, to a new one, which reflects the intended strategy for the future. These aspects of process and transition management will be discussed in Chapter 5.

## Show me your organization chart, and I will tell you what strategy you have

The organizational structure should relate to the benefit you are seeking in your international strategy. In principle, therefore, the question of organization cannot and should not be answered before we have a clear and shared view on what our strategy is and what it will be in the future. In that sense, the paradigm of 'structure follows strategy' (Chandler, 1984) may to a certain extent apply to the international domain as well.

If one were to look at the organigram of Vedior International in the temping industry in 1998, most of us would come to the obvious conclusion that a multinational strategy drives the company. Each country in Europe has its own Vedior management team which bears responsibility for that country's strategy and profit and loss, and is not directly linked to the other country's organizations. 3M based its European organization on product lines. If you realize that 3M manages over 60,000 different products, a division of labour and assets on the basis of product lines across borders may make a lot of sense to get the required focus and differentiation.

Given that international strategy and its balance of global and local aspects are shaped largely by the cost and network benefits, we would expect to find the desired emphasis on the internationalization benefits in the organizational set-up. The organization chart should deliver the desired strategy and objectives. If you decide to go for cost benefits in your organization, it looks sub-optimal to go for a country-by-country organization. If you want to deliver network benefits to your clients, isolated and independent country subsidiaries would not be our suggested organizational approach.

When we ask managers to show us their organization charts, we may expect some of them to reply: 'Yes, but that is not the way we work really'. This means that either they are not working according to the official organization chart, or that people think the reality is a bit more complex than the statement suggests. It can happen that the real decisions are not made in the way that the organization chart prescribes, and communication flows differently across units and individuals. But if the chart does not represent how the company operates, should we not adapt the chart? As a strategy is designed to achieve specific objectives, if what you do in real life is not represented in your organization chart, it seems that your organization is not supporting your strategy, or is it?

This is conceptually simple, but in practice not always easy to develop, prioritize and implement. It requires you to know where the benefits and priorities are, and then align the organization's view and perception on these benefits. But especially in today's fast moving landscape, benefits may change over time, and you may have to adopt a different strategy, requiring you regularly to redo the structure.

Organizations are 'living organisms' and 'associations of people': it is not just a matter of optimizing an equation (on cost or network benefits or anything else) within certain conditions as though it were linear programming. Inventing the next catchy name for the ideal organizational blueprint – *transnational, supranational, the N-form or metanational* – may be exciting and inspirational, but the challenge is mostly to get the organization and its people to 'work' that way.

It is this complexity that makes our point valid to discuss and manage. Our message is intrinsically simple: among the range of determinants and preconditions for structuring your international activities, the globalization potential and strategic priorities undoubtedly should affect the type of organization that you are trying to build. You should at least return to the basic 'dominant strategic logic' in your specific context at a given moment.[1] It is hard enough to organize your activities and people the way you want and get the different teams to deliver the expected output. Having the focus right from the beginning is therefore almost a precondition for success. Would we not all like to make our organization efficient, effective, customer driven, flexible, entrepreneurial and innovative? Knowing that you probably will not be able to make all this happen at the same time, focusing your organization on one of these characteristics could make a big difference.

In a way, we may agree with those who claim that it does *not* work that way: structure should not *follow* strategy. The risk of the 'structure after strategy' adage is that it reduces the structure to a passive translation of yesterday's strategy, lagging behind the developments in the company. *Show me your organization chart and I will tell you what strategy you have* may therefore not be an attractive proposition, since it brings out the rustiness or lack of adaptation and focus in an organization. But this is also an invitation to use the structure in a proactive way.

The organizational structure may allow us to create a tension or gap between how we have been operating in the past, our history, ingrained habits and reflexes, and where our analysis and vision for the future tells us the emphasis *should* be. Organizational design, therefore, should become a strategic tool and an exercise of *change* management, and a reflection of the strategy (we will elaborate on this in Chapter 6).

The general principle remains that the strategic priorities in internationalization should define the organizational model, which is why we have spent so much time questioning the strategic requirements in your specific case. We now turn to some key issues in translating these into an appropriate organizational set-up and suitable organizational dimensions.

## Which dimension to push?

Global organizations fit global strategies, multinational strategies go with multinational organizations. How and along which dimension should an organization be structured then?

Global organizations are intended to transcend country borders, with no division on the basis of geographies.

> A global organization should feature a fluid, boundaryless structure that has only modest respect for divisional barriers. (Marquardt, 1999)

Units and managers in the units have a global responsibility, for example for a certain product (line) or a function, or other bases such as customer segments, or processes. In that sense, the boundaries in a truly 'global' organization are not defined by geography but by these other dimensions. The question is what dimension?

Multi-local or multinational organizations on the other hand are an assembly of independent national or local organizations, with little or no coordination between them. The key organizational dimension in these organizations is geographical.

Research confirmed that the organizational dichotomy between 'global' and 'multinational' organizations is still very valid (Harzing, 2000). Recently, some authors have been introducing alternative categorizations on the basis of a broader range of global and local characteristics (Calori et al., 2000). That is probably because, in reality, more creative solutions than the pure global or multinational structure and a more balanced mix and division of power throughout the organization are often called for.

Multinational organizations are particularly appropriate when the globalization potential is limited. If there is no or limited added value in coordinating activities across countries, the case of a small international playing field, it makes sound business sense to adapt your local activities and organization as much as possible to the specific requirements of the local clients, as we still see in many 'international' companies, such as Vedior International mentioned earlier.

But the key question remains, why have an international strategy in the first place? If there are hardly any cost or network advantages in the international market, we may not need to be international at all. This is a very valid comment, but, even then, there is still something to gain in international markets. You should capitalize as much as possible on the *learning opportunities* across markets in multinational businesses, especially in multi-local businesses where there is maximum diversity. The geographic dimension in your organization keeps the focus on local responsiveness, while some form of cross-border coordination allows for knowledge exchange and learning to happen.

Not only can the multinational organization create an opening for cross-border learning, it often also gives a platform for future globalization. When market limitations start to fade and cost or network advantages can develop further, the multinational strategy and organization allows a quicker transition towards a more globally oriented strategy and organization in order to reap the emerging benefits. It gives you a head start in the anticipated globalization wave in the industry. We will return to the aspects of organizational change in Chapter 5.

In any event, a multinational organization should be designed and managed according to the learning objectives. It is worth asking yourself whether your current decentralized structure stimulates cross-border learning. Certain organizational vehicles in multinational structures may not fit that profile. Several, especially newly internationalizing, organizations use an 'international division' as their organizational device in a multi-local set-up. This structure divides the activities between the domestic and foreign or international market, a geographic dimension if you wish. But if you expect to learn from your international experiences, would it not be wise to link this learning back to the domestic activities as well? And if you expect to get cost advantages in the longer term, should you separate home from foreign operations? While the international division may be a useful step in developing an international company, hardly any benefits will be fully delivered by separating domestic and foreign activities. For most industries and companies, a division on the basis of domestic versus non-domestic does not have a sound business foundation in the long run and serves mainly a transitional purpose.

This is the conclusion that Tractebel came to in 1997 when it merged with its international division Powerfin. The use of Powerfin as a separate vehicle had helped to get the initial internationalization going: it separated the more risky international investments, with their own requirements in terms of people, management, systems and resources, from the profitable, stable activities of Tractebel's domestic subsidiary Electrabel, and helped to convince the shareholders to embark on international projects.

Five years later, however, the division of Powerfin and Tractebel/ Electrabel was no longer required, and could only hinder benefits from cost, network or learning materializing to their full extent. Powerfin was subsequently integrated into Tractebel. In the next phase, one may wonder if integrating the learning of Tractebel back to the domestic activities of Electrabel, which would probably imply merging the two, would not make a lot of sense. This very point is possibly one of the reasons why EDF (France), while contemplating the requirements of its aggressive internationalization strategy, was not considering a separate listing of their international activities as a priority at this stage in the game (*Le Figaro*, 2 March 2001).

In cases where there are cost and network benefits, a more globally oriented strategy and organization may be required. Which dimension to choose in coordinating activities across borders will depend initially on where the globalization potential is and at what level.

---

Along which dimension exists the greatest potential for cost or network benefits?

■ Products?

■ Functions?

■ Competence?

■ Client industry?

■ Key accounts?

---

Usually organizations use more than one of these dimensions: they have a combination of product/functional and geographic responsibilities. However, we believe that, at any given point in time, there is probably only one or maybe two dimensions that can be on top at the same time. What matters is which of the dimensions actually dominates: where are you putting the *real* emphasis?

If the real globalization potential is actually at the level of the functions (R&D, production, sourcing), a functional organization might be worth considering. If the product range of the company is too diversified and requires more differentiation across business lines, the product (line) dimension could be put on top of the functional or geographic dimension. Other organizations see most of the benefit they seek at the level of competencies, key accounts or client industries: networking and learning are probably more important than cost in those cases. SAP, the German ERP-software producer, recently restructured its global activities, particularly in consulting, according to 'vertical markets' or client industries, very much in line with the earlier adaptation towards industry solution units or industry verticals by IBM.

When IBM was shaken up by low profitability in May 1994, it installed 'client industry verticals' as a key dimension, first for the European division and later for their entire global organization. An 'industry vertical' was intended to take care of all their clients in a given industry, for example banking, insurance, health care, transport, mostly on a regional, European basis, and others such as oil exploration and travel on a global basis.

This type of organization would allow IBM to reap network benefits, offering clients a worldwide service, and to nurture the learning about specific client needs as much as possible. It may not have been the best way to deliver sufficient cost benefits in R&D, purchasing or production. While industry verticals made sense for marketing, sales and services, it made less sense for the upstream activities in the value chain. But this was part of the message: IBM's strategic imperative at that time was to move in the direction of knowledge-based strategic services and consulting.

Several other organizations have similarly embarked on variations of 'international account management programmes' (key account, international key account or global account programmes), expecting the customer dimension to lead in the near future. While not all of these had a true international character (some companies designed account programmes per country), research confirmed that adapting and focusing the structure for (global) account management (including the assignment of specific staff and account managers, reporting processes and incentive schemes) is considered a key condition for success and increasingly so (Montgomery et al., 1999).

However, insufficient attention is usually paid, based on a careful Cone analysis of the customer's and your own business, to the underlying real benefits that we aim to supply and whether the organization of mere account management systems and functions will be sufficient to realize those benefits. Our sense is that some key account programmes fail because they are not integrated into the entire organization, but others fail because they *should* fail, in so far as there is no real added value to find (see also our discussion on slogans in Chapter 1).

The IBM example also illustrates how important it is to understand where exactly to find what benefits, at the finest level of detail. Differentiation along the value chain, activities, processes or tasks unlocks the potential for reaping the benefits exactly where they are. It does of course make the organizational structure and management of international activities more complicated, and will require substantial coordination to secure cross-border and cross-functional optimization.

## What really matters is reality

Which dimension is on top is not always clear from looking at the chart. What counts is not which dimension comes first in descending the chart from top to bottom. It is more meaningful to know which dimension rules in reality. What makes the organization and the people 'tick'? How do different parts and units really interact? What are the real communication lines? Who is really calling the shots? Who gets most reward and admiration? How are managers remunerated and promoted? Sometimes it is the strength of personalities that matters in understanding how the company really works.

It is not because we have a vice president production, next to a VP R&D and Marketing, reporting to the CEO that the functional dimension is key. If profit and loss responsibility is ultimately in the hands of the product line managers, who report to the different VPs on different functional aspects, and the de facto strategic decisions are taken by the product line management team, the dominant dimension will clearly be with the latter.

Not only are we talking here about the broader organizational 'rules of the game', we are also entering into the grey zone between the 'official' organization and 'informal' culture. When there is a gap between the dimension pushed by the modus operandi and that pushed by the chart, it means that either the chart is *running behind* the way things really work, in which case the organization chart should probably be adapted to the reality or it remains useless, or the chart is *running ahead*, in which case the chart can be used as a leverage for changing the modus operandi and culture and other conditions for successful change need consideration (as further elaborated on in Chapter 5).

## The danger of the ever-returning silos

As change is the only constant in organizations, they must avoid getting stuck with a given dimension. Even the best choice at a given point risks becoming sub-optimal later. There the danger of building 'silos' becomes apparent. While organizational units should take up key responsibilities in defining their strategy, in most instances, the coordination of activities across units would still be fruitful for all parties involved, if only for the learning and exchange of practices and knowledge across units. The paradox of international organizational development implies that once the appropriate divisionalization has been put in place, on the relevant criteria, as much effort and energy will be needed for implementing mechanisms and systems to transcend the divisions. Most people are well aware of the risks of geographical silos, probably because they have already lived through some of the shortcomings of this set-up. Nevertheless they seem less vigilant about functional or product silos they may put in place in their attempt to shift the power away from the country organizations, which is the problem of the ever-returning silo.

In case of a functional organization, there is a risk of dissecting the value chain into isolated activities, without sufficient cross-functional coordination. The installation of the Trio teams in Alcatel was an attempt to improve the coordination between the R&D department, the production department, and the product line responsible for the final product and its sales. This team set-up should avoid any of the departments passing on the bug in times of R&D delays, production problems or frustration in the sales force with a low response from the market. The problem of the Trio remained the coordination across country organizations.

Especially in businesses where clients want cross-border offerings, product line unit managers risk being overly focused on their products. 3M Europe installed a product line organization to improve the effectiveness and efficiency of its European country-based organization. By so doing, however, it left the demand of international clients for a single contact and contract with 3M Europe largely unanswered. The question is, which imperative deserved to be superior in those days: efficiency and product focus or client focus?

## What will fall between the cracks?

Regardless of the dimension chosen, you can be sure that ultimately things will fall between the cracks. The question is what and how much of it will fall between the cracks and between which cracks? If you turn upside down the objective to maximize the benefits, one could say that the purpose is to limit the loss of Conelearn benefits. How many economies of scale will you lose in R&D if you spread R&D over different product lines? How important are cross-border offerings in the total turnover, and how do they weigh against the importance of locally tailored offerings? How big is the risk of losing opportunities for cross-fertilization and learning between different product lines?

Typically, the lost opportunities to learn and share within and across organizational units are underestimated. Whatever dimension you push, Nonaka and Takeuchi (1995) predict that a company's ability to create, store and disseminate knowledge across the organization will be crucial for staying ahead of the competition. Knowledge creation and sharing should not only happen within the organizational units, created on the basis of the most relevant dimensions. The future competitive edge of global masters will be embedded in their ability to manage their best practices and knowledge, across country borders for multinational organizations, across product lines for global product line organizations, or across functions for global functional organizations.

Especially for multi-local businesses, the knowledge exchange and the ability to create and share knowledge between different markets could be the added value of their international presence. A lot of service businesses may not intrinsically have a strong globalization potential (cost and network axes) but could benefit mainly from their international exposure through the exchange of practices, and clash of ideas (our learning axis). Not surprisingly, state-of-the-art international knowledge management systems were typically developed first in consulting businesses (for example Andersen, Price Waterhouse, McKinsey), financial services businesses (for example Skandia) and other service and information businesses.

Effective international knowledge management requires the systems, processes and organizational culture for people to give to and take from their international colleagues, within or between units. While technology platforms may support a free flow of ideas and experiences, in most instances they will not be sufficient. The management attitude and awareness, and appropriate incentives, sometimes considered the 'soft' aspects, are usually the hardest to develop.

You should focus at any given point in time on the main sources of potential advantage, whether cost, network or learning, knowing that other, more marginal aspects will not be covered for the moment. And which benefit is key and which one is more marginal will change over time. That is why organizational structures should evolve from one dimension to another: as efficiency and cost are dealt with in the product organization, you may want to move towards a client organization in order to capture the increasingly important networking benefits and knowledge sharing and creation while hoping to retain the efficiency of the former product organization.

## Beyond the centralization–decentralization dilemma

There is often a tendency to constrain the debate on organizational structures to a choice between centralization or decentralization: should we not concentrate decision-making? At what level? To what extent would centralization jeopardize local responsiveness? But do we not risk reinventing the wheel in every country organization when we decentralize decision-making power? While the centralize–decentralize dichotomy may be an appealing starting point in management discussions to simplify the decision-making cycle, it runs the risk of overlooking alternative coordination and integration mechanisms.

Although it may seem helpful to physically centralize decision-makers in order to facilitate coordination, it is not always the most efficient and practical route for linking activities and people. There are alternative ways to integrate activities across borders. The current state of technology offers an array of tools to support coordinated decision-making and stimulate communication between key managers around the organization.

The range of possible coordinating mechanisms is rather wide: there are structural and formal mechanisms, such as organization structure, formal authority, formalization, planning and control, and less formal mechanisms, such as lateral relations, informal communication and socialization through culture and incentive mechanisms. Research has indicated that there is a growing interest in more subtle mechanisms, probably because formal mechanisms are found to be unidimensional and lack the need for differentiation and nuance (Bartlett and Ghoshal, 1987b; Martinez and Jarillo, 1989).

The challenge with the informal type of devices is that they depend a great deal on the willingness of managers to participate, and fall back on the voluntary cooperation of people. In that sense, these mechanisms are harder to control, and offer fewer guarantees for effective coordination. The recent debacles in the foreign subsidiaries of high-tech companies such as Real Software and Lernout and Hauspie Speech Products, both from Belgium, have again exposed the issue of control: in both cases, the lack of coordination and control from headquarters on the overseas subsidiaries led to major surprises about the breadth and depth of the local client base and financial resources. The history of internationalization is filled with these *accidents de parcours* (chance mishaps), a less recent one being the debacle at Barings in Singapore that brought down the whole investment bank. Central management's wish to give independence to the local management and for informal coordination failed and had to be complemented and substituted with much more rigorous coordination and control systems.

Formal structures, however, generally do not do the job in and of themselves either. They too only work to the extent they are run by people who understand and share the purpose and are willing to cooperate. Therefore, we sometimes put it in this paradox: 'a matrix only works for companies that do not need it' (and maybe the same can be said about most other organizational types!). People and cultures who have a natural tendency to share and coordinate with the relevant experts and colleagues in their company do not need a formal matrix structure to impose this way of working, while those who do not have this tendency will hardly find motivation to start doing so in the hierarchical structure.

Very often, a mix of formal and informal mechanisms will be necessary. Exactly what mix will depend on what the objective and intended benefit of the coordination actually is. It is not hard to imagine that the type of coordination that ensures economies of scale is probably intrinsically different from those mechanisms that stimulate cross-border learning. At the risk of generalizing, we could state that the optimal degree of formal coordination probably declines as you move from cost, over network to learning benefits. This is illustrated in Figure 4.1. In the early 1980s Procter & Gamble Europe started using Euro Brand Teams (EBT) as a way to improve coordination across European country organizations. These teams brought together relevant decision-makers from all over Europe in order to reflect on the marketing strategy of P&G in Europe, and look for ways to realize synergies. A similar approach emerged within 3M: the European Management Action Teams (EMATs) in the late 1980s were the first step towards cross-country coordination of sales and marketing strategies of 3M in Europe. In both examples, the teams were a useful phase in the organizational development in Europe, but were not a sustainable, long-term solution. The teams lacked the authority to decide on strategies for Europe and could only act as information and vision-sharing groups, while the final authority remained in the hands of people not participating in the teams, for example the country MDs (managing directors) within 3M Europe. The full synergies of cross-border coordination were only realized when the formal authority problem of EBTs and EMATs had been solved.

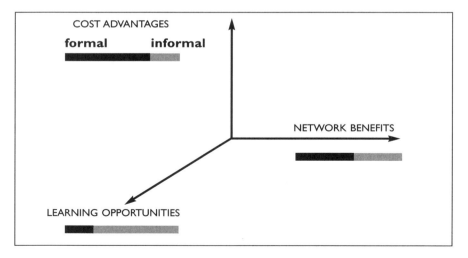

**Figure 4.1** Conelearn framework: how to balance formal and informal coordination?

Eureko, as a cross-border insurance alliance, held back for years on formal coordination to facilitate the cross-border learning. As the emphasis of certain partners shifted towards cost benefits (and to a lesser extent network advantages), the recent merger between two of the partners, BCP from Portugal and Achmea from the Netherlands, clearly signalled a way to install manifest power and decision structures and hence more formal coordination. Their challenge remains to leverage the size of their operations, mainly for efficiency reasons, and in the meantime to allow for more informal mechanisms to (continue to) share and exchange know-how in the new company and with the alliance partners.

## Implications for headquarters and subsidiaries

The preceding observations have important implications for the relationship between company headquarters and subsidiaries. How should the centre rule and what role should the subsidiaries play?

Bartlett and Ghoshal (1986) identified four potential types of roles for subsidiaries on the basis of the competence of the local subsidiary and the importance of the local market, for example because of market size: *the strategic leaders*, *contributors*, *implementers* and *black holes* (Figure 4.2). Strategic leaders are highly competent subsidiaries covering an important local market. Contributors have an important capability, but do not control

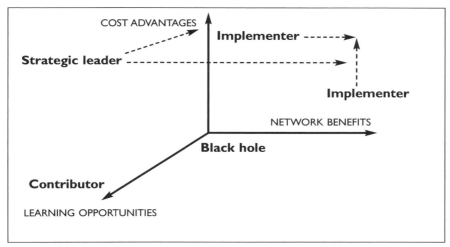

**Figure 4.2** The Conelearn framework and the role of subsidiaries
*Source:* Based on topology of Bartlett and Ghoshal, 1986

a substantial market. The implementers have no distinctive competence, and are not in a market of particular importance, but offer the company the opportunity to capture economies of scale or scope that are crucial for the company's global strategy. Black holes are worrisome as they deliver in an important market but offer no added value to the company.

Reinterpreting the role of the local subsidiaries from a Conelearn point of view, you may want to look for *strategic leaders* and *contributors* when seeking international learning: they may have a competence that you want to benefit from in the whole organization. Additionally, *strategic leaders* cover a weighty market: this market could be key because it is large and may help to capture cost benefits, and/or clients have substantial operations in that market and need the services and products there too. *Implementers* are useful just to implement the standardized strategy which has been set: they are supposed to deliver cost and/or network advantages. The *black holes* will deliver you none of these benefits.

Classifying the subsidiaries on this basis should allow you to check to what extent the local organizations could be ready to take up the role you have defined for them in your international strategy and objectives. With a lack of contributors, you may have to rethink the learning objectives you have; too many contributors could make the cross-border coordination and integration of activities a complex matter.

The organization around Centres of Excellence, found in Nestlé (Bouttelier et al., 2000) or Alcatel for example, is based on the strength and expertise of different subsidiaries in various areas. Their role in managing the learning and know-how of the company across borders is crucial to leverage the international presence of both organizations in terms of efficiency and innovation.

Birkinshaw (2000) has questioned such an approach as being based too much on a headquarters view and instead has developed an argument for a subsidiary-based perspective on these issues, in an attempt to recognize and foster entrepreneurship. This argument seems to fit particularly well with a focus on the learning axis, emphasizing the importance of local initiatives, diversity and innovations, but will probably remain less appropriate when cost synergies or network advantages for clients are the main international benefits being sought.

It is probably no coincidence that this line of argument seems more attractive at a time when many 'traditional' multinationals may have reached the limit of the international playing field potential on the first two axes or have perhaps come to realize that pushing it further may run the risk of 'overglobalizing'. A return to the more entrepreneurial, often locally differentiated, roles of country managers seems to be attracting real interest

(see Quelch, 1992; Quelch and Bloom, 1996), even in what were traditionally perceived as global organizations such as Coca-Cola (*Financial Times*,
6 March 2001) and McDonald's or global newcomers such as AOL, MTV
and CNN International.

## The role of regional headquarters

In light of the intensifying regionalization of the economy, and the
increasing value for companies to think in terms of regional strategies, as
discussed before, several multinationals with global coverage have
introduced regional headquarters. Those headquarters mediate between the
global headquarters, perceived to be too far from the particular market to
understand the local requirements, and the local subsidiaries. We have seen
US and Japanese multinationals, such as P&G, 3M and Toyota, set up
European headquarters, and US and European multinationals, such as Otis,
ABB and Seagram develop Asian headquarters (Schütte, 1996).

While this may seem to be an interesting solution for the traditional
headquarters–subsidiary tensions, because it is a halfway solution, it may
not necessarily achieve what is expected. It does help to regionalize the
strategies; it could be a useful catalyst for coordination between local
country organizations at a manageable level; and it allows the strategy to be
tailored to the regional market needs. But it also confounds decision-
making and increases the complexity of strategy coordination between the
three levels; it risks getting squeezed between global headquarters and the
local subsidiaries, especially when the regional headquarters was intended
only for coordination and lacks decision-making power; and it may turn into
a halfway solution that brings none of the benefits to their fullest extent.

In-depth research has shown that regional headquarters are, however,
useful organization units within multinationals, and are expected to become
stronger in the future (Schütte, 1996). Also, regional headquarters were
important but not dominant in shaping the multinational's regional perspective, and had only a negligible influence on the creation of synergies
between local subsidiaries. Staff at RHQ generally feel more linked to the
global headquarters than to the region and are mostly expatriates from the
home country. This highlights the risk of duplicating the headquarters at
regional level, while wasting opportunities to reap regional synergies.

We have the impression from our observations that the role of regional,
and especially European, headquarters, differs among US and Japanese
multinationals. American companies see it as a way to integrate their
European activities more actively, and improve efficiency and effectiveness.

P&G and 3M felt that their local subsidiaries in Europe could reap significant Conelearn benefits from working together, and used the European head office to do that. Japanese multinationals, such as Toyota or Matsushita, felt that their product lines needed to be tailored better to the European market. Thus, regional headquarters can play a role in coordinating country organization or in tailoring strategy to a particular regional market.

The added value from regional headquarters lies particularly in their ability to stimulate regional strategies and find a more creative and manageable solution for the globalization–localization tension. If we look at the global integration process within P&G and 3M, and the regionalization in Toyota and Matsushita, the role of the regional headquarters was key in this process. In either case, the role of the regional staff changed dramatically over time: often from advisory to line responsibility. In some instances, the European headquarters were even abolished or became virtual: this could indicate either that regional head office had not delivered the benefits that were expected, or that the role had been fulfilled and could now be taken over by global head office and/or local subsidiaries on a virtual basis.

# SECTION 3

# On Managing the Process of Internationalization

So far this book has dedicated much of its argument to emphasizing the importance of identifying and *analysing* the benefits of internationalization that a strategy should be after – the why question – and *specifying* what organizational vehicle is best suited to realize these benefits – the what question. We deliberately classified the 'strategy' question under the 'why' part in order to emphasize the importance of formulating the objectives, drivers and benefits and classified the organizational question under the 'what' part, in so far as its focus on charts and structures does not answer the more important implementation and process questions, to which we will turn now. However complex these analytical steps may be, we would argue that they may constitute the easiest part. When all the arguments and analyses have been said and done, the real issues are about to show up. These issues are related to implementation – the how question.

■ In the implementation phase we concentrate on reaping the benefits of globalization. At this stage you will realize how many of the potential benefits in the international playing field will actually show up and why

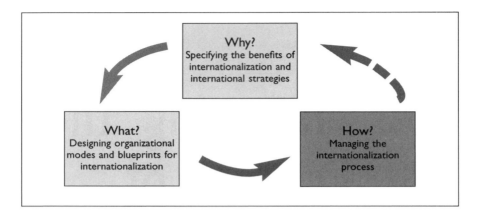

**Figure S3.1** The how of internationalization: managing the process

they do not materialize as expected. It is also at this point that the management of the *process* becomes critical. We therefore treat process management as the third cornerstone of successful internationalization (see Figure S3.1). Critical in this part of the exercise are the management challenges in overcoming the many barriers and pitfalls for implementing 'what you decided on'.

■ In addition, we consider process management aspects of internationalization at another, probably even more important and holistic level: we firmly believe that the management of the *overall agenda* as an integrated system, the interaction and integration of strategy, organization and implementation, is even more critical. The foundations of successful internationalization and globalization, as with other strategic challenges, lie in managing the loop and interactions between all its different aspects in a combined and continuing process, and not simply as a logical sequence of stages. It is not a mechanical procedure whereby you simply move 'from why, to what and then to how'. Long-term success is often deeply rooted in the management of the complex iterations and careful manoeuvring throughout this loop. It is a ongoing process of analysis, organizational change, management of people and teams, adapting the strategy to changes in the market, rethinking the organization, overcoming barriers for implementation, and back. You may want to enter the loop and iterations at different starting points (as illustrated in Figure S3.2).

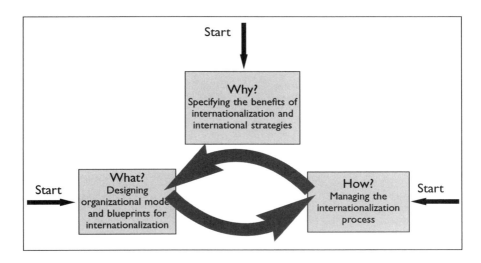

**Figure S3.2** Managing the iterations in the why–what–how loop of globalization

In Chapter 5, we will highlight some of our findings on how to move *from theory to action*, the 'simple' implementation process. We will discuss some of the strategy and organization implementation challenges in an international environment, indicating the common internal barriers we have come across in our research, and suggest ways to overcome them. In Chapter 6 we will return to the broader picture and reinforce the point of an iterative process through the loop: how to move *from action back to reflection and management of the entire process*.

Many of these issues will be very familiar, some will undoubtedly have been dealt with easily through the overall management style and culture in your company, others you may have overlooked and find useful to think through.

We do not believe that we, or anyone else, can tell you unambiguously how to manage internationalization and give you the magic formula for a successful process. Particularly since the purpose is to gain a unique advantage over your competitors, we are not able to give you a grand formula that produces uniqueness either, and, if we did, that uniqueness would quickly evaporate or be copied anyway. As clearly stated at the outset, our attempt with this book was to inspire and support your own reflection on some of these critical issues in the key processes that we identified.

## CHAPTER 5

# Managing the Implementation Process

Internationalization is more than just deciding on the strategic and organizational blueprint you should go for. Yet, we see a continuing tendency to underestimate the importance of working through *how* to put the blueprints into action. More specifically, the critical issue usually is how to get from here, the current strategy and organization, to there, the desired strategy and organization. This may seem simple, too simple. But a manager with experience in the globalization of a major multinational from Asia said: 'Those that planned it, saw it too easy.'

In the management literature, as well as in many real-life internationalization discussions, the tendency is to search for the model that is expected to guarantee international success. It goes without saying that top management invests significant time and money (including consultants' time) in deciding on the ideal strategic and organizational model for internationalizing; it is less common to dedicate sufficient time to the implementation challenges, and the required management tasks in getting it done. We strongly believe in the value of considering the implementation aspects before, during and after the start of the process. This means that you should try to anticipate the barriers that you may encounter along the path, identify the steps to take to overcome the obstacles and install the supporting mechanisms.

How often is one or the other internationalization decision treated just like another investment opportunity? The principal decisions have been made at the top, on the basis of a net present value calculation, EVA (economic value added) or whatever other financial or accounting measure, and the implementation is delegated to a task force, expatriate managers, a corporate HR (human resource) team, international division or external advisors who should find you the right acquisition target, the best market for you to enter or the right people to do it for you. It is not just a matter of getting the figures right, making the grand plan, agreeing on the go-ahead, freeing up the required financial resources and then just executing what has been decided on.

Of course it is helpful to have somebody who speaks different languages, who can take orders, arrange delivery in foreign markets, and send the invoices. But will you be getting the cost, network and learning opportunities that we have identified? Does internationalization just take off on the basis of a few ad hoc international deliveries? Can you expect the internationalization to manage itself and the organization to develop smoothly towards foreign markets? Apparently, it does not work that way.

When did you last hear or read about a multinational deciding to restructure their international activities, and setting up regional head-quarters to coordinate or centralize a number of functions? You staff headquarters in Brussels or London to coordinate marketing campaigns and pricing in the different national markets or decide to centralize production and streamline product range, as a European specialty chemicals company recently did. They calculated how many million euro they could save in the next five years by doing so. But immediately, you could see local marketing and production managers refusing to give up local product specialties, claiming headquarters did not know their market and finding twenty-five excuses to run their own campaigns, and deviate from the central pricing and specification list. Another chemicals company launched a European pricing scheme, and found its local sales people protesting heavily against it. How come that these and many other managers seem so reluctant to adapt? Why don't they just implement the new European strategy if it makes so much sense?

The net result is the same: the 'plan' (assuming there was one) does not work. You expected things to be easy once the principal decision was taken, and you left the execution to others, or you neglected what could go wrong. You thought it was conceptually rather simple, but experienced how hard it was to implement. Our suggestion is that you prepare explicitly for things to go 'wrong' or be 'difficult': you will most certainly encounter obstacles that keep you from installing the appropriate international strategy and organization. You must think of all the reasons why it may not work the way you foresee it, before the implementation.

## Identifying internal barriers

Bearing in mind that the market limitations on the cost and network side often strongly reduce the globalization potential and define the boundaries of the international playing field, now we must add a number of internal and company-specific aspects which complicate the implementation of an international strategy and organization. In effect, these limit the realizable benefits as indicated in Figure 5.1. Several organizational characteristics potentially mortgage your company's ability to realize certain benefits to their full extent or at the foreseen time.

Internationalization and globalization indeed imply change. Often it is more than just change: it is strategic transformation, sometimes even a revolution. Such a change in the organization tends to collide with structural counter forces and inertia, resistance and frustration of all kinds, shapes and forms.

In our research we identified two broad categories of internal barriers to internationalization: the *organizational structure*, and the *people* in the organization. With organizational structure we refer to many different aspects: communication and reporting lines, culture, systems and processes (for example appraisal or IT systems), or the history and modus operandi of the company. We will first discuss the nature of both types of barriers, and then indicate a number of key conditions for overcoming them.

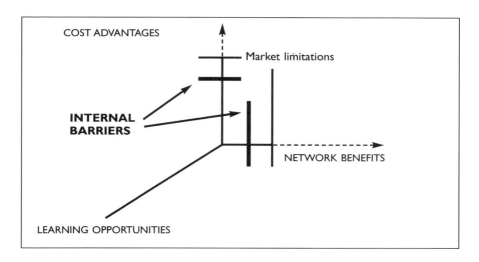

**Figure 5.1** Internal barriers linked with the real globalization potential

## Organizational structure

We emphasized in Chapter 4 how important it is to align the international organization with your strategy or vice versa and draw a chart that fits the intended benefits of internationalization. We also indicated that drawing the boxes and lines on paper is rarely the real problem. Different aspects and derivatives of the old blueprint, such as culture or systems, may hamper getting the new structure to work in reality.

■ *Communication* and *reporting lines* are typically embedded in the organizational structure and culture. When transferring ideas or coordinating development projects internationally, you need people in the different locations to talk to each other and communicate effectively. The lack of these communication lines or the old habits embedded in people's behaviour can inhibit the coordination of activities, and jeopardize cost, network or learning benefits. The problem is much more complicated than a change in the blueprint might imply, because reality is often poorly captured even by the old organization chart.

■ The *organizational culture*, which is an expression of how the organization really works, can thus be an even greater block to make the international strategy work, while it can be a powerful enabler for those organizations who have change, flexibility and cooperation built in. A culture that thrives on independence, empowerment and self-managed teams may find it burdensome to incorporate increased coordination of activities. The culture of Philips, Alcatel and IBM was deeply rooted in the individual country organizations and getting people to optimize resources on an international scale took time. It required building a different culture. 3M Europe, on the other hand, had a very different culture, based on innovation, sharing of know-how and cooperation, which allowed it to make the required organizational shifts much more quickly (see the later discussion on 'Shock therapy or slow and steady').

■ Each company has its unique way of doing business. Its modus operandi, closely intertwined with the culture, is often the result of the history, years of experience, trial and error of different policies, personal influence from key actors, and other forces. The operational mode is almost by definition in tune with the past and present, and not necessarily with future objectives. Letting all of this evolve towards the new international status may take time, and it will certainly require attention.

- The installation of performance measurement and HR appraisal *systems*, or the IT infrastructure is grounded on a number of parameters, which may not have much to do with the internationalization criteria that should be guiding the future strategy. Many companies lack the accounting and reward systems necessary for accurately following up on internationalization. Many multinationals experienced the difficulty of comparing financial data across their national subsidiaries, because of different accounting practices and systems. Formal planning and project management systems could lack the international perspective required for getting the benefits. The decision cycle for investing in foreign markets possibly differs from the traditional way of ruling operations.

- Similarly we noticed that the profit and loss responsibility often lagged behind the emerging international reality and strategic objectives. While P&G and 3M continued to build a pan-European organization, the profit and loss remained initially in the hands of country managers. This made it difficult for local managers, whose success was measured on their own bottom line, to accept decisions that were taken on a European level and were good for all of Europe, but bad for specific countries. It is hardly surprising that the new pan-European strategy does not catch on when all the benefits are captured centrally and the local managers, who remain responsible for profit and loss, barely get to see any of them and indeed often only see increased costs (in the short term).

We detected quite innovative incentive mechanisms for securing the implementation of a pan-European strategy. To avoid the question 'who gets what', a multinational in the ice-cream business proposed giving the benefits back to the local organizations. The local managers were asked what marketing efforts they would embark on with an extra budget of 5 million euros, and, obviously, they had plenty of ideas to boost their local sales. The figure mentioned represented the potential efficiency gains from coordination and centralization of the production units. If the local units were willing to give up their production and leave that to headquarters, they could directly benefit and get an extra marketing budget. Despite the success of such a creative trick in this particular case, we still question such an approach as a long-term solution, as you should be trying to implement a new strategy built on a cross-border logic, instead of an old country-by-country structure.

Similar issues have come up in several central purchasing or global sourcing exercises. We experienced the frustration of the management with newly centralized purchasing departments in several companies. Local management was very reluctant to give up its purchasing authority, because they did not see the benefit, and often it was not even clear whether one existed or how big it was, especially as, even if there was a benefit, *they* did not get it anyway.

Even assuming that the rationale for a new international strategy and organization is clear, you cannot expect the culture, operational methods or systems to change to the new organizational set-up automatically and overnight. Internationalization is more than just turning a switch in your day-to-day operations, hence the importance of managing the implementation process.

In the early stages of internationalization, the organizational structure typically shows up as a barrier through the 'international division'. This unit holds responsibility for the non-domestic activities, and in most cases was set up to explicitly differentiate home from foreign markets (if it does not differentiate, why was it detached in the first place?). It shifted some of the challenges in internationalizing, to secure cost, network or learning benefits, to the internal relations between the international division and the rest of the organization.

Should we expect the international division to be a barrier or an enabler for the internationalization benefits in the long term? While it made sense to separate the home activities from the foreign ones in some of the cases we studied, we also saw how debatable its role was in reaping the benefits in the longer term, and how quickly the organization ran into the issue of linking the domestic with the international assets (this organizational issue has been observed in various other contexts as well).[1] Powerfin, as the internationalization division of Tractebel, was a useful vehicle to overcome the shareholders' fear of risking money in foreign markets, but was made redundant soon after it was acceptable for Tractebel itself to bet on international activities.

The structure and its characteristics often become more of a barrier in the later phases of internationalization and globalization. Multinational corporations often have to deal with sensitive balancing acts between geographies, product areas, functions and other dimensions in order to get the maximum cost, network or learning benefits. In various parts of the organization, conflicts can arise between what the ideal structure for the established multinational should be, the blueprint, as defined in Chapter 2, and how things have 'always' been, for example how, traditionally, the business has been run.

## Circumventing the structure

A frequently used method we observed was to circumvent the structure through 'overlay' structures, or 'ad hoc teams'. Coordination teams, such as the Euro Brand Teams in P&G, European Marketing Action Teams in 3M, or Trio's in Alcatel, were set up to cross the lines in the organization chart, whether based on geography, functions or any other dimension. Other teams typically had a de facto limited time horizon, such as the Y2K or Euro Teams. The idea is to overrule the normal reporting lines, and select relevant people who should coordinate and work together on a specific topic.

These substructures often indicate what the current structure lacks and where the shortcomings are. 'Overlay' structures try to superimpose the characteristics of a potential 'future' structure over the 'current' one. They create a tension in the organization, as, by definition, they bypass the current structure and its reporting lines. It is their purpose to go 'against' the current organization. The challenge is to convert this tension into a positive energy for more structural changes.

In many instances, the 'ad hoc teams' acted as devices for learning how to deal with constantly changing organizational designs and adapt the formal organization chart, and identify which systems or cultural aspects were blocking genuine change. The EMATs of 3M were experiments that prepared for the shift in the structure from geography towards product groups.

There is an interesting paradox at work here in the sense that teams should work as hard as possible to make themselves redundant. Regardless of the *ex ante* time scale, they should be of a temporary nature only. They either become part of the new structure or they accomplish their mission, for example the successful implementation of the euro, and everybody reverts back to the existing organization. The worst thing that can happen to a team is that the existing structure is confirmed while you structurally undermine the organization through 'permanent cross-unit teams'. As a manager observed, paraphrasing a well-known saying: 'It is OK to confuse the organization for some time, but it is not OK to keep it that way for too long.'

When the 'overlay' structures or teams become permanent, they become the new structure, hence they are no longer 'overlay', and you should let the old structure go.

Because many of the teams ran into the logic of the existing structure, and if they did not, maybe they were not necessary in the first place, they risked failure and eventually dying out. This form of redundancy is obviously not what the teams and their management should look for. They risk only increasing the reluctance for change, feeding the frustration of several people and building up inertia. Hence the management of the teams, and their expectations become key: it is essential that these teams do not fail and jeopardize authentic change in the longer run.

The success of the overlay structures depends a great deal on how they are used and managed. We should realize that teams and substructures are meant to serve the future strategic objectives, and are often running ahead of the current organization chart. In other words, they fall outside the normal routine and should be managed accordingly. Therefore, there is a limit to how many substructures an organization and its people can deal with and control.

Teams should serve a clear purpose. If you know what the substructures should do, such as temporarily bypass the structure around a specific issue or serve as experiments for true changes in the structure, and how they should contribute to the overall strategic agenda, chances are you may get something out of it.

The current organization chart is after all only a temporary snapshot of an organization in flux. The strategic question is not only what your current organization chart is, but also what the next one should look like, and how you can get there. The organizational and strategic development of your activities is a continuing process, whereby you manage the transition from the current strategy and organization to the next one. And the use of a substructure and ad hoc teams represent a different change path than the overnight alteration of the structure. Whatever the speed of transition, nevertheless it remains critical to have certain conditions in place, as we demonstrate below.

## People

Typically, internationalization gets pushed from the top of the organization, but its success depends as much on the people who have to implement it. Although we will argue later that it requires the commitment of top management, this does not mean that you can ignore involving the many layers throughout the organization. We have seen many internationalization processes get stuck or become counterproductive because of a typical pattern showing that each time we moved down a step in the organization, we could sense a lesser degree of involvement and knowledge. Yet the real benefits were supposed to be realized throughout the organization. It should be no surprise that in such a situation frustration and resistance can set in. Therefore, as people are to be the engine or driving force behind the process, a lack of involvement, sharing and communication quickly leads to people becoming the main internal barriers rather than drivers.

Even when the structural conditions for international change have been met, you can run into *people* as the main barrier. You may find a few people positioned as roadblocks, preventing the realization of the true benefits. A manager testified: 'We get messages from the top, but it is not happening at the bottom.'

Imagine you want to offer the international network as a selling point to your clients, and you dress up your organization in order to manage international sales contracts, but find your local salespeople blocking any cross-border sales. You want R&D to benefit from scale as much as possible, and centralize it in a global R&D lab. And still the local product managers want to tailor products to their local needs and have engaged local developers to do so, as happened in a chemicals company we observed. The not-invented-here syndrome on the 'receiving' end keeps your marketing department from benefiting from the exchange of advertising themes. Or as we heard in one case: 'Local staff are very reluctant to change. They should not insist so much on doing things their own way' (notice the emphasis on 'they').

In the best case, your sales or R&D people slow down globalization and have difficulties coping with the cross-border coordination, because they lack the perspective, experience, competencies, skills, or the capacity to handle the complexity of international operations. Such problems erupted vividly at Alcatel when it was trying to cross the borders with its new product development concepts, under the name of Trio and Product Life Cycle, which it had already successfully introduced to bridge the traditional silos of R&D, marketing and production within different countries.

As one manager in Procter & Gamble witnessed in the early days of the company's European integration process:

> As a junior person, I was in a very difficult position. The European headquarters expected me to get the country manager in line, and the country manager expected me to hold off the headquarters. This situation was very bad, because the conflict ended up at too low a level ... only strong people could handle the situation.

There are few substitutes for life experience through cross-border teamwork, intensive international training or expatriation as a way to gather the international management skills required. This is where international training, management development or management exchange and rotation programmes may prove valuable.

However, the opposition to change goes beyond 'just not knowing how to deal with it'. It is expressed in a variety of ways. Here are some popular phrases we came across:

It will be too difficult!

We will make a fool of ourselves!

I don't understand why we are the ones to take on international experiments.

Let us come back to reality!

In principle you are right, but …

It is obvious that the person with these great internationalization ideas is not a practitioner!

Let us form a committee.

Let us sleep on it.

We are not going to rush into this, are we?

We have tried it before.

It is against my experiences.

Then everything we have learnt until now will be antiquated.

You don't quite understand the problem.

It cannot be sold.

You will never be able to sell that idea to the management.

The others won't accept it.

If we follow your internationalization proposal, it will be your responsibility.

We don't have the staff required for internationalization.

We are too busy!

We must keep in mind that we are working with people.

We are not educated for this.

We don't have the necessary facilities for internationalization.

And we are confident that you can add a few dozen of your own creative excuses.

People tend to have all sorts of reasons for blocking change: some of these are rational, others emotional, many a mixture of both. You can hardly expect your local R&D managers to share ideas with their colleagues, if their bonus depends on how many local innovations they managed to bring out. Emotional aspects often get in the way when people face change: inertia is a very natural characteristic of an organization.

## How to overcome the barriers?

While you may initially be discouraged from looking at all the reasons why internationalization may never bring what you hoped it would, it may save you a lot of trouble to *think ahead* and *anticipate* what the barriers could look like. Expect things to be difficult and go wrong, and allow yourself to adapt your path to avoid, bypass, minimize or overcome the obstacles. Your strategy should include ways to deal with the barriers. Good preparation may be half the solution. Acknowledging and anticipating the existence of real and imagined barriers eliminates half of the work in overcoming them.

However, mere identification of the structural and human barriers, while essential, will not be enough. You will probably have to work on these in order to overcome them. This requires managing a complicated process, which should at least pay attention to the following conditions:

- Committing top management

- Developing a clear and shared rationale

- Involving the relevant actors

- Supporting with systems and processes

- Securing the necessary resources and competencies

- Building an international mindset

- Deciding on the time frame.

## Top commitment

If the top management of the company does not take the internationalization seriously and sends out this message, we can hardly expect the people who have to implement it in the field to feel that international assets are worth spending time and energy on. Internationalization will sooner or later require top management to stand up: it cannot be handled lower down in the organization alone as it will force a rethink of the strategy, organization and processes of the whole company.

You may delegate the development of key aspects of international operations to lower levels but the overall agenda cannot be run and managed in the field only. The creation of an 'international division' may allow a dedicated team to concentrate on foreign activities, and permit a clearer division of labour, but do not expect these people to manage the broader strategic agenda of internationalization.

Philippe Bodson, CEO of Tractebel, championed the internationalization of his utility group. He sent out the message that money was no longer a constraint as long as the international projects were bringing something to the table. The international team he put together had his full support, and could count on their CEO to defend the projects to the board.

A large player in the services sector in Europe, who had engaged in a joint venture with a local partners to implement a successful service concept in a local Asian market, realized that, in order to implement the concept, it needed to change the entire organization of the local partner. For the local project managers it was important to have the commitment of the top of the organization back home but it was not their role to manage the broader strategic context.

## A shared rationale

Organizational structures and operational processes can easily be changed on paper, but making them effective will require people to understand the changes and believe in the international mission. You need to convince people why the new way of doing things is a step forward. They need to *see* and *agree* on the benefits you are after and that they should be after too. Their perception of the situation, and a broad consensus on what it is your company should do and how, can make a big difference in managing the process. This obviously increases the need for communication, which is different from 'telling them', and leadership in the internationalization process.

Hammerly, Executive VP International of 3M in 1991, toured the European country organizations together with Hanson, VP Europe, to explain the international reorganization to the local teams, to convince them that this was beneficial for all, and listen to their reactions, questions and frustrations, and anticipate their potential contribution in the new organization. Together, they had more than 80 extensive interviews with all the top managers involved.

## Involvement

As a result, one could say that the local management of 3M experienced this strategy-making process as a 'due process' (Kim and Mauborgne, 1993): they felt it was an open process, consistent, fair, sensitive to obstacles and allowed for their input. People should feel part of these decisions as much as possible. The wider and deeper the involvement of the entire organization in the reflection and formulation, the more the 'implementation' or 'action problem' will evaporate, as illustrated in Figure 5.2. This often requires time. However, the time you invest in the joint 'formulation' process, you will probably gain in the implementation and communication process.[2]

'Those that implement the plans, must make the plans' is what one top executive at Texas Instruments proclaimed. If people feel part of the international strategy and have an affinity with the worldwide operations, they will more easily and willingly invest in it, adapt to it and learn from it. You need to give people a chance to buy in to the new philosophy, as your internationalization will call for their capabilities, support and energy.

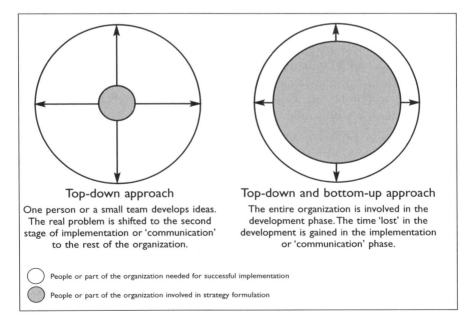

**Figure 5.2** The importance of involvement in development and implementation phase

## Systems and processes

Managers in established or new multinational subsidiaries need to be motivated to execute the international strategy of the company. Incentives can be rendered through matching compensation, monitoring systems, rewards, and profit and loss responsibility. Typically this is an area that gets attacked much too late. In most situations we have seen, systems and incentives have been lagging behind, rather than leading or at least keeping pace with the required changes in strategy and organization.

While Procter & Gamble has gone a long way to integrate its activities across Europe and has been steadily progressing in making that happen, the profit and loss responsibility remained for a very (maybe too?) long time in the hands of the country managers. This has been slowing down several of the organizational and cultural changes that were necessary throughout the years. Other organizations have also been avoiding the overhaul of profit and loss and incentive schemes, in the hope that waiting longer would make it easier. But in fact, with hindsight, it may have been easier to change these earlier on in the process.

## Resources and competencies

It is key to enable people to manage the complexity of international operations and put them in a position to deal with the trade-offs, dilemmas and pressures. They need the skills and competencies to handle this personally and the organizational instruments, such as the staff, IT, and other resources, to deal with conflicts and frictions (Malnight, 1995).

## Mindset

Internationalization is very much a mentality, a way of looking at domestic and overseas operations (Bartlett and Ghoshal, 1992). Thirty years ago, Perlmutter (1969) emphasized the different mindsets of managers in leading an international network: either they focus on the domestic market (ethnocentric), have a host country orientation (polycentric) or are orientated towards the global market (geocentric). We would encourage you, even in local businesses, to think internationally, to broaden your mindset, and not limit your perspective just to the competitor and evolutions next door.

If people in your company lack this international perspective, the risk of them not understanding the pressures, problems, challenges and opportunities is considerable. Opening the mindset beyond the domestic market will support the international mission. Jack Welch, GE's legendary CEO, said:

> The real challenge is to globalize the mind of the organization. Until an organization captures the intellects of other areas, it really does have a problem. Until you globalize intellect, you have not really globalized the company. (*Fortune*, 2 October 2000)

Although GE has been doing business in Asia for a hundred years, Welch claims it is only just beginning.

One way to create this routine is through experience: research has indicated that internationally experienced managers succeed faster in making the company international (Reuber and Fischer, 1997). Building this cadre of internationally minded managers is crucial and takes a long time. Percy Barnevik, who led ABB through its phase of globalization in the 1980s and 90s, said: 'It can take 10 years' (*Financial Times*, 8 October 1997).

Sometimes, the company has already moved a long way on the internationalization path before top jobs are offered to foreigners. Within Nokia, for example, only recently has the number of non-Finns grown significantly.

> And while most of the company's operations around the world still have at least a Finn or two in leadership roles, key jobs are increasingly going to people who did not grow up in a sauna. (*Fortune*, 1 May 2000)

However, a global mindset will require more than internationally experienced managers. While a home basis or bias may remain and is even desirable as part of your corporate culture, we ultimately need to fully integrate 'international' into the company and no longer distinguish between people, ideas, products and anything else coming from home or international markets. The best manager or researcher should be recruited and promoted and the best idea should be implemented, wherever it comes from.

Try to incorporate this reflex to think wide and ahead: it is not sufficient that you are still making money today, a successful international strategy is about the success of tomorrow and the day after it. A culture that constantly pushes people to look beyond today's success and the competitor next door, and tries harder to serve existing and new clients is a great asset for a company, especially in the face of a strategic transformation such as internationalization.

## Shock therapy or slow and steady?

Should you move quickly to overcome the barriers, or do it slowly? The pace of your initiatives in overcoming the barriers can, in our opinion, have a significant impact on their success.

A growing stream of research on corporate transformation raises the question of whether transformations should be effected quickly or slowly. Working with a model of radical change and punctuated equilibrium, Tushman and Romanelli (1985) posit that corporate transformations, because they affect all the fundamentals of an organization, should occur quickly. Organization systems, they argue, are tight configurations of reinforcing patterns, and tweaking the system to achieve change simply does not work. On the other hand, some argue that a slower pace, requiring as much as ten years, makes more sense. They argue that changing requirements for skills and, even more importantly, the need to build and retain trust require a more patient approach (Chakravarthy and Gargiulo, 1994; Kim and Mauborgne, 1996).

Both approaches were observed in the companies we researched (for more detail see De Koning et al., 1997; Verdin and Van Heck, 2000a). P&G, for example, had followed a twenty-year-plan, building trust, organizational capability and ensuring changes happened positively with a substantial amount of limited experimentation. By contrast, 3M Europe opted for shock therapy in globalizing its strategy and organization. The change was implemented quickly, even ahead of schedule, possibly even to the surprise of employees and customers. Many employees had been involved in discussions about the problems that would arise if the company failed to integrate; nearly everyone agreed that integration was the way to go. With widespread support for the changes, the general sentiment was that dragging out the awkward in-between stages would be too distracting for everyone. Arguably, both approaches were successful for the companies involved in a given context.

The example of 3M is not really representative of a typical 'shock therapy'. Most of these quick turnarounds we observed could take place because the pressure from the market or shareholders had become unbearable. Disappointing results in consecutive years, shrinking market share, unsatisfactory product development pipelines and so on often created the circumstances and external pressure to make the transformation happen quickly, often combined with a change in top management. The crisis atmosphere created the feeling in the organization that 'something needed to happen' and gave little room for resistance to develop. In very exceptional cases, and probably 3M is one of those, top management managed to create an 'internal' crisis, that set up the context for everybody to realize that there was no other way out but to change. Especially in times when the relevant figures (turnover, profit, market share and so on) do not show a dramatic fall in competitiveness, is it very difficult to get the organization aligned for 'shock therapy'. What is required then is probably a very strong 'organizational culture' to substitute for the external pressure.

Despite being polar extremes, both the 'shock therapy' and the 'slow and steady' approach have one thing in common: they minimize the trauma and confusion associated with fundamental change. In the shock therapy, because the changes are implemented rapidly, people can settle down to learn the new systems relatively quickly, often supported by new people. The change may be cathartic, but any confusion and trauma is short lived. Under the slow and steady approach, most changes occur following discussion, debate and experimentation. Relatively little resistance is created and, where it does arise, the organization can take the time to counter or bypass the resistance that might otherwise blossom. One way of adjusting, used by P&G for example, was to implement changes in subsidiary roles and responsibilities at the same time that general managers were due for normal rotation. This opportunity arose quite frequently because the established personnel policy called for a two- or three-year-term rotation.

Other companies opted for a medium pace of change. They seemed to experience all the trauma and confusion of the short-term fundamental change, without the benefit of a quick shock to overcome organizational resistance. On the other hand, the change was too rapid to allow a true evolution of attitudes, responsibilities and capabilities among managers. The result was a greater tendency to retreat to the old structure, making little or no progress towards internationalization or cross-border integration. We observed that these companies often got stuck in the middle of the two types of change processes because management had not explicitly or implicitly made the necessary choice or balanced the trade-offs and choices, and therefore were not able to manage the critical weaknesses inherent in either approach.

For example, for years Philips, Alcatel and IBM had been trying to 'tilt their matrix' and foster more cross-border cooperation in Europe without significant success. It took a severe crisis to finally make major inroads into the stifling power of the country baronies. These companies seemed to have become 'stuck in the middle' for quite some time. Other companies such as Unilever have been going back and forth between centralization and decentralization in rather short-term swings of the pendulum, without gaining the benefits of organizational learning, or being able to achieve the true benefits of either choice, probably at high cost to their performance and market presence (see Figure 5.3).

The medium-paced processes were often a sign of doubt, unclear strategic direction and lack of support for overcoming the barriers. The organization did not have the focus on getting it right straight away, neither had it the patience to build the resources and competencies and learn along the way. One could agree that it represented a lack of overall process management.

Which of these routes will be most effective in a particular situation largely depends on the specific circumstances of the case, including how powerful the likely resistance will be. The slow and steady approach is preferable for companies whose challenge lies primarily in natural inertia or resistance in the system, the organization as the main barrier, rather than active hostility from the people who are operating in it. In the latter case, an initial programme of incremental change may provide the basis for a more important or crucial change to take place later. In other companies, a direct approach, tackling the core of the company's habits head on, is essential to break with the past and the usual way of doing business. In these cases, making changes too slowly may allow a chance for parts of the organization to build resistance.

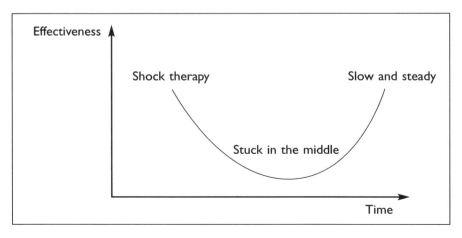

**Figure 5.3** Shock therapy versus slow and steady

An alternative line of thinking, less common in the literature but probably supported by a lot of practical experiences and (casual) evidence, would argue that, whatever the need or preferred time span, organizational change remains a tremendous and unrealistic agenda, not because of the time span or poor process management, but because it is often severely constrained by the rather limited capacity for change in many organizations (Tibau, 2001).

Whatever path you choose it has to be carefully prepared and monitored. In the absence of such preparation, the shock therapy route becomes 'quick and dirty' and destructive rather than putting a better alternative in place, while the slow and steady route involves high costs for little result, leading to frustration and even more resistance to internationalization in the future.

Each approach also has a relatively distinct need for supporting mechanisms and side conditions in the change process. Slow approaches to globalization rely heavily on a shared rationale and the involvement of key people, and allow for a gradual build up of the necessary systems, processes and competencies through learning and experimentation. They do require strong top commitment in order to ensure progress is made and they raise the stakes for flexibility. The shock therapy often coincides with a change in top management, clearly committed to the new agenda, and thrives on the momentum of a clear rationale.

In some circumstances, the selection of the time frame for changes may be sharply constrained by the pressures of the external environment, the pressures from the market, the speed of deregulation, the competition, the client demands, or the company's financial condition. The dimensions of the international playing field, and especially the relative positioning of your company in the playing field, give important indications on how urgent the globalization agenda really is. If sudden major changes are taking place in the size of the playing field, for example as a result of deregulation or technological breakthrough, as in European telecoms or high-tech industries, or if a company is on the verge of bankruptcy or under severe shareholder pressure, slow change may not be an option (Strebel, 1994). When the pressures from the cost or network side are modest, or only slowly mounting, a step-by-step approach could be preferred, as in the case of the Eureko Alliance in the European insurance industry.

For a local company 'stuck' in an intrinsically more global industry, shock therapy may be the way to do it. Daimler and Chrysler opted for shock therapy and 'jumped' to become a global player, as a company that had been (too?) slow in becoming 'truly' global. However, the subsequent debacle, especially in the US operations, seems to indicate that the conditions for a successful shock may not have been in place.

## CHAPTER 6

# Beyond 'Implementation': Managing the Overall Agenda

From local or multinational champion to global master is a long trajectory that requires tactful and thoughtful management. Rare are the companies that manage to become truly global in one big leap, whatever press reports or dramatic acquisition stories may make us believe. Witness Daimler (buying into the US through the acquisition of Chrysler), Whirlpool (buying into Europe through the Philips' domestic appliances business), Pharmacia and Upjohn (merging) or Renault (taking a stake in Nissan in Japan), or even some of the dot com companies which quickly evaporated or ran into a series of troubles. Even when the benefits of internationalization have been well defined, the matching organizational structure constructed, and the temporary barriers and resistance have been avoided, internationalization requires more (see Figure S3.2 earlier in this section).

It is not a one-shot deal. You successfully handled your initial international orders, you bought a foreign company, you restructured your organization geographically to cross-border product units, you just decided to set up a global manufacturing network: does all this make you a global company? In most instances, neither the overall strategy nor the organization are fully adapted to the emerging international status after the acquisition, the restructuring or the latest investment in plant and equipment. And even if they were, you should constantly rethink the why–what–how interaction of your strategy.

Established multinational corporations planted their flag in different parts of the world a long time ago and went through the internationalization loop several times. And yet, most are still searching for the right balance of standardization in their strategy and organization. They wonder if they should gain more from their global presence on the cost, network or learning dimensions and how to balance the requirements for country, geographic or market focus with the demand for scale, network and knowledge management, each requiring the emphasis on different organizational dimensions.

When we consider internationalization and globalization to be primarily a *process*, we mean that it needs to be managed as:

- an integrated and consistent picture

- often following a non-linear course

- offering ongoing learning experiences

- a really strategic trajectory

- that should always be business driven

- and a continuing process.

## The whole is more than the sum of the parts

The main reason we divided the internationalization question into different parts in our discussion so far is to make the reflection on a complex challenge more manageable and transparent, and focus sufficient attention to each of the different strategic, organizational and managerial aspects. The advice is not to 'divide and conquer' the process of managing internationalization: on the contrary, conquering international markets and businesses requires managing internationalization as an integrated system, not as a series of divided and isolated sub-questions.

The questions of where the benefits are, what the organization should look like and how to ensure implementation are not three separate issues: they are one and the same issue. The answer to one question will influence the others, there needs to be consistency between the benefits, strategy, organization and management process, and, in the end, they either reinforce each other or else they contradict. Should we follow Jürgen Schrempp, CEO of DaimlerChrysler, when he blames all the problems on implementation while still proclaiming that 'our strategy as such is still brilliant' (*New York Times*, 2 December 2000)? Most probably, the implementation problems are not the only issue, and question the overall feasibility of the strategy and organization as well, as much as they highlight the importance of effective process management.

The key to success lies in connecting the strategic, organizational and managerial aspects of internationalization whereby the whole is more than the sum of the parts. We emphasized before how the organization should reinforce the strategy which in itself is rooted in the analysis of where the benefits are, and how the implementation process should be focused on getting the strategy and organization in place, but if well managed will allow for feedback and correction on these aspects.

It is exactly the role of top management to manage this broader picture and incorporate and integrate each of the different elements into a successful internationalization path. They should safeguard against reducing internationalization and globalization to a purely analytical exercise, merely drawing boxes or lines in organizational blueprints, sheer 'implementation problems' or a series of isolated actions. Top management should secure the broad strategic agenda of the company; they need to ensure clear strategic and organizational direction. It is their responsibility to keep track of the full picture, understand the threats and opportunities and initiate action accordingly. They are ultimately the ones who have access to the resources, knowledge and power to manage this process.

## Consistency

Very often, this will require giving in on the 'analytically ideal' strategy or organization. Consistency across the process may be more important than getting it 100% right the first time on each of the individual aspects. We have come across companies that successfully went for sub-optimal solutions but made the best of it and managed according to realistic expectations. Tractebel had to live with projects in Hungary and Ireland, while it had initially hoped to win the bid for some of the regional electricity companies in the UK. Yet, the overall process, including expectations, strategy and management, was focused on getting the most out of the international projects. A consumer goods company we referred to earlier went for alliances and joint ventures in order to enter certain countries, while it would really have liked to buy its partners but could not do so for several reasons.

This should not make internationalization problematic for these companies, on the contrary, we have seen many of them prosper. The top management of these companies was fully aware of what they were doing and trying to achieve, and were willing to work with the consequences of it.

Gillette realized that it was giving up certain, potentially important segments of the market by standardizing its products and marketing around the globe. Its business system and organization were focused on selling, some would argue overly, standardized razor blades in a universal way around the global. It is no surprise to Gillette that its penetration in developing markets is lower than in other markets and highly variable across countries: that is how it was set up. And this is partly a natural consequence of or reason for its heavy investments in the research and development of new razor blades: its economics force Gillette to write off huge R&D and marketing budgets over the largest (homogeneous) output possible.

This partly explains why we see as many different international strategies and organizations as we see companies in a given industry. This diversity does not imply that only one of them is right, and the others got it wrong. It just tells us that there is no single best way to do it. But some are *smarter* and more effective than others and it is possible to learn from the mistakes that others have already made. If you manage to align your view of an appropriate strategy with the organization and management, you may be better off than your competitor, who has not set the right expectations and managed the process accordingly.

While Vedior International seemed to have (had) a hard time getting its French acquisition in line with the overall European strategy of the company, and in selling its European business proposition to the financial markets, some of its competitors, such as Adecco and Creyf's Interim, may have been more successful in managing the internationalization and globalization process, both in their own way – the first with a rather similar, the second one with (at least initially) a very different strategy and implementation process.

## Overshooting today's benefits of globalization

Sometimes, it may make sense to go beyond the logic on one of the internationalization aspects, in light of the overall process. You may, for example, want to reach for overglobalization, according to today's analytical criteria as illustrated in Chapter 2, because you expect the market rationale to evolve quicker than your own organization can, or because you see it as a way to catch up and get the momentum going. Overplaying today's benefits is not necessarily a sin, when you realize how it fits into the overall picture and manage the broader process consistently.

At times, top management senses that internationalization or globalization adds value in the longer term, even though, at the beginning, they can only vaguely describe what the expected benefit really is. They have a vision that the benefits will be there, some day, somehow, and anticipate the process of internationalization in their own organization to be difficult and long. Sometimes getting started is the only way to find out how important internationalization is. And the only way to get started may be to create the perception that major benefits will show up soon.

Although the current playing field does not (yet) justify the current dimensions or spread of internationalization, the perspective on the overall process and the anticipated barriers may constitute good reasons to start early. You believe that the playing field will change faster than the organization ever can, hence you may need to anticipate the market evolutions. This increases the pressure on monitoring the benefits and developing a vision on what will happen or can happen.

Philippe Bodson, when he became CEO of Tractebel, knew that liberalization of electricity would not happen in 1992 and would take at least ten more years to happen. But he was sure that preparing his company for it would take at least that long. That is why he was so keen on Tractebel's internationalization back in 1992: liberalization was not happening yet, but it would come, one day. 'The idea was clearly that the deregulation and privatization would come, but nobody knew really when it would come. We decided to prepare ourselves for it.' And when it did come, Tractebel needed to be ready for it.

Nevertheless, the best visions remain grounded in sound analysis and understanding of the current status in the industry. Visions are not just dreams, if they are disconnected from reality, they may quickly turn into nightmares. To understand what is likely to be important in the business in five to ten years, undoubtedly it is sensible to understand what is happening in the business today. And it will be important to adapt the internationalization process in all its aspects to the ambitions and their market context.

Another reason that companies *purposely* overshoot the current benefits of internationalization and the resulting global–local balance in their strategy is to shake up the organization and overcome the internal barriers. The Ford Mondeo project, not quite a success in reality against its initial objectives, was nevertheless a major experience for the company and a catalyst for overcoming the internal barriers encountered in previous attempts to build a more global strategy and organization. Overglobalizing helped to *jump the internal barriers*. It was an action that may not have made sense when evaluated on the criteria of one aspect only, as it went beyond the globalization potential, but had its rationale in the overall picture. The (temporary) overglobalization forced appropriate changes in the structure and way of working and thinking of people. In addition, as one senior manager said about the project: 'We learned a lot' (we hope Ford did learn as this can quickly become a 'catch-all' to justify any project that has gone wrong!).

Overshooting does not necessarily imply that you will actually reach that degree of globalization you seem to be aiming for, as in the Mondeo case where corrections were made in the strategy and organization later, to better align with the actual shape of the international playing field. However, correcting too early runs the risk of falling back to the starting point and undoing the changes you intended to achieve by overshooting.

## Beyond the Cartesian logic

Notwithstanding the structure of this book, internationalization is *not* a matter of moving from why, to what, to how in one straight line. This view would turn internationalization into a sequential chain of analyses to be done, decisions to be made and changes to be implemented. Let us be realistic: mostly it will be a messy process, which has little resemblance to the Cartesian logic of moving step by step. It is exactly because you do not and cannot manage it in such a systematic way, following our logical sequence, that we emphasize the importance of making the overall agenda more explicit and transparent.

While our framework may help to structure the disordered nature of internationalization discussions, we do not want to force you into rigidly going through the why–what–how loop in a logical sequence. It would be naive to expect you to start in the why-box, before moving into the what and how of internationalization, either in reflection or in action. One of the instances where we saw a company think through its globalization rather systematically and act accordingly was in Procter & Gamble Europe. Its in-depth analysis of the benefits led from a gradual integration of functional strategies, starting with the areas where the benefits were most obvious, such as R&D and purchasing, to the development of differentiated organizational mechanisms and the appropriate management of different integration speeds in a carefully managed globalization process. And even here, one could argue that this represents a rationalization after the facts, as implied in the words of the European Vice President R&D who had been a driving force in this process for about 20 years: 'At the time, it was an act of faith.' He daringly added: 'By now it has become a religion!'

### It is not important where you start

Rarely is the internationalization debate initiated with the question of where 'the beef' of international operations really is or should be. DAF Trucks missed out on the cost and network benefits of internationalization and consequently got hit in its bottom line, ultimately to be pushed into bankruptcy. The company lagged behind the competition which had worked out the requirements of internationalization and acted accordingly. Similarly many other companies found that their expectations in terms of lower costs or additional revenues from international presence did not materialize. This often led to a flawed international strategy and organization.

Deutsche Bank scaled back its earlier international operations in the US, after the initial aggressive expansion, because of the big losses it suffered. With hindsight, one could say that the investments were simply too large: they went way beyond the benefits that it could achieve in the short to medium term. Network benefits, for example, would need to be built up slowly and would need time to accrue. The takeover of Bankers Trust represents a new attempt by Deutsche Bank, the results of which remain to be seen. ABN AMRO, advertising heavily at some point as the 'Global Network Bank', is stepping back now, and starting to focus on 'selected markets' only: geographic markets such as (parts of) Europe, the US mid-west, and Brazil in retail banking, or specific segments such as investment banking where it most recently acquired part of the ING-Barings operations in New York, while at the same time selling European American Bank, an early banking joint venture in the New York area together with an alliance of other European banks which it later acquired in full, to Citigroup.

In reality, many of the issues, problems and challenges show up in other parts of the loop, such as the what and how. Indeed, a problem in one area may reveal an underlying issue in another and this process and its identi-fication may take quite some time. The frictions in the organizational set-up of 3M, or people's resistance to change in the chemicals company we observed, initiated the globalization logic and triggered reflection on why, what and how aspects. This did not mean that the debate was out of place, neither did it imply that the discussion was less relevant. On the contrary, it encouraged these companies to look at the broader perspective and shed light on each of the aspects contained in it.

Messing up in one area may lead to the right corrections if the other areas are properly managed and, above all, the full picture of the why–what–how is constantly revisited and re-evaluated. And to know exactly where things seem to get off track, you may find it useful to detect whether the strategic, organizational or management logic is in alignment.

Saatchi & Saatchi, the UK advertising agency, thrived on the expected globalization of businesses, and was very active on building a cross-border network through acquisitions to deliver clients advertising campaigns on a worldwide basis. However, the organizational tensions, based on decentralized authority, could never deliver this benefit to the agency's clients. Luckily, the lack of appropriate organization was compensated for by a strong presence in local or national markets where most clients were still operating on a national level anyway! *If the organization is not able to implement a strategy which was wrong or way out of line in the first place, you may end up doing reasonably well!*

3M's European Marketing Action Teams (EMATs) could not ensure the coordination of marketing strategies around Europe: the teams lacked the authority and appropriate management instruments, and the local country managers resisted giving up their own objectives for the good of other countries or the whole of Europe. The experience with the EMATs led 3M to rethink the strategy and organization, based on a clearer picture of the expected benefits, and the VP International and VP Europe went on a confidence-building tour around the European country organizations.

Sometimes, even the organization of your client may raise the issues around your internationalization. The international contracts in the temporary work services industry confronted the temp agencies with the lack of underlying benefits for them and the client organization. The client organizations were mostly still managed in a decentralized way, despite some attempts to centralize purchasing contracts. Thus, national subsidiaries refused to adhere to the centrally negotiated contract with the temp agency because they failed to see the benefit (and rightfully so!) and continued buying from their preferred local temp supplier. The resistance in the client subsidiaries initiated a debate on the underlying benefits for clients to have international contracts for temping and hence for the temp agencies to have international networks.

Conversely, the basis for success can lie in any part of the loop. A successful process of implementation may show the way for the real business economics and appropriate organizational approach. We saw several companies that just happened to internationalize, without a grand plan or any preset objectives. They had not analysed their strategy or organization in any great detail. They just internationalized 'by doing': 'J'agis, puis je réfléchis' (I act, then I think).[1] However, they found that the internationalization benefits were much more limited, sometimes more compelling but different from those expected, leading them to reconsider the strategy, organization and implementation process. Their process management fitted the market, their own organization and culture and became a source of their international success. A well-managed 'opportunistic strategy' will, nevertheless, sooner or later trigger the question about the real benefits and the appropriate organizational instruments.

Tractebel, the Belgian utility group, had no grand plan when it started embarking on international electricity generation and distribution projects in 1992. There was the belief that European deregulation in electricity, whenever it came, would force the company to look beyond the domestic market and become more competitive. There was the commitment from top management that internationalization was the way ahead, and there was a team dedicated to international projects, but no theoretical reflection on how big the playing field was, and what type of organization best fitted the ideal strategy. It literally started by 'looking in *The Wall Street Journal*' for international opportunities. In so doing, however, the company built up its learning, understood what it required and what it could get out of it, put all the additional conditions in place and adapted its strategy and organization along the way. Now, political complications aside, it seems as though Tractebel is reinforcing its real network and scale benefits closer to home.

The initial rationale for setting up the Eureko Alliance for several of its initial or later partners can be considered as mainly defensive. The partners were happy to join forces on some international projects as it allowed each of them to focus on and protect their strong domestic position. The alliance partners were taking a kind of call option on further internationalization in the industry which was very much expected but uncertain in terms of shape and timing in the wake of Europe 1992. As they moved on, the partners saw more clearly the slowly releasing benefits on the cost, network and learning side, and also experienced the difficulty of managing these benefits across borders in the Alliance governance structure. While the initial structure was not based on an *ex ante* in-depth analysis of where the benefits were, and what the strategy and organization should look like, the functioning of the Alliance quickly brought up the why and what questions more explicitly. The trial (and sometimes error) strategy of the Alliance led to a dramatic restructuring of the partner structure, including a full-scale merger of some of the leading parties involved.

## Beyond the grand plan

Internationalization is generally a long process that requires patience for the benefits to be realized. We do not expect everything to be right from the beginning, or to happen exactly the way it was planned. The company must be committed, but avoid being overly rigid; as we sometimes say: 'only fools *never* change their mind!'

Internationalization is a moving target. The complexity and attraction lies in the rapidly developing markets, competition and regulation. A constant reflection on how the industry is evolving, and how these changes will affect your business, should prevent you from falling behind. Other parameters can also change, and indicate a different internationalization approach: a change in the management team, a shifting client base and new technologies could demand a new set-up. Anticipating the market requires even more flexibility, as you may want to adapt as you go, and may find that your expectations on the globalization of the market were not completely accurate. Being open and adapting the course as you learn from experience and observe changes in the environment remains key.

You may consider setting up the internationalization as a learning experience from the start: you have no expectations as to what internationalization should bring. You 'give it a try' and 'see what happens', you prepare yourself for 'trial and error'. You use internationalization as an active instrument for the continuous upgrading of a company's knowledge and competence base. The only expectation you have is to learn from a few international projects, and you are willing to swallow whatever it takes. However, you must recognize that you cannot run internationalization like an investment fund. In the financial markets, you may be able to change your positions for a marginal cost, but this may be less valid in industrial projects. That is why internationalization is strategic and timing remains key.

It also implies that the internationalization process that is implemented along these lines may have to be managed like an 'innovation' process, with all its implications: you may need a portfolio of potential projects, have a process for selecting and monitoring their progress and provide the management culture and follow-through to make it happen. You do not say: 'We just decided to internationalize, now just go and do it' (this argument has been clearly developed in the context of strategic innovation management; see Williamson, 1999).

The opportunistic companies that were succesful had one thing in common: they were well aware that true internationalization would require a whole lot more than just selling in a different country. They built up learning in the process, chased experience and adapted their overall approach and expectations to that philosophy. A lot of opportunity driven internationalizations are turned into fully fledged international strategies later, after the companies ensured that processes, management, strategy, structure, people and culture evolved accordingly.

In that case, the need for monitoring the environment and evolutions in the market is even more necessary. An emerging internationalization strategy should adapt promptly to key internal and external developments, and allow for leveraging and capturing unique opportunities in the market.

One food company had aggressively internationalized, through acquisitions and alliances, mainly on an opportunistic basis. Most of the activities were run initially on a country-by-country basis. However, as the portfolio grew, the question arose as to what the added value of this portfolio really was for the client or shareholders. This retrospective reflection led to regrouping the activities in geographic areas, and evaluating the alliance strategy in some countries, as it turned out that these did not deliver the expected benefits.

You may want to develop into a flexible learning organization as you become increasingly involved in international operations. Again this requires commitment: you need to adopt a long-term view and top management needs to support the risk-taking and trial and error implied. Failure then has to be accepted as part of company policy, in fact, you may want to push the limits of failure. It is mainly from the mistakes that you can learn what works and what does not.

The Eureko Alliance had been developing its ideas on potential cross-border benefits along the same lines. While the initial aim had been to reap the potential synergies between the various national partners and leverage know-how and expertise, it turned out that the alliance structure did not necessarily enable them to acquire the cost or network benefits. This was a typical example of learning-by-doing: as a result, two of the partners decided in July 2000 to merge their activities and go for more of the cost synergies between countries, under the structure of a new Eureko NV, while the other partners decided to move on as the Eureko Alliance Partner Company on learning and selected joint projects.

Even with a grand strategy, companies need to be prepared for learning and opportunities along the way. Internationalization is a dynamic process that needs following up, managing, evaluating and fine-tuning. Bob Shapiro, CEO of Monsanto, observed: 'Restructuring a company to become global is like designing an airplane while flying it.'

## You will never be the same company again

Internationalizing is a strategic decision calling for much investment of time and money. The management of internationalization is no more, no less than a strategic project: it is about irreversible, long-term investments. Be careful, however, that your company does not end up, as others have, calling their internationalization moves 'strategic' because they are not paying off.

A free trial of internationalization does not exist. While companies may not need to invest resolutely in international operations from day one, and can or should grow in their international involvement, we cannot imagine a company being 'just a little bit' international in the long run. You cannot say that only the people in the international division are international or that the organization is only 25% international. Of course, you can have 25% of your turnover, profit or people in foreign markets. However, organizations that aim to get the most out of their worldwide presence will have to think international in every part of their organization. To use the words of Meyer Feldberg from Columbia Business School: 'International business is everyone's business' (*Financial Times*, 21 August 2000). This can take time, and is a lengthy process that the organization and its people should go through.

Internationalization should not be seen separately from any other strategic issue: the overall strategy and organization should be included in the picture. It is not a decision that is taken in a vacuum, but needs to be grounded in the overall strategic ambitions and objectives of a company. How strategic do you want internationalization to be: are you willing to question fundamentally the whole business and organization because of the internationalization? The fundamental shift in how different functions in Eli Lilly, the US pharmaceutical company, were performed had been defined as globalization, without it being the objective. It was simply part of a broader strategic repositioning of the company (Malnight, 1995).

You must expect the international operations to affect the whole value chain and force you to adapt all your processes. Even if you started internationalizing through a few international orders, you will quickly realize that internationalization is not just a few salespeople handling these orders. In the end, successful internationalization will fundamentally change the way business is done everywhere: you will never be the same company again.

Wal-Mart's operations in Germany have had a hard time adopting to the American retailer's business system. The outsourcing of in-bound logistics to external parties in Germany led to complete sourcing chaos, the tight management control from the US made the local German management extremely nervous and the cost of shop renovation turned out to be five times higher than in the US. An analyst commented on this situation: 'The German case is raising questions about the broader international strategy of the group' (*Financial Times*, 14 October 2000).

But Wal-Mart has never been stopped by one or two mistakes, domestically or internationally. It took years to turn its Canadian acquisition into profit, it failed in Thailand, succeeded quite well in Mexico, while Argentina is still in the balance. But wherever it went, whatever it did, it drew on its experiences and moved on stronger and better equipped for the next round of competition (Govindarajan and Gupta, 1999).

The more you go down the learning axis, the more significant the long-term impact will be on your organization. While the cost and network axes refer mainly to the configuration and spread of your international activities, the learning axis will ultimately question the whole *raison d'être* of your organization and its strategy. Learning often starts rather innocently, but quickly tests the whole organization. The purpose of the third axis is precisely to put the whole business model to the test in different markets, and adapt it according to experiences and lessons learnt.

Internationalization can then become even more critical, as it triggers broader strategic questions and changes in the organization. It puts the question of what the real overall strategy or real source of sustainable advantage is high on the agenda. Sometimes the real objective is to make a strategic transformation occur – refocus on value added for the client, restructure distribution channels, revisit the product range and brand portfolio, stimulate innovation or focus on shareholder value – and well-managed international projects are just the way to achieve that. International initiatives allow a company to start from scratch. Hence, they can set the example for how you want to do business in the whole organization.

Globalization at Eli Lilly was not an objective in itself, rather it was the cumulative result of a series of adjustments within and across individual functions, which represented a fundamental adjustment to how the company operated globally (Malnight, 1995).

In 1994 IBM pushed the 'industry verticals', the client industry, as a key dimension for its international organization. However, this dimension probably did not match the criteria for selecting the appropriate organization dimension, as we discussed earlier, because the client industry may not have been the dimension that could liberate most of the cost or network benefits. It remains to be seen whether it was in the end the best way to stimulate cross-border coordination, as many clients ended up in a category of clients named 'others' because they did not belong clearly to any of the industry verticals. Moreover, all of that happened while academics and practitioners were questioning the relevance of the notion of 'industry' and 'sector'. It was nevertheless a strong message to the IBM organization that it wanted to do away with the traditionally decentralized geographic organizational structure in a dramatic way and was shifting its focus from products to services. In that context, the selected dimension helped to create the global focus and awareness.

Thus globalization can help companies to face a restructuring that was necessary anyway. In our opinion, that is exactly what happened with many of the mergers and takeovers on the European scene, in the face of Europe 1992 and the euro. For example, in the financial services industry there were ample national and cross-border M&As and alliances between traditionally national banks and insurers. Many of the restructuring or internationalization initiatives may, in reality, have ended up as a vehicle for domestic restructuring and cost cutting that could or should have taken place without the European or 'international threat' but could not because of external, as well as internal, barriers (evidence on true economies of scale and scope in the sector is scarce; Langohr, 1998; Walter, 1999).

This may not be a bad idea as such, as long as you realize what you are doing and have the overall picture in mind. Sometimes it helps to have the strategic discussions on these elements brought up by the challenges in the international markets. If you know what you are after, preparing for the future benefits, overcoming internal barriers or overall corporate transformation, it is important that you adapt the expectations, strategy and organization to it. The downside of internationalization as a catalyst for change is that the argument could be used to justify failed international projects.

Philippe Bodson knew very well that Europe 1992 would not open up the utility market overnight, but he was confident that it would initiate regulatory measures for deregulation. Electrabel, the domestic electricity company of the Tractebel Group, would need to rethink its position in an open electricity market. And in fact, the whole Tractebel Group needed tightening up as an industrial group, rather than a purely financial holding. Both agendas were initiated or at least reinforced by the international projects that Tractebel realized around the world from 1994 onwards. Tractebel managed to position itself as a competitive player in foreign, liberalized or opening markets, such as the US, Latin America and the Middle East. The internationalization made the company think about its future role in the market, and its core competencies.

The domestic activities will in the long run have to be an integral part of the internationalization. Splitting up domestic and international activities does not seem to make a lot of sense to us. The virtuous circle is closed when you manage to bring the internationalization back home.

A company such as Tractebel is currently in the middle of this process. Tractebel still has two faces: it is a highly competitive, leading company in the markets abroad; and has the image of a conservative monopolist in the domestic market as Electrabel. The group has not managed so far to integrate fully the learning that it built up through its international experiences into its domestic organization. Therefore we would argue that *internationalization starts in the home market, and it should be taken back home.*

## Internationalization should make a real difference

As we have noted, internationalization is or should be a business-driven process. While it can happen by accident, it may be done for the sake of internationalization in the first place, or seem like a natural extension to the domestic activities of a national champion, the only way to get it right in the long term is to know where the beef is or is not, and what type of strategy, organization and management it requires. Internationalization will sooner or later force a company to have the logic and rationale in place. How soon the benefit aspect becomes critical in the overall process will depend on the strategic imperatives in the industry, the market requirements and your company position: in short on the size and growth of the international playing field and your own position within that field.

A good internationalization process, and how the opportunities and problems show up, does not automatically follow the logical sequence of why, what and how. Nevertheless, sooner or later along the process of internationalization, you will need to know what you have achieved and whether you want to achieve more. How can you decide on a strategy, align the organization and get the right management support in place if you do not know where the added value is to be expected? In any successful internationalization or globalization process, you will at some point be confronted with the question of whether you want to make a difference as an international company.'If it does not make cents, it does not make sense!'

Benefits are not just out there waiting to be immediately grasped. You may not became poor by doing a good deal. Selling high or buying low is never a bad idea. And it is always good for the momentum in the organization if you manage to get something out of it in the short term. But internationalization generally requires more than just 'a good deal' or a few quick wins. You rarely achieve everything at once. True internationalization will only lead to long-term sustainable success and add genuine shareholder value if you are committed to make it work and willing to take a long-term perspective.

A stop and go policy will therefore not be sufficient, as illustrated in the case of Goodyear. Goodyear slashed the workforce in one of its plants, relocated most of its production to Mexico and Brazil and moved some of the redundant personnel to another operation 300 miles away. Ten months later, it reversed course and rehired 700 people in order to relaunch the production in that particular plant. However, the staff remain constantly fearful that the company may switch again tomorrow (*Business Week*, 24 April 2000). Was Goodyear operating for the short or the long term?

Marks & Spencer, the UK retailer, expanded its activities to France but was unsuccessful, as the entry scale was not big enough to reap the cost advantages of international presence. Commitment, and maybe deep pockets, could in the long run have led to sufficient scale and hence the internationalization benefits it had hoped for. On top of this, M&S quickly discovered how different the UK market is from the French. This, in combination with the tough competition at home, led M&S to withdraw totally from the French market.

This is all the more reason to *manage the process for the benefits*: be clear on what you want to achieve, follow up the progress and ensure that the benefits materialize. How will internationalization make a difference to you and your clients? A financial services company once wrote to me: 'In connection with the European unification, we decided to adapt our organization structure to operate more efficiently in all countries where we are active in the field of financial services. In practice, however, you will not notice anything of these changes.' Although we understand what they meant, it beautifully illustrates the importance of the benefits: if nobody notices that you are international or globalizing, you are probably not capturing the benefits you should be going for. Identifying the benefits is one thing, realizing them is another. Securing those benefits from internationalization will never or only in exceptional cases be automatic or go according to plan.

- Even for the most 'obvious' benefits on the cost side such as *economies of scale*, it requires a lot of sustained effort to make them materialize. When scale in R&D is pointing towards internationalization, then make sure that your R&D is effectively used in the international operations, and is driving business success over a larger output or volume. Too often, companies have reinvented the wheel in different places, because the R&D efforts were not well coordinated and managed across the borders, a pertinent risk in industries where the R&D pressure is intensifying such as the pharmaceutical or car industry. We have witnessed a lot of potential cost benefits simply evaporate in duplication, conflict or just waste. In some cases, the management and focus required in R&D may actually point towards diseconomies of scale or creativity intensive efforts, as in some parts of software development or specific stages of drug development in the pharmaceutical industry.

- In the case of *network benefits*, it is not sufficient simply to have the international network or launch an advertising campaign. The network should be organized and managed so that the clients experience added value in working with you in different countries. Saatchi & Saatchi had the international network that could potentially deliver benefits to international clients. However, it was managed in a decentralized way, so that the communication and coordination between the various national offices was inadequate to deliver all the network benefits to the customer. The lack of organizational capabilities jeopardized Saatchi & Saatchi's opportunity to achieve a competitive edge over local advertising agencies. In some locations, Saatchi & Saatchi was maintaining competing agencies, as Publicis proudly confirmed that it would, after buying Saatchi & Saatchi in Europe.

▪ However, the real challenge lies in making sure that you cash in on the *learning opportunities*. The hype around the critical role of knowledge management is in sharp contrast to the difficulty of making information, know-how and expertise flow within your company. And the international dimension multiplies this challenge: think of the diversity of cultures, social habits, languages and so on. One organization that we followed for years was set up explicitly to validate the international learning, and therefore created a dedicated team and division for managing the knowledge, as many companies have come to do, only to realize how hard it is to deliver concrete benefits.

Therefore, it is important to *focus* on the benefits that you want to achieve from internationalization. Be obsessed about them. Repeatedly ask yourself the question, whenever you make choices and decisions: how will this allow us to reap the benefits? How will it deliver the cost or network benefits or open up scope for learning? It will be hard enough to realize the benefits when you are focused on them, so you cannot afford to be distracted, or count on capturing the benefits automatically.

If the benefits are obvious, it will be crucial to *prioritize* them. Overarching benefits may imply that the internationalization rationale is so compelling that you cannot afford to miss out on it, if you want to keep up with the competition. Gaining all three types of benefit at the same time is nevertheless overly ambitious. The type of organization, strategy and management that will deliver cost or network benefits is, in our opinion, intrinsically different from the set-up that allows international learning. You may not be able to do all things right at the same time, so better try to do the right things first.

In so doing, you must keep track of the progress made: how many benefits have actually been gained so far, and what remaining potential is there? Managing for the benefits prompts you to *monitor* and *evaluate* constantly where you are on the internationalization path. Especially if you were not able to identify in detail or quantify the benefits, it is necessary to check and countercheck how much of the potential was actually internalized.

What is your monitoring process: how frequently does your top management revisit the decisions it took, and measure how far you are in reaching the internationalization objectives? Generic financial measures, such as growth in turnover or profit are followed up, but how long ago did you actually gauge the amount of international benefits you really managed to gain and how many you missed?

## Learning makes a difference

The ability to learn in an international context is often still an underestimated benefit of internationalization and globalization. Frequently, this aspect of globalization gets far less management attention and focus than the ability to cut costs or build a network for your clients.

Having observed internationalization and globalization happen (and not happen!) in several companies and industries, we have the impression that the initial attraction to foreign markets is because it allows them to sell existing products. It is then about transferring products and physical assets across borders. Similarly, international restructuring and globalization in established multinationals is often initially about the allocation of physical assets in different locations: where to produce, where to do research and where to provide the services. What drives this is often the search for cost efficiency and better client offering (network).

In the next phase, the attention may shift towards the potential benefits of moving *intangible* assets, such as copying what you have elsewhere or teaching subsidiaries how to improve the system, expertise or knowledge. This is not only about moving machines or products around, it is also about transferring ideas, insights and people. The type of learning in this context can be 'forced', such as 'headquarters have sent us to a training course or want us to follow a manual', or of a more 'receptive' kind, such as 'one party sends the message, the other party receives it' (Segal-Horn and Faulkner, 1999, p. 243).

A study has indicated that this type of transfer of know-how and best practices across borders within the same company is already a very complex phenomenon (Szulanski, 1996). No single formula exists for making it happen: it would be too easy to blame it on people's motivation to share and compare only. It depends on the characteristics of the organization, the type of know-how and the ability of people to learn and unlearn. Some of the key difficulties identified in this context include:

- the recipient of the know-how and best practices lacks the capacity to absorb the know-how, or to understand the practices: because he or she does not have the know-how, it is hard to absorb it.

- the 'relationship' between the sender and receiver of the know-how was poor: this is often an organizational issue, not a personal aspect.

- the recipient lacks the motivation to use the information and know-how received: the well-known 'not-invented-here' syndrome.

The life cycle of knowledge is often described in four stages (Nonaka and Takeuchi, 1995): the origination or socialization stage whereby people create tacit knowledge by working with each other; the externalization stage whereby the tacit knowledge is articulated explicitly; the combination phase whereby explicit knowledge is integrated into a knowledge system; and an internalization phase whereby the knowledge that was made explicit is internalized by individuals again. A lot of the knowledge management initiatives in the international context have explicitly focused mainly on the combination (and externalization) stage.

It becomes more difficult when we move from static knowledge management where we share what we have, to a dynamic concept where we learn from each others' experience and hence build new insights and ideas, which is more origination than combination. This is what some people call 'strategic learning', as a complement to the 'systemic and technical' learning (Segal-Horn and Faulkner, 1999, p. 239). The learning opportunities, our third axis, are based on the notion that two brains are smarter than one. While initially it may be hard to make two different brains work together, when it does happen, the result will probably be much richer and more powerful. The Mondeo development teams on both sides of the ocean cross-fertilized any future joint R&D activities in Ford beyond Mondeo, however painful their first cooperation was. With hindsight, the Ford Mondeo project also catalysed the development of a global mindset, which can facilitate any future global projects in Ford.

Making sure that your company becomes more competitive and really benefits from operating in a diverse environment will obviously not happen overnight. It requires specific organizational capabilities and a culture that not all companies control.

Even in the most local of industries, where the international playing field is not large enough to justify internationalization for cost or network benefits, one may still spot opportunities to share and learn across borders. If you believe that managing diversity can be beneficial, you may actually want to increase the diversity rather than avoid it. This is clearly a different way to look at internationalization and globalization than the widely applauded approach of 'one size fits all'. Without wishing to downplay our message of 'managing the internationalization to explicitly benefit from it', we believe that there are huge learning opportunities for *any* organization. *Each* company should embark on a journey like this. The difficulty, however, will be in locking in the potential for learning: while all companies *could* potentially benefit, not all of them *will*.

Given that an organization's ability to learn will largely depend on its people, we should re-emphasize the importance of 'managing the process' when moving down the third axis. In a learning environment that thrives on the management of intangibles, the process through which experience, lessons learned, knowledge and expertise is managed, brought together and leveraged will be even more key. The organizational mechanisms of network or web and vehicles that incorporate learning, the exchange of ideas and expertise and the drive for innovative business opportunities will also be intrinsically different. No system will deliver the benefits of confronting good ideas in the hope that even better ideas come out, at best, the systems can offer support.

Several key factors are necessary for learning to take place: a commitment from top management that there is an opportunity to improve the value proposition; a culture and mindset that allows for trial and error; an alertness for potential barriers in the people and the organization; the monitoring systems to follow up the learning captured; a continuous feedback on the benefits to the organizational set-up and process (and back); involvement from the key actors; and a willingness to learn along the path of globalization and internationalization.

## It is a never-ending story

We believe globalization is a process that requires several, often continuing iterations through the internationalization loop: it is about analysing and understanding what is going on in the market, it requires monitoring how benefits are changing; it is about adapting and preparing the organization, forcing you to rethink the role of subsidiaries and continuously change the balance of informal and formal coordination mechanisms; it is about anticipating the barriers, avoiding them, spotting new types of resistance and managing the people and organization in order to deliver the benefits. In the best case there is a clear starting point in internationalizing but probably there will never be a real end point.

Look at how established multinationals, such as P&G, 3M, Philips, Alcatel, Unilever, Ford or Toyota, keep adjusting in order to balance the organizational power, wondering what coordinating mechanisms to apply and what the role of regional headquarters should be, and struggling with the shifting power within the organization from one level to another – tilting the matrix, as they say. Although these issues tend to present themselves in a slightly different way in each of these companies, they are not intrinsically different from the sort of issues that local companies are dealing with when internationalizing.

There was a time when 3M was just a local company. Internationalization in this company did not happen overnight but has been a long process of trial and error. There used to be products labelled 'rejected, ok for international', when international operations were of minor importance to the company. Now it is an international company with a worldwide presence that is constantly assessing its international strategy and organization in terms of the global–local balance. Although the development of its activities requires a different way of handling these challenges, 3M also needs to understand what the cost and network benefits are, how important they are, how they are changing, and how to manage the process from an international company to a globally integrated company.

Procter & Gamble has gone through similar types of development and process. Internationalization did not start yesterday in this company either: it evolved from a company 'where expatriation to the international operations was like being sent to Siberia' to a globally integrated company that continues to think about how to balance the global and local focus in its strategy and organization.

The same thing applies to Alcatel, Philips, Matsushita, ABB, Nestlé and so on: the questions of what international strategy and organization to use and how to manage the process of running an international company is a daily reality.

The three underlying questions to be reflected on remain much the same for these established multinationals:

■ *Why* integrate across borders? What benefits can you gain from increased cross-border coordination of activities: are you looking for cost-cutting, improved customer delivery and service, or cross-border learning and knowledge management and creation? What strategy will deliver these benefits?

- *What* international organization will support gaining the benefits: how global should your organization be, and which organizational mechanisms will allow you to make that happen?

- *How* do you manage the process of integration: how do you turn a decentralized, geographically oriented organization into a fully integrated, global organization? What is key in this process?

The difficult challenge is ultimately how to build a truly global master, where not only products and services but more importantly know-how, people, competence and capabilities flow. These can and should go in all directions to achieve critical mass, pushing each other constantly to upgrade and improve your capacity to create value.

## CHAPTER 7

# From Local Champions to Global Masters: Conclusion

It's impossible to avoid the risks completely. But sensible managers, and prudent investors, can at least avoid the obvious mistakes. (Peter Martin)

Having guided you through the 'internationalization' loop and some key reflections around the why, what and how of internationalization, now we want to recap the key highlights in the strategic reflection on internationalization.

We will also put our conclusions on managing internationalization within the context of the globalization debate, a debate that has raised certain expectations, probably beyond feasible and desirable proportions. We will indicate some potential causes for the turn of events in the global landscape and the limited degree of globalization within some corporations, as we indicated in the introduction of the book.

Ironically, we think the best way to summarize the key learnings may be through a number of 'provocative questions', 'statements' and 'one-liners'. We realize that this may seem to contradict our warnings in Chapter 1 that one-liners lack depth and one needs to go beyond the surface. The key objectives of this book and this conclusion are to invite, support and give guidance to a strategic reflection on internationalization, and provocative questions and statements may actually help us to do that. They should *stimulate* the discussion, not *be* the discussion.

## Why globalization is NOT happening in your company

Why is globalization not happening? In the Introduction, we used this question as a way to force us to think at a finer level of detail beyond the slogans (and counter-slogans). We also gave you a checklist of globalization problems. We are now better equipped to evaluate and improve a concrete internationalization process in a given company context in a more productive way. Rather than spending all our energy on outlining blueprints and optimal paths, we found it more productive to reflect on why we have not progressed as far as we should have and what will prevent us from getting there in the future.

Therefore we propose to revisit the main points and steps developed in this book from this seemingly negative angle, which in practice may prove more productive as a lead into a constructive discussion and implementation process. Why is globalization or internationalization not happening (as much as we would like, in the way we had envisaged) in *our case*? We suggest that you use this question as a way to start a reflection process in your own specific context, rather than try and develop the next grand plan or organizational blueprint.

There are two main reasons why we think this approach is more productive in practice. The first reason is a rather methodological one and goes to the heart of 'the strategy paradox'; it is also a key message of this book: we cannot tell you what *your* strategy should actually look like or how exactly it should be implemented. *The only generalization that can be made is that it is hard to generalize.*

Since there is no grand recipe or generic route to success, the only thing we can realistically do is point to pitfalls and errors to avoid and try and understand and learn from past experiences and mistakes, in our own and in other companies.

The second reason is a much more practical one. If possible mistakes and obstacles are clearly identified and anticipated, we firmly believe that we are in a much better position to avoid them, to remove or overcome them in due course, as long as the basic objectives and visions are shared with the relevant people in the organization (in principle as large a group as possible). The more people that are involved in developing our strategy and anticipating these barriers, the more the implementation problem evaporates. The best way to avoid problems is to ask yourself explicitly what could go wrong and hence be prepared to avoid the most likely mistakes and opposing forces.

The main structure developed in this book, centred around the 'why' (Section 1), 'what' (Section 2) and 'how' (Section 3), then serves as a clear

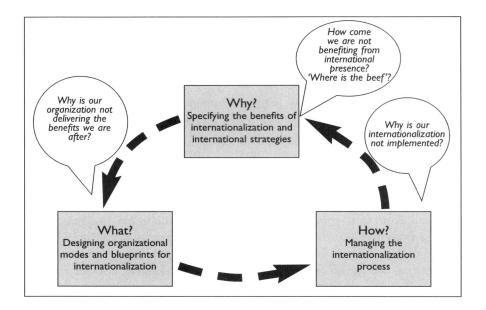

**Figure 7.1** Why is globalization not happening in our company?

framework to classify the different types of problem, and structure a constructive discussion about overcoming them. Below we outline, as an illustration of what can come out of this process and by way of a recap, the many reasons why internationalization is not happening or not working (Figure 7.1):

- We are not clear on the benefits of globalization
- We have not adapted our organization to deliver these benefits
- We have not followed up the implementation of globalization.

### No clear view of the business benefit

Internationalization may not have happened yet, because the benefit that we are after is *not clear*:

- We may not have clearly identified what we are after by internationalizing: *where is the beef*? Should we be surprised that we are not gaining the benefits that we have not identified or cannot see? We should be in a position to detect the benefits when and if they emerge, and monitor the market and business environment closely enough for that.

■ We do not share the same perception about what is happening. There is more than analytics and scientific reality in the process of becoming an international company. An important factor is the perception of individuals, and ultimately the shared perception of the organization of what we are striving for. It is hard to get everyone to work for the same objective if we do not share the same *vision* for the future world and our own future in that world.

In the hype of internationalization and globalization, a lot of us seemed to take the benefits for granted. But are they really there? We tend to think that *globalization is not a one-way street.*

Maybe not all companies are or should be globalizing, to the same extent, at the same time. The key is to understand where the benefits are and how big they are, and how fast they are emerging, *for you.*

We may have overestimated the benefits because:

■ Market convergence is not happening at the speed we were assuming or anticipating. This seems to be the real situation in many markets or segments.

■ Our expected cost advantages are not supported by the economics of the business.

■ The cost advantages cannot materialize because market limitations (external barriers) are not evaporating as quickly as expected so that *our* potential benefits are barely worth the costs of overcoming or pushing these barriers. While market limitations such as transportation costs, trade barriers and consumer differences are falling, this should not affect all companies in the same way, it depends on the industry you are in and your positioning and strategy and it may not happen as fast as we thought it would. We recommend that you *distinguish between the level and rate of market integration.* It is not because market limitations are falling that all markets are global in one big leap. Do not confuse the rate of change in internationalization opportunities with the absolute size of the already available potential.

■ The network advantages that we can theoretically see are not very important for most of our (more attractive) clients.

- If we push for global cost or network advantages, we risk marginalizing ourselves to rather small (albeit sometimes growing) global segments.

In short, internationalization and globalization are not happening within our company, because maybe it *should not* be happening: either because the relevant international playing field is more limited than we thought, or because we have no clear and shared vision as to what we are after.

Markets may not be as homogeneous as we expected them to be by now: the high level of integration within the US market may appear more as the exception rather than the rule in terms of relevant business models in a global context. And even in the US, there are clear indications of a trend away from 'national' or 'standard' strategies towards more rather than less differentiation on a local and regional levels, or towards differentiation based on other than geographic criteria.

## Inappropriate organizational vehicles or structures

Are we sure that, starting from the benefits and the appropriate strategy, we are organized for these benefits?

- We tried the wrong vehicle(s) (alliances, FDI, or other) or selected the wrong market(s) for internationalizing. They were not adapted to the main strategic benefits that we wanted to realize in the long run.

- Our organization does not show where the strategic priorities are, or focuses on too many priorities at the same time.

- The organization is based on the wrong 'dimension' or on 'dimensions' of the past, and is not pointing towards future priorities.

- Our organization is too complex (too many dimensions) or changes too often.

You may want to ask yourself:'How will our organization allow us to deliver the benefits we are after?' Organizational blueprints of the past will not allow you to create and capture the benefits of the future.

In addition, 'blueprint thinking' is not very helpful without the proper attention to the transition path and management of the process.

## Getting stuck along the process

Globalization has not happened because there were too many roadblocks along the way and we mismanaged this transition and change process.

### Too many internal barriers

Even if we are clear as to where we want to go and have organized accordingly, we will have to deal with quite a few roadblocks that hinder us along the way. Some of these barriers are:

- the structures, systems and incentives that were used in the past are less optimal for the future objectives of the organization, as indicated above.

- cultural barriers: the organizational culture (as well as the different national cultures, but that is an external aspect) could prevent an easy change towards globalization.

- internal political barriers: whether you are in a process of internationalizing or restructuring an already international organization, you will be fighting old and building new centres of personal organizational power. A major blockage for many multinationals in their attempts to improve the cross-border integration of activities were the 'country baronies' that they had carefully built up in their earlier internationalization moves. Local management had a hard time giving up their local decision-making power 'for the good of the whole company', a continuing battle in many organizations today.

- the intrinsic resistance to change in an organization and its people. You cannot reprogramme an organization overnight, there is legacy from the past you will have take into account. The reluctance to change may stem from a genuine difficulty in changing the way the organization and its people work, as well as excuses for 'no change'. One of the popular excuses for not changing the strategy and organization are the remaining, *imagined* or *real*, cross-border differences and lack of market convergence, irrespective of the potential benefits of globalization. A bottle is always half full and half empty at the same time.

## Mismanaging the process

Overcoming the barriers calls for well-conceived and sustained process management, as emphasized in Chapter 5, based on the following elements:

- A shared, long-term vision and rationale:

  - What is the vision of where we are going? To what extent is this vision based on a sound and careful analysis, or is it just daydreaming, which goes back to the question of 'the beef'?

  - How has this vision been shared? It is rarely sufficient to '*communicate*' the view from the top to the bottom of the organization. '*We told them, didn't we*?' Building the shared rationale will require a broader, sustained involvement from the key actors in *making* the plans, *and* in *implementing* them. Careful attention should be given to the form and context of this 'communication' so that it is really shared and action-provoking.

- Top commitment: we cannot expect the overall globalization process to be managed lower down in the organization.

- The required resources, systems and tools: without the budgets and, as importantly, the human resources, experience and know-how, we will have a hard time making the globalization happen.

- A clear view about the type of process or change path we have engaged in: are we going for shock therapy or the long view? Do we have all conditions in place for either of these routes?

- Momentum: while we may have or want to build up our strategy and organization in the longer term, it will remain key to capitalize sufficiently on short-term successes in order to keep the process going. Make sure we do not forget to catch the 'low hanging fruit' or 'quick wins'.

- Follow-through: globalization is an ongoing *process*, it should not be handled as a one-shot deal, without proper follow-up and monitoring.

In the end, globalization should be managed as a consistent and iterative process between strategy, organization and management. *Where* you start this process is not as important as *when* you start it. It is never too late to start, but the best time is *sooner* rather than later.

Internationalization is a *management* challenge: it is a process of change and transformation. It involves changing *objectives*, on paper and in the heads of people, redesigning the *organization*, on paper and in reality, and changing the way you *manage*, on paper and on the shop floor. Some of the paper changes can be outsourced to consultants or delegated to staff; the changes in the field, however, will require *top management* to stand up, manage the broader agenda and lead the process of change.

## Globalization is strategic

While we feel strongly about the need for specifying the benefits of globalization and are sure that, in some cases, internationalization is not a matter of survival, we are at the same time convinced that internationalization *should be happening in all companies.*

Internationalization should therefore be an intrinsic part of your *strategy*. It is strategic for everyone.

*Globalization is strategic* because it forces us to question fundamentally the way we go about our own business, what our key sources of success are and how we will maintain or even grow them in the face of competition from home and abroad. This point reaches beyond the immediate (or long-term) benefits on the cost or income (or network) side as represented in our Cone(learn) framework. Even when we have reaped the benefits or they are small, there is still a lot to gain out there. Internationalization is about leveraging what you have, duplicating your world-class experience in different markets, but it is increasingly also a dynamic, interactive and iterative process with lots of opportunities to 'learn', 'share' and 'innovate', and hence *become* world class. Obviously, this requires a different set of strategic priorities, organizational vehicles and management approaches than internationalization for cost or network reasons, as was represented by the third axis in the Conelearn framework. So, globalization is strategic for everyone, but for different reasons.

Those who reduce globalization to 'one-size-fits-all' approaches have clearly missed or will miss most of the message. In our opinion, there are as many opportunities for localization, leveraging diversity, maximizing rather than minimizing differentiation, developing multi-whatever strategies, even and especially in markets where homogenization is still a long way off. You may even want to institutionalize this diversity in your own organization and management. The global masters will be those companies that succeed in managing different degrees and speeds of internationalization and globalization across different units, departments, functions, products, client segments, processes or any other dimension. Internally as well as externally, *globalization is probably more about managing diversity than about standardization.*

We believe that genuine globalization will leverage or invite you to build your capacity in managing complexity and diversity, and approach markets and segments with a sense of nuance and attention to detail. The best way to summarize positively the journey we have been through in this book could sound like this:

If you are world class, what are you waiting for!
If you are NOT world class, what are you waiting for!

# Notes

## Preface

1   *From Local Champions to Global Masters: With Tractebel as an Illustration*, produced and distributed by Videomanagement/FTKnowledge, in English, French, Spanish, Portuguese and Dutch, for more info see: www.videomanagement.com.

## Introduction

1   The index weighs the percentage of foreign assets over total assets, with the percentage of foreign sales over total sales, and foreign over total employees.

2   Famous statement by Achille Van Acker, legendary Belgian socialist politician in the 1940s and 50s.

## Section 1

1   *Business Week* (24 April 2000) reported on the fear for globalization and its effect on the growing divergence between the richer Western countries and poorer Third World countries under the title 'Backlash behind the Anxiety over Globalization', as just one example.

2   Real Software, a successful ERP software company headquartered in Belgium with a fantastic growth record, was severely punished on the Euronext for an American acquisition that turned out to have very few long-term client relationships and was rumoured to have built up its turnover mainly on the back of the Y2K hype.

## Chapter 1

1   We realize that this list of slogans is not exhaustive, neither could we prevent the slogans overlapping in one way or another.

2  It is also scary to see that even the macroeconomic debate is tempted to fall back on broad generalizations and one-liners for defending or opposing the globalization of economies (*International Herald Tribune*, 5 December 2000, 'Exposing Anti-Globalization Myths').

3  You have surely heard the slogans in other contexts as well, when justifying the consolidation in the industry, or explaining the next M&A. Regardless of the context they were used in, however, the slogans, in the best case, are still only telling one part of the truth.

4  An article in *Fortune* on 15 May 2000 beautifully illustrates how often simplistic generalizations and projections from one market (US) to another (Europe) raise expectations that Europe should only have three car manufacturers.

5  Iberdrola, the second largest electricity company in Spain, merged with Endesa, the number one in Spain, in order to be big enough to compete internationally (*The Economist*, 21 October 2000). Many of its European competitors have embarked on a similar route, for example Tractebel (Belgium) that we will discuss in more detail in other chapters of the book.

6  The M&A hunger of British and German law firms, in their quest for size, and the interest of the big five consultants and auditors to link up with a law services arm, has shaken up the Continental European law service industry, with lots of mergers and de-mergers, buyouts or buy-ins of partners, for example in Belgium (*De Standaard*, and *Financieel Economische Tijd*, August and September 2000).

7  We can refer to research that the EC has organized around the benefits of the 1992 programme. While it had been predicted that scale economies would represent one third of the benefits of the integrated market, more recent research by the EC indicates that not all of these economies of scale have materialized. We will elaborate on the limitation on economies of scale later, and touch on the managerial aspects and requirements.

8  Several studies on the effect of the Delors programme on the European economy and business indicated that the impact was less far reaching than foreseen (see *Study on the Extent of Realisation of Economies of Scale due to the Internal Market Programme*, Commission of the European Communities, 1996).

9  For a more fundamental discussion on the strategic impact of the euro introduction for non-financial services companies, see Verdin and Van Heck (1999a). While our concerns have not always made us popular and it took some time to prove us right, the current debate on the euro seems increasingly to support our insights (*International Herald Tribune*, 8 September 2000).

10  See *Financial Times*, September 2000.

11  Researchers found that, in reality, a much smaller portion of the ventures that were meant to be international from the start really were (Reuber and Fischer, 1997).

## Chapter 2

1  The phenomenon of the learning curve, and the link between growth (output) and profitability (and hence also cost) has been a major factor in the development of the domain of strategic management itself, as, for example, in the BCG and other portfolio matrices (Hax and Majluf, 1996, p. 276).

2  It is interesting to observe that while alternative typologies have a more elaborate and nuanced view on types of international strategies, one can still distinguish larger groups of strategies which are typically more global, some others more local or multi-local, some more regional (as we will discuss later) and some other strategies that are more transitional (in the process of regionalizing or globalizing) (Calori et al., 2000).

3  In fact, for the fans of an analytical approach, you could draw *globalization isobars* in the Cone axes. Each point of those isobars represent strategies that have the same 'degree of globalization/standardization', with a varying balance of cost advantages and network benefits. This means that graphically the optimal international strategy is defined by the point where the globalization isobar touches the international strategy playing field, with the given mix of network benefits and cost advantages. A similar degree of globalization could be achieved through more focus on network benefits, and less emphasis on cost advantages and vice versa. The difficulty with this strategy could be that it goes beyond the network benefits that the company can realize, due to localization pressures, while it underdevelops the potential cost advantages.

4  This is in sharp contrast with Jeannet's (2000) observation that the globalization pressures would be identical for all directly competing firms. In our opinion, it is debatable to expect the pressures to show up at industry level only, at a time when the notion of industry has become more obsolete in itself – especially in strategy making (Hawawini et al., 2000; see also Rumelt, 1991).

5  Presentation by P. Rowley, Group Finance Director, Kingfisher, 'Key lessons from King-fisher's pan-European expansion', European Finance Executives, Versailles, 10–12 April 2000.

6  This picture is based on an in-depth case study by one of our students.

7  But of course, how to define a 'region' may depend on the industry and market characteristics. For a more in-depth discussion on the forces creating fracture lines, see Calori et al., 2000.

8  The Integration–Responsiveness (IR) grid of Prahalad and Doz (1987), and its expansion into the IRL (Integration–Responsiveness–Learning) grid by Bartlett and Ghoshal (1987a), are intended to balance the globalization and localization pressures in international operations, and their impact on the appropriate international strategy and organizational stereotype (global, multi-domestic, international or transnational). The Integration–Responsiveness decision is represented mainly as a trade-off, which effectively reduces it to an unidimensional instrument. In fact, recent empirical research confirms that representing the pressures as two independent constructs is misleading (Venaik et al., 2000, p. 1).

9  Various authors have identified where the pressures for globalization are coming from, such as Yip (1989) and Jeannet (2000), and have linked this to the required type of international strategy. Their classification of pressures tended to include what we call catalysts, or disappearing barriers, for globalization (such as government actions and falling trade barriers, or internationalizing suppliers) without expanding on the underlying benefits. They also tended to focus on cost and network benefits, rather than the learning, in their frameworks.

10  The Configuration–Co-ordination matrix of Porter (1986a) disconnects the geographical coverage from the international coordination decision, while we consider these to be intrinsically intertwined.

11  The organizational stereotypes of global, multi-local and transnational organization, (Bartlett and Ghoshal, 1987), the IR trade-off in international strategy models (Prahalad and Doz, 1987) and the archetypes of Bartlett and Ghoshal (1986) that specify the role of the international subsidiaries are intrinsically rich, but risk stereotyping the discussion.

12  Yip (1989) and Jeannet (2000) explicitly talked about *industry* pressures. We disagree with Jeannet when he says: 'In that sense, the global logic spiderweb would be identical for all directly competing firms'.

13  Internationalization decision trees, as in Root (1994), are often set up on the basis of operational criteria such as the size of the market, the government policy, the fiscal and legal environment and so on.

## Chapter 4

1    Referring to the familiar concept which has been developed as a guide or an exploration for the shaping and management of a diversified corporate portfolio (for example in Prahalad and Bettis, 1995).

## Chapter 5

1    In times of organizational and strategic change, the broader issue is when to set up a separate unit or division, and when to (re-)integrate into the existing organization. When GE pioneered the set up of SBUs (strategic business units) in order to streamline its organization into a more strategically oriented one in the 1970s, it initially chose to use an overlay structure, so as not to upset the existing organization (too much). Obviously, the benefits of such an approach will be structurally limited. Similarly, the debate around innovations in large companies is filled with arguments for and against internal corporate venturing. At the height of the initial e-commerce and e-business boom, for example, many companies considered setting up a separate unit, often largely independent, only to reintegrate them quickly with their 'core activities' as it prevented reaping many of the real benefits which were as prevalent internally as externally on the market.

2    In the strategy domain, it is increasingly accepted that the involvement of key people in the strategy process will lead to a better, shared, implemented and functioning strategy.

## Chapter 6

1    Famous statement by Achille Van Acker, legendary Belgian socialist politician in the 1940s and 50s.

# References

Aaker, D.A. and Joachimsthaler, E. *Brand Leadership*, (New York: Free Press, 2000) 351 pp.

Abell, D.F. 'Competing Today while Preparing for Tomorrow', *Sloan Management Review*, Spring 1999, 73–81.

Ahlberg, J., Garemo, N. and Naucler, T. 'The Euro: How to Keep your Prices up and your Competitors down?', *The McKinsey Quarterly*, **2**, 1999, 112–19.

Aliber, R.Z. and Click, R.W. (eds), *Readings in International Business: A Decision Approach*, (Cambridge: MIT Press, 1993) 521 pp.

Arnold, D., Birkinshaw, J. and Toulan, O. *Implementing Global Account Management in Multinational Corporations*, Marketing Science Institute, Report 2000–103.

AT Kearny 'Language, Cultural Barriers and Social Constraints are Keeping Euro-insurers from Capturing Savings of at Least Five Billion Euro in Non-life Alone', Presentation of results of European insurance survey, May 2001, www.atkearny.com.

Barney, J.B. 'How a Firm's Capabilities Affect Boundary Decisions', *Sloan Management Review*, Spring 1999, 137–45.

Bartlett, C. and Ghoshal, S. 'Tap your Subsidiaries for Global Reach', *Harvard Business Review*, November–December 1986, 87–94.

Bartlett, C. and Ghoshal, S. 'Managing Across Borders: New Strategic Requirements', *Sloan Management Review*, Summer 1987a, 43–53.

Bartlett, C. and Ghoshal, S. 'Managing Across Borders: New Organizational Responses', *Sloan Management Review*, Fall 1987b, 7–53.

Bartlett, C. and Ghoshal, S. 'What is a Global Manager?', *Harvard Business Review*, September–October 1992, 124–32.

Bartlett C. and Ghoshal, S. *Transnational Mangement*, 3rd edn (Boston: McGraw-Hill, 2000a) 880 pp.

Bartlett, C. and Ghoshal, S. 'Going Global: Lessons from Late Movers', *Harvard Business Review*, March–April 2000b, 132–42.

Beamish, P.W., Killing, J.P., Lecraw, D.J. and Crookell, H. *International Management*, (Homewood, IL: Irwin, 1991) 546 pp.

Beamish, P.W., Morrison, A. and Rosenzweig, P. *International Management: Text and Cases*, 4th edn (Boston: McGraw-Hill, 1999) 326 pp.

Beinhocker, E.D., 'Robust Adaptive Strategies', *Sloan Management Review*, Spring 1999, 95–106.

Birkinshaw J., *Entrepreneurship in the Global Firm*, (London: Sage, 2000) 154 pp.

Birkinshaw J. and Hood, N. *Multinational Corporate Evolution and Subsidiary Development*, (Basingstoke: Macmillan – now Palgrave, 1998) 392 pp.

Blackwell, N., Bizet, J.P., Child, P. and Hensley, D. 'Shaping a Pan-European Organization', *The McKinsey Quarterly*, **2**, 1991, 94–111.

Blackwell, N., Bizet, J.P., Child, P. and Hensley, D. 'Creating European Organizations that Work', *The McKinsey Quarterly*, **2**, 1992, 31–43.

Bleackley, M. and Williamson, P. 'The Nature and Extent of Corporate Restructuring within Europe's Single Market: Cutting through the Hype', *European Management Journal*, **15**(5): Oct 1997, 484–97.

Bleeke J. and Ernst, D. *Collaborating to Compete*, (New York: John Wiley & Sons, 1993) 284 pp.

Bleeke, J., Isono, J., Ernst, D. and Weinberg, D. 'The Shape of Cross-Border M&A' and 'Succeeding at Cross-Border M&A', *The McKinsey Quarterly*, **3**, 1990, 15–26 and 46–55.

Blomqvist, H.C., 'Operationalizing International Competitiveness: What Are We Really Measuring?', Proceedings of the University of Vaasa. Discussion papers 109, (Vaasan korkeakoulu Vaasa Finland, 1990) 19 pp.

Boutellier R., Gassman O. and von Zedtwitz, M. *Managing Global Innovation: Uncovering the Secrets of Future Competitiveness*, 2nd revised edn, (Berlin, Springer Verlag, 2000) 635 pp.

Brandenburger, A. and Nalebuff, B. *Co-Opetition: A Revolutionary Mindset that Combines Competition and Co-Operation: The Game Theory Strategy that's Changing the Game of Business*, (New York: Doubleday, 1996) 290 pp.

Bryan, L., Fraser, J., Oppenheim, J. and Rall, W. *Race for the World – Strategies to Build a Great Global Firm*, (Boston, MA: Harvard Business School Press, 1999) 364 pp.

Buelens, F. *Globalisation and the Nation-State*, (Cheltenham: Edward Elgar, 1999) 185 pp.

Calori, R. and Lawrence, P. '1992 – Diversity Still Remains – Views of European Managers', *Long Range Planning*, **2**, 1992, 33–43.

Calori R., Atamer, T. and Nunes, P. *The Dynamics of International Competition*, (London: Sage, 2000) 239 pp.

Campbell, A. and Alexander, M. 'What's Wrong with Strategy', *Harvard Business Review*, November–December, 1997, 42–51.

Carr, N.G. 'Hypermediation: Commerce as Clickstream', *Harvard Business Review*, January–February, 2000, 46–7.

Caves, R.E. *Multinational Enterprise and Economic Analysis*, 2nd edn, (Cambridge: Cambridge University Press, 1996) 1–23.

Chakravarthy, B. and Gargiulo, M. 'Corporate Renewal Initiative – Organizing for Hyper-Competition: The Legitimation of Corporate Leadership', INSEAD Working Paper 94/16/OB/SM, 1994, 22 pp.

Chandler, A.D. Jr. *Strategy and Structure: Chapters in the History of the Industrial Enterprise*, 13th impression, (Cambridge, MA: MIT Press, 1984) 463 pp.

Chen, N. 'Intra-national versus International Trade within the European Union: Why do Borders Matter', Working Paper, ECARES, Brussels, 2000.

Choi, S-Y., Stahl, D.O. and Whinston, A.B. *The Economics of Electronic Commerce*, (Indianapolis: Macmillan Technical Publishing, 1997) 626 pp.

'Christopher A. Bartlett on Transnationals: an Interview', *European Management Journal*, September 1992, 271–6.

Collis, D. 'A Resource-based Analysis of Global Competition: The Case of the Bearings Industry', *Strategic Management Journal*, Summer 1991 (Special Issue), 49–68.

Commission of the European Communities, 'Study on the Extent of Realisation of Economies of Scale due to the Internal Market Programme', 1996.

Daniels, J.D., and Radebaugh, L.H. *International Business – Environments and Operations*, 7th edn (New York: Addison-Wesley, 1995) 788 pp.

D'Aveni, R. 'Strategic Supremacy through Disruption and Dominance', *Sloan Management Review*, Spring 1999, 127–35.

De Bettignies, H.C., Lecture notes, in: Schneider, S.C. and Barsoux, J.L. *Managing Across Cultures*, (New York: Prentice Hall, 1997) 267 pp.

De Koning, A., Verdin, P. and Williamson, P. 'So you Want to Integrate Europe : How do you Manage the Process', *European Management Journal*, June 1997, 252–65.

De Koning, A., Subramanian, V. and Verdin, P. 'Regional Organisation: Is it the Way for the Multinational?', Proceedings of the International Conference on Economic Integration and Corporate Development: Europe and Latin America. (Montpellier, France: ESKA, 2000) 499–513.

De la Torre, J. and Neckar, D.H. 'Forecasting Political Risks for International Operations', *International Journal of Forecasting*, **4**, 1988, 221–41.

De la Torre, J., Doz, Y. and Devinney, T. *Managing The Global Corporation: Case Studies in Strategy & Management*, 2nd edn (Boston: McGraw-Hill, 2000) 580 pp.

De Montbrial, T. and Jacquet, P. *Ramses 2001. Les Grandes Tendances du Monde*, (Paris: Dunod, Rapport Annuel Mondial sur le Système Economique et les Stratégies, 2001).

Dermine, J. and Hillion, P. *European Capital Markets with a Single Currency*, (Oxford: Oxford University Press, 1999) 376 pp.

Doremus, P.N., Keller, W.W., Pauly, L.W. and Reich, S. *The Myth of the Global Corporation*, (Princeton, NJ: Princeton University Press, 1998) 193 pp.

Douglas, S. and Wind, Y. 'The Myth of Globalization', *Columbia Journal of World Business*, Winter 1987, 19–29.

Doz, Y.L. and Hamel, G. *Alliance Advantage: The Art of Creating Value through Partnering*, (Boston, MA: Harvard Business School Press, 1998) 316 pp.

Doz, Y.L., Williamson, P.J., Asakawa, K. and Santos, J. 'The Metanational Corporation' INSEAD Working Paper No 97/60/SM, 1997, 32 pp.

Dunning, J.H. *The Globalization of Business*, (London: Routledge, 1993) 467 pp.

Dussauge, P. and Garrette, B. *Cooperative Strategy: Competing Successfully through Strategic Alliances*, (New York: Wiley, 1999) 236 pp.

Dyer, J.H. and Nobeoka, K. 'High-performance Knowledge-sharing Network: The Toyota Case', *Strategic Management Journal*, **21**(3), Special Issue, March 2000, 345–67.

Eisenhardt, K.M. 'Strategy as Strategic Decision Making', *Sloan Management Review*, Spring 1999, 65–72.

Evans, P. and Wurster, T.S. 'Getting Real about Virtual Commerce', *Harvard Business Review*, November–December 1999, 85–94.

Foreign Policy, 'Measuring Globalization', *Foreign Policy*, January–February 2001, 56–65.

Galbraith, J.K., 'The Winner Takes All … Sometimes', *Harvard Business Review*, November–December 1995, 44–6.

Garette, B. and Dussauge, P. 'Alliances versus Acquisitions: Choosing the Right Option', *European Management Journal*, **18**(1) 2000, 63–9.

Ghemawat, P., and Ghadar, F. 'The Dubious Logic of Global Megamergers', *Harvard Business Review*, July–August 2000, 65–72.

Ghoshal, S., Bartlett, C.A. and Moran, P. 'A New Manifesto for Management', *Sloan Management Review*, Spring 1999, 9–20.

Gomes-Casseres, B. 'Joint Ventures in the Face of Global Competition', *Sloan Management Review*, Spring 1989, 17–26.

Govindarajan, V. and Gupta, A. 'Taking Wal-Mart Global', *Best Practice*, 4th Quarter 1999, 14–25.

Govindarajan, V., and Gupta, A. 'Analysis of the Emerging Global Arena', *European Management Journal*, **18**(3) 2000, 274–84.

Graham, E.M, 'Market Structure and the Multinational Enterprise: A Game-theoretic Approach', *Journal of International Business*, 1st Quarter 1998, 67–83.

Grant, R. *Contemporary Strategy Analysis – Concepts, Techniques, Applications*, 3rd edn (Oxford: Blackwell, 1998) 461 pp.

Grosse, R.E., *Thunderbird on Global Business Strategy*, (New York: Wiley, 2000) 362 pp.

Hamel, G. and Prahalad, C.K. 'Do you Really have a Global Strategy', *Harvard Business Review*, July–August 1985, 139–48.

Harzing, A.W. 'An Empirical Analysis and Extension of the Bartlett and Ghoshal Typology of Multinational Companies', *Journal of International Business Studies*, 1st Quarter 2000, 101–20.

Hawawini, G., Verdin, P. and Subramanian, V. 'Is Profitability Driven by Industry or Firm-Specific Factors? A New Look At The Evidence', INSEAD Working Paper No. 2000/80/FIN, 2000, p. 32.

Hawawini, G., Verdin, P. and Subramanian, S. 'The Home Country in the Age of Globalization: Does it Matter for Firm Performance', Working Paper, Solvay Business School, ULB, Brussels, 2001, 32 pp.

Hax, A.C., and Majluf, N.S. *The Strategy Concept and Process – A Pragmatic Approach*, 2nd edn (London: Prentice Hall, 1996) 440 pp.

Hirsch, S. 'An International Trade and Investment Theory of the Firm', Oxford Economic Paper, July 1976, 258–70.

Hirst, P. and Thompson, G. *Globalisation in Question*, 2nd edn (Cambridge: Polity Press, 1999) 318 pp.

Hofstede, G. 'Cultural Dimensions in People Mangement – The Socialization Perspective', in: Pucik, V., Tichy, N.M. and Barnett, C.K. *Globalizing Management*, (New York: John Wiley, 1992) 139–58.

Hofstede, G., *Cultures and Organisations: Software of the Mind*, (New York: McGraw-Hill, 1991) 279 pp.

Hout, T., Porter, M.E. and Rudden, E. 'How Global Companies Win Out', *Harvard Business Review*, September–October 1982, 98–108.

Humes, S. *Managing the Multinational: Confronting the Global–Local Dilemma*, (New York: Prentice Hall, 1993) 406 pp.

Humphrey, J., Lecler, Y. and Salerno, M. *Global Strategies and Local Realities – The Auto Industry in Emerging Markets*, (Basingstoke: Palgrave, 2000) 304 pp.

IMD, *IMD World Competitiveness Report*, (Lausanne: IMD, yearly).

Jeannet, J.P. *Managing with a Global Mindset*, (London: Prentice Hall, 2000) 245 pp.

Jeannet, J.P. and Hennessey, H.D. *Global Marketing Strategies*, 2nd edn (Boston, MA: Houghton Mifflin, 1992) 899 pp.

Jennings, J. and Haughton, L. *It's not the Big that Eat the Small … It's the Fast that Eat the Slow – How to Use Speed as a Competitive Tool in Business*, (New York: HarperCollins, 2001) 288 pp.

Kaiser, K. and Stouraitis, A. 'Value Creation through Corporate Restructuring: European Divestures', *European Management Journal*, **13**(2) 1995, 164–74.

Kanter, R.M. *World Class: Thriving Locally in the Global Economy*, (New York: Simon & Schuster, 1995) 416 pp.

Katrishen, F.A., and Scordis, N.A. 'Economies of Scale in Services: A Study of Multinational Insurers', *Journal of International Business Studies*, 2nd Quarter 1998, 305–24.

Kay, J. and Hannah, L. 'Size and Scale (1), (2) and (3)', 2000, www.johnkay.com.

Kim, C. and Mauborgne, R. 'Making Global Strategies Work', *Sloan Management Review*, Spring 1993, 11–27.

Kim, C. and Mauborgne, R. 'The In-roll and Extra-roll of Multinational's Subsidiary Top Management: Procedural Justice at Work', *Management Science*, 1996, **42**(4), 499–515.

Kim, C. and Mauborgne, R. 'Value Innovation: The Strategic Logic of High Growth', *Harvard Business Review*, January–February 1997, 103–12.

Kim, C. and Mauborgne, R. 'Strategy, Value Innovation, and the Knowledge Economy', *Sloan Management Review*, Spring 1999, 41–54.

Kinnear, T.C., 'Brave New World', in: *Financial Times, Mastering Strategy – The Complete MBA Companion in Strategy*, Chapter 4 Strategy and Globalization, (London: Prentice Hall, 2000) 107–11.

Kobrin, S. 'An Empirical Analysis of the Determinants of Global Integration', *Strategic Management Journal*, **12**, 1991, 17–31.

Kogut, B. 'Designing Global Strategies: Comparative and Competitive Value-Added Chains', *Sloan Management Review*, Summer 1985, 15–28.

Kogut, B. 'What Makes a Company Global?', *Harvard Business Review*, January–February1999, 165–9.

Krugman, P.R. *Pop Internationalism*, (Cambridge, MA: MIT Press, 1997) 240 pp.

Krugman, P.R. and Graham, E.M. *Foreign Direct Investment in the U.S*, 3rd edn, (Institute for International Economics, 1995) 232 pp.

Langohr, H. 'Big is not Best in Euroland', *The Banker*, 148, 1998, 27–8.

Lawrence, P. and Lorsch, J. *Organization and Environment: Managing Differentiation and Integration*, Rev. edn, (Harvard Business School Press, 1986) 279 pp.

Levitt, T. 'The Globalization of Markets', *Harvard Business Review*, May–June 1983, 92–102.

Lorange, P., Roos, J. and Bronn, P.S. 'Building Successful Strategic Alliances', *Long Range Planning*, 1992/6, 10–17.

Lyons, M.P. 'Joint Ventures as a Strategic Choice: A Literature Review', *Long Range Planning*, 1991/4, 130–44.

Malnight, T. 'Globalisation of an Ethnocentric Firm: an Evolutionary Perspective', *Strategic Management Journal*, **16**, 1995, 119–41.

Malnight, T. 'The Transition from Decentralized to Network-based MNC Structures: An Evolutionary Perspective', *Journal of International Business Studies*, **27**(1) 1996, 43–65.

Markides, C.C. 'In Search of Strategy' and 'A Dynamic View of Strategy', *Sloan Management Review*, Spring 1999, 6–7 and 55–63.

Marquardt, M.J. *The Global Advantage – How World-Class Organizations Improve Performance through Globalization*, (Houston, TX: Gulf, 1999) 266 pp.

Martinez, J. and Jarillo, C. 'The Evolution of Research on Coordination Mechanisms in Multinational Corporations', *Journal of International Business Studies*, 3rd Quarter 1989, 489–514.

McCallum, J. 'National Borders Matter: Canada–US Regional Trade Patterns', *American Economic Review*, 1995, 615–23.

Mintzberg, H. and Lampel, J. 'Reflecting on the Strategy Process', *Sloan Management Review*, Spring 1999, 21–30.

Mitchell, C. *A Short Course in International Marketing Blunders*, (Novato, CA: World Trade Press, 2001) 192 pp.

Montgomery, D.B., Yip, G.S. and Villalonga, B. 'Demand for and Use of Global Account Management', *Marketing Science Institute*, Report 99–115, 1999.

Morrison, A.J., Ricks, D.A. and Roth, K. 'Globalization versus Regionalization: Which Way for the Multinational?', *Organizational Dynamics*, **20**(3) 1991, 17–29.

Nonaka, I. and Takeuchi, H. *The Knowledge-Creating Company – How Japanese Companies Create the Dynamics of Innovation*, (New York: Oxford University Press, 1995) 284 pp.

Ohmae, K. 'Managing in a Borderless World', *Harvard Business Review*, May–June 1989, 152–61.

Parker, B. *Globalization and Business Practice – Managing across Boundaries*, (London: Sage, 1998) 655 pp.

Perlmutter, H. 'The Tortuous Evolution of the Multinational Corporation', *Columbia Journal of World Business*, January–February 1969, 9–18.

Piggott, J. and Cook, M. *International Business Economics – A European Perspective*, 2nd edn (New York: Longman, 1999) 429 pp.

Porter, M.E. *Competition in Global Industries*, (Basingstoke: Macmillan – now Palgrave, 1986a) 581 pp.

Porter, M.E. 'Changing Patterns of International Competition', *California Management Review*, Winter 1986b, 9–40.

Porter, M.E. *The Competitive Advantage of Nations*, (Basingstoke: Macmillan – now Palgrave, 1990) 855 pp.

Praet, P. and Wigny, A. 'What the Euro Means for Non-financial Business', *Single Currency in Practice*, October 1997.

Prahalad, C.K. and Bettis, R.A., 'The Dominant Logic: Retrospective and Extension', *Strategic Management Journal*, **16**(1) 1995, 5–15.

Prahalad, C.K. and Doz, Y. *The Multinational Mission*, (New York: Free Press, 1987) 290 pp.

Prahalad, C.K. and Oosterveld, J.P. 'Transforming Internal Governance: The Challenge for Multinationals', *Sloan Management Review*, Spring 1999, 31–9.

Quelch, J.A. 'The New Country Managers', *The McKinsey Quarterly*, **4**, 1992, 155–65.

Quelch, J.A. and Bloom, H. 'The Return of the Country Manager', *The McKinsey Quarterly*, **2**, 1996, 30–43.

Rangan, S. 'Seven Myths regarding Global Strategy', in: *Financial Times, Mastering Strategy – The Complete MBA Companion in Strategy*, Chapter 4 Strategy and Globalization, (London: Prentice Hall, 2000) 119–24.

Reeb, D., Kwok Chuck, C.Y. and Black, H.Y. 'Systematic Risk of the Multinational Corporation', *Journal of International Business Studies*, 2nd Quarter 1998, 263–79.

Reich, R.B. 'Who is Us ?', *Harvard Business Review*, January–February 1990, 53–63.

Reisenbeck, H. and Freeling, A. 'How Global are Global Brands?', *European Business Report*, Summer 1993, 12–17.

Reuber, A.R., and Fischer, E. 'The Influence of the Management Team's International Experience on the Internationalization Behaviors of SMEs', *Journal of International Business Studies*, 4th Quarter 1997, 807–25.

Ricks, D.A. *Blunders in International Business*, 3rd edn (Oxford: Blackwell, 1999) 184 pp.

Root, F.R. *Entry Strategies for International Markets* (revised and expanded edition), (New York: Lexington Books, 1994).

Rose, A.K. 'One Money, One Market: The Effect of Common Currencies on International Trade', *Economic Policy*, **15**(30) 2000, 7–46.

Roth, K. and Morrison, A.J. 'An Empirical Analysis of the Integration-Responsiveness Framework in Global Industries', *Journal of International Business Studies*, 4th Quarter 1990, 541–65.

Rothenberg, R. 'An Interview with John Quelch', *Strategy+Business*, **20**, 3rd Quarter 2000, 8.

Roure, J., Alvarez, J.L., Garcia-Pont, C. and Nueno, J.L. 'Managing Internationally: The International Dimensions of the Managerial Task', *European Management Journal*, **11**(4) 1993, 485–92.

Rugman, A.M. and Hodgetts, R.M. *International Business: A Strategic Management Approach*, 2nd edn (London: McGraw-Hill Series in Management 2000) 637 pp.

Ruigrok, W. and Van Tulder, R. *The Logic of International Restructuring*, (London: Routledge, 1995) 344 pp.

Rumelt, R. 'How Much Does Industry Matter?', *Strategic Management Journal*, **12** 1991, 167–85.

Sarkar, M.B., Cavusgil, S.T. and Aulakh, P.S. 'International Expansion of Telecommunication Carriers: The Influence of Market Structure, Network Characteristics, and Entry Imperfections', *Journal of International Business Studies*, 2nd Quarter 1999, 361–82.

Schlie, E. and Yip, G. 'Regional Follows Global: Strategy Mixes in the World Automotive Industry', *European Management Journal*, **18**(4) 2000, 343–54.

Schneider, S.C. 'National vs Corporate Culture: The Implications for HRM', *Human Resource Management*, Summer 1988, 231–46.

Schneider, S.C. and Barsoux, J.L. *Managing Across Cultures*, (New York: Prentice Hall, 1997) 267 pp.

Schütte, H. 'Between Headquarters and Subsidiaries: The RHQ Solution', Paper presented at the EIAB Conference, Stockholm, 1996.

Segal-Horn, S. 'The Internationalization of Service Firms', *Advances in Strategic Management*, **9**, 1993, 31–55.

Segal-Horn, S. *The Challenge of International Business*, (London: Kogan Page, 1994) 251.

Segal-Horn, S. and Faulkner, D. *The Dynamics of International Strategy*, (London: Thomson Business Press, 1999) 286 pp.

Smith, R.C. and Walter, I. *The First European Merger Boom has Begun*, (Center for the Study of American Business, 1991).

Stanat, R. and West, C. *Global Jumpstart – The Complete Resource for Expanding Small and Midsize Businesses*, (Cambridge: Perseus Books, 1999) 198 pp.

Steinfield, C. and Klein, S. 'Local versus Global Electronic Commerce', *Electronic Markets*, **9**(1–2) 1999, 6.

Stonham, P. 'Demergers and the Hanson Experience. Part One: The Prelude', *European Management Journal*, **15**(3) 1997, 266–74.

Stonham, P. 'Demergers and the Hanson Experience. Part Two: Demerger Tactics', *European Management Journal*, **15**(4) 1997, 413–22.

Strebel, P. 'Choosing the Right Change Path', *California Management Review*, Winter 1994, 29–51.

Szulanski, G. 'Exploring Internal Stickiness: Impediments to the Transfer of Best Practice within the Firm', *Strategic Management Journal*, **17**, Special issue, Winter 1996, 27–44.

Taylor, W.C. 'Whatever Happened to Globalization?', *Fast Company*, **27**, 228.

Tibau, J. 'Fundamental Organizational Change: An Achievable Goal or Condraction in the Terms', in: Van Tilborgh C. and Duyck, R. (eds) *Management Jaarboek 2001*, (Vlaamse Management Associatie (VMA) en Academici Roularta Media (ARM), 2001 forthcoming).

Tushman, M. and Romanelli, E. 'Organizational Evolution: A Metamorphosis Model of Convergence and Reorientation' in Cummings, L. and Staw, B. (eds), *Research in Organizational Behavior*, (Greenwich, CT: JAI Press, 7, 1985) 171–222.

UNCTAD *World Investment Report*, (New York, UNCTAD, yearly) 268 pp.

UNCTAD *Division on Transnational Corporations and Investment Transnational Corporations and World Development*, (International Thomson Business Press, 1996) 581 pp.

UNCTAD *World Investment Report 1999: Foreign Direct Investment and the Challenge of Development*, (yearly) (New York: UNCTAD, 1999) 541 pp.

US Congress – Office of Technology Assessment 'US–Mexico Trade: Pulling Together or Pulling Apart', ITE-545, Washington DC, 1992.

US Congress – Office of Technology Assessment 'Multinationals and the National Interest: Playing by Different Rules', OTA-ITE-569, Washington DC, 1993.

United Nations *World Economic and Social Survey*, (New York: United Nations, yearly) 296 pp.

Usunier, J.C. *International Marketing: A Cultural Approach*, (New York: Prentice Hall, 1993) 494 pp.

van der Padt, A. 'Wat Betekent 'Europa 1992' voor de Strategie van DAF?' – 'What is the Meaning of "Europe 1992" for the Strategy of Daf?', *Bedrijfskunde*, 1990/2, 167–72.

Venaik, S., Midgley, D.F. and Devinney, T.M. 'An Empirical Examination of the Dimensionality of the Integration–Responsiveness Framework', INSEAD Working Paper 2000/53/MKT, 2000, 29 pp.

Verdin, P. 'The Euro and Market Convergence', in: *Financial Times, Mastering Strategy – The Complete MBA Companion in Strategy*, Chapter 3 Strategy and the General Business Environment, (London: Prentice Hall, 2000) 100–2.

Verdin, P. and Bogaert, R. 'Een Organisatie Gebouwd op Snelheid of een Structuur Gebaseerd op Middelen. De Wisselwerking tussen Structuur en Succesvol Innoveren' – 'An Organisation Built on Speed versus a Structure Based on Resources. The Interaction between Structure and Successful Innovation', in: Van Tilborgh, C. and Duyck, R. (eds) *Management Jaarboek 2000*, (Vlaamse Management Associatie (VMA) en Academici Roularta Media (ARM), 2000) 56–62.

Verdin, P. and Van Heck, N. 'The Euro and Corporate Strategy: Reflections on the Implications of the Single Currency for the Strategies of Non-Financial Companies', *European Management Journal*, August, 1999a.

Verdin, P. and Van Heck, N. 'The Euro: Operational Hype or Strategic Relevance', *European Management Journal*, **17**(4) 1999b, 356–67.

Verdin, P. and Van Heck, N. 'Knowledge Integration Across Borders: How to Manage the Transition?', in: Conceiçao, P., Gibson, D., Heitor, M. and Shariq, S. (eds) *Science, Technology and Innovation Policy. Opportunities and Challenges for the Knowledge Economy,* edited by, International Series on Technology Policy and Innovation, Vol. I, (IC2 Institute, University of Texas at Austin and the Center for Innovation, Technology and Policy Research, Instituto Superior Technico, Lisbon, Quorum Books: Westport, CT, and London, 2000a) 41–68.

Verdin, P. and Van Heck, N. 'Strategy and the Euro: The Impact of the Single Currency on Company Strategy', in: Ooghe, H., Heylen, F. and Vander Vennet, R. (eds) *The Economic and Business Consequences of the EMU*, 24th Flemish Scientific Economic Congress, March, 17–18, 2000, (Dortrecht, Holland: Kluwer Academic Publishers, 2000b).

Vernon, R. 'International Investment and International Trade in the Product Cycle', *Quarterly Journal of Economics*, May 1966, 190–207.

Vernon, R. 'The Product Cycle Hypothesis in a New International Environment', *Oxford Bulletin of Economics and Statistics*, Nov 1979, 255–67.

Vernon, R. 'Research on Transnational Corporations: Shedding Old Paradigms', *Transnational Corporations*, February 1994, 137–58.

Vernon-Wortzel, H. and Wortzel, L.H. *Strategic Management in the Global Economy*, (New York: John Wiley & Sons, 1996), 592 pp.

Walter, I. 'Financial Services Strategies in the Euro-zone', *European Management Journal*, **17**(5) 1999, 447–65.

Walter, I. and Murray, T. *Handbook of International Management*, (New York: John Wiley & Sons, 1988), 672 pp.

Welch, L. and Luostarinen, R. 'Internationalization: Evolution of a Concept', *Journal of General Management*, Winter 1988, 34–55.

Williamson, P.J. 'Strategy as Options on the Future', *Sloan Management Review*, Spring 1999, 117–26.

Williamson, P.J., Doz, Y.L. and Santos, J. *From Global to Metanational: How Companies Win in the Global Knowledge Economy*, (Boston, MA: Harvard Business School Press, forthcoming).

Yip, G. 'Global strategy … In a World of Nations?', *Sloan Management Review*, Fall 1989, 29–41.

Yip, G. 'New Strategic Challenges Facing the Global Company', in: Simon, D.F. (ed.), *Corporate Strategies in the Pacific Rim: Global versus Regional Trends*, (New York: Routledge, 1995) 77–103.

Yip, G. and Madsen, T.L. 'Global Account Management: The New Frontier in Relationship Marketing', *International Marketing Review*, **13**(3), 1996, 24–42.

## Cases

3M Company, The: Integrating Europe (A), (adapted version of the case of Ackenhusen, M., Muzyka, D. and Churchill, N.), by Van Heck, N. and Verdin, P. (KU Leuven-INSEAD, 1994) 20 pp.

3M Company, The: Integrating Europe (B), (adapted version of the case of Ackenhusen, M., Muzyka, D. and Churchill, N.), by Van Heck, N. and Verdin, P. (KU Leuven-INSEAD, 1994) 11 pp.

3M Company, The: Integrating Europe (C), (adapted version of the case of Ackenhusen, M., Muzyka, D. and Churchill, N.), by Van Heck, N. and Verdin, P. (KU Leuven-INSEAD, 1994) 13 pp.

3M Europe: The Nordic Region, by Rotch W. (Case Reference No. UVA-C-2109, Darden Business School, University of Virginia, 1994) 28 pp.

ABB's Relays Business: Building and Managing a Global Matrix, by Bartlett C.A., (Case Reference No. 9-394-016, Harvard Business School, 1994) 29 pp.

Alcatel Access Systems Division (A): Lessons from the Past, by Verdin, P., De Meyer, A. and Bogaert, R. (Case Reference No. 300-126-1, INSEAD, 2000) 22 pp.

Alcatel Access Systems Division (B): Building for the Future, by Verdin, P., De Meyer, A. and Bogaert, R. (Case Reference No. 300-127-1, INSEAD, 2000) 18 pp.

Alcatel Access Systems Division (C): The Virtual Company – Adsl, by Verdin, P., De Meyer, A. and Bogaert, R. (Case Reference No. 300-128-1, INSEAD, 2000) 8 pp.

Alto Chemicals Europe (A), by Kashani, K. (IMD, 1991) 13 pp.

Alto Chemicals Europe (B), by Kashani, K. (IMD, 1991) 3 pp.

Alto Chemicals Europe (C), by Kashani, K. (IMD, 1991) 3 pp.

A Note on Knowledge Management, by Garvin, D.A. and March, A. (Case Reference No. 9-398-031, Harvard Business School, 1998) 20 pp.

Banco Comercial Português (1993), by Doz, Y., De Pomme, C. and Taubman, C. (Case Reference No. 11/93-4216, INSEAD-THESEUS, 1993) 46 pp.

BIS Banking Systems (A) Heading for the 1990s, by Verdin, P.J. and Van Heck, N. (Case Reference No. 300-052-1, INSEAD, 2000) 19 pp.

BIS Banking Systems (B) Distribution Strategy, by Verdin, P.J. and Van Heck, N. (Case Reference No. 300-053-1, INSEAD, 2000) 16 pp.

Daf in 1991: Preparing for the Post-1990 Era, by Ricart, J.E., Verdin, P. and de Haan, F. (Case Reference No. 392-041-1, IESE, 1992) 16 pp. In: Ghoshal, S., Mintzberg, H. and Quinn, J.B. (eds) *The Strategy Process*, European Edition, 2nd edn (Prentice Hall, 1995) 155–68.

European Temporary Work Services Industry in 1989: Preparing for the Nineties Background Note, by Rius, D., de Haan, F. and Verdin, P. (Case Reference No. 392-040-5, IESE, 1992) 20 pp.

European Temporary Work Services Industry in 1994, by Verdin, P.J. and Van Heck, N. (Case Reference No. 300-051-1, INSEAD, 2000) 21 pp.

European Truck Industry in 1990: Preparing For The Post-1992 Era Background Note, by De Haan, F., Thomas, H. and Verdin, P. (Case Reference No. 392-039-5, IESE, 1992) 24 pp. In: Ghoshal, S., Mintzberg, H. and Quinn, J.B. (eds) *The Strategy Process*, European Edition, 2nd edn (Prentice Hall, 1995) 137–54.

Electrolux: The Acquisition and Integration of Zanussi, by Ghoshal, S. and Haspeslagh, P. (Case Reference No. 390-037-1, INSEAD, Fontainebleau, 1990) 31 pp.

EMI and the CT Scanner (A), by Bartlett C.A. (Case Reference No. 9-383-194, Harvard Business School, 1983) 10 pp.

EMI and the CT Scanner (B), by Bartlett C.A. (Case Reference No. 9-383-195, Harvard Business School, 1983) 13 pp.

Eureko Alliance Case A: Building a Pan European Network in Insurance and Banking, by Verdin, P. and Freeman, K.E. (Case Reference No. 399-008-1, INSEAD, 1999) 28 pp.

Eureko Alliance Case B: Building a Pan European Network: Achievements and Future Challenges, by Verdin, P. and Freeman, K.E. (Case Reference No. 399-009-1, INSEAD, 1999) 35 pp.

Eureko Alliance Case C: Eureko May 1998: Latest Developments, by Verdin, P. and Freeman, K.E. (Case Reference No. 399-010-1, INSEAD, 1999) 4 pp.

Honda (A), Christiansen, by E.T. and R.T. Pascale (Case Reference No. 9-384-049, Harvard Business School, 1984) 9 pp.

Honda (B), Christiansen, by E.T. and R.T. Pascale (Case Reference No. 9-384-050, Harvard Business School, 1984) 8 pp.

Honeywell Europe (A), by Schneider, S.C., Hansen, L. and Wittenberg-Cox, A. (Case Reference No. 492-004-1, INSEAD, Fontainebleau, 1992) 23 pp.

Honeywell Europe (B), by Schneider, S.C., Hansen, L. and Wittenberg-Cox, A. (Case Reference No. 492-005-1, INSEAD, Fontainebleau, 1992) 9 pp.

I.S.S. – International Service System A/S, by Ackenhusen, M. and Ghoshal, S. (Case Reference No. 394-019-1, INSEAD, Fontainebleau, 1994) 34 pp.

Knowledge Management at Arthur Andersen (Denmark): Building Assets in Real Time and in Virtual Space, by Dutta, S. and De Meyer, A. (Case Reference No. 397-001-1, INSEAD, Fontainebleau, 1997) 21 pp.

McKinsey & Co: Managing Knowledge and Learning, by Bartlett, C.A. (Case Reference No. 9-396-357, Harvard Business School, 1996) 21 pp.

Nexia International, by Reney, M.-C. and Koza, M.P. (INSEAD, Fontainebleau, 1997) 15 pp.

Note on the Motorcycle Industry – 1975, by Buzzell R.D. and Purkayastha, D. (Case Reference No. 9-578-210, Harvard Business School, 1978, revised 1987) 20 pp.

Philips Group – 1987, by Yoshino M.Y. and Aguilar, F.J. (Case Reference No. 9-388-050, Harvard Business School, 1988) 20 pp.

Philips and Matsushita: A Portrait of Two Evolving Companies, by Bartlett, C.A. and Lightfoot, R.W. (Case Reference No. 9-392-156, Harvard Business School, 1992) 23 pp.

Procter & Gamble Europe: Vizir Launch, by Bartlett, C.A. (Case Reference No. 9-384-139, Harvard Business School, 1984) 16 pp.

Procter & Gamble Europe: Ariel Ultra's Eurobrand Strategy, by Verdin, P., Bartlett, C.A. and De Koning, A. (Case Reference No. 300-085-1, INSEAD/HBS, 2000) 25 pp. In: Bartlett, C. and Ghoshal, S. (eds) *Managing Across Borders: The Transnational Solution*, 2nd edn, (Harvard Business School Press, 1998) ??? pp. and in: de la Torre, J., Doz, Y. and Devinney, T. (eds) *Managing the Global Corporation: Case Studies in Strategy and Management*, Section III 'Managing Global Operations', Unit 9 'Managing the Global Marketing Function', 2nd edn, Boston: McGraw-Hill, 2001) 349–64.

Product Development for Line Transmissions Systems within Alcatel NV, by Bonheure, K. and De Meyer, A. (INSEAD, Fontainebleau, 1992) 18 pp.

Ryanair – The Low Fares Airline, by O'Higgins, E. (Case Reference No. 399-122-1, University College Dublin, 1999) 30 pp.

Saatchi & Saatchi Plc., by Ghoshal, S. and Avis, A. (Case Reference No. 190-029-1, INSEAD, 1990) 34 pp.

Skandia AFS, by Bartlett, C.A. and Mahmood, T. (Case Reference No. N9-396-412, Harvard Business School, 1996) 20 pp.

Telefonica: The Making of a Multinational, by Casanova, L. and Meseguer, M. (Case Reference No. 300-003-1, INSEAD, Fontainebleau, 2000) 28 pp.

Tractebel (A): Heading for the 1990s, by Van Heck, N., Vercaemst, P. and Verdin, P. (KU Leuven, 1999) 27 pp.

Tractebel (B): The Internationalisation of a Big Group from a Small Country by Van Heck, N., Vercaemst, P. and Verdin, P. (KU Leuven, 1999) 17 pp.

Tractebel (C): Evolution of the Group until its 10th Anniversary by Van Heck, N., Vercaemst, P. and Verdin, P. (KU Leuven, 1999) 7 pp.

Vedior International's European Strategy: The French Revolution, by Verdin, P.J. and Van Heck, N. (Case Reference No. 300-050-1, INSEAD, 2000) 19 pp.

Volvo Trucks Europe, by Lambin, J.J. and Hiller, T.B. (Lovanium International Management Center, Belgium, 1994), in: Montana, J. (ed.) *Marketing in Europe*, (London: Sage, 1994), 608–22.

Wal-Mart Stores Inc., by Bradley, S.P. (Case reference No. 9-794-024, Harvard Business School, 1994) 22 pp.

Xerox: Building a Corporate Focus on Knowledge, by Dutta, S., Van Wassenhove, L. and Biren, B. (Case Reference No. 600-015-1, INSEAD, Fontainebleau, 2000) 27 pp.

# Index

## Company names

This index of company names is provided for information, not because these companies have been discussed in any detail.

3M (Europe), 73, 83–4, 120, 127, 130, 142, 143, 154–5, 164–5, 178
ABB, 6, 34, 84, 119, 133, 178
ABN AMRO, 70, 164
Achmea, 96, 131
Adecco, 31, 161
Alcatel, 127, 132, 142, 145, 147, 155, 178
Allianz, 91
Allstate International Insurance, 8
Amazon.com, 51–2, 72
American Express (Amex), 68, 70
American Online (AOL), 7, 29, 133
Arthur Andersen, 40, 128
  (now Accenture)
AT&T, 68
Axa, 91, 96

Barings
  see ING (Group)
BBC, 69
BCP, 96, 131
Belgacom, 9
BIS Banking Systems, 45
BNP, 38
Body Shop, The, 66–7, 89
Boeing, 27
Boo.com, 52
Brantano, 66–7, 89
British Steel
  see Corus
British Telecom (BT), 68

C&A, 33
Carrefour, 40, 96, 103
Caterpillar, 45
Cibox, 31, 79
Citigroup, 164
CNN International, 69, 133
Coca Cola, 6–7, 71, 72, 84, 133
Colruyt, 40
Compaq, 31, 79
Concert, 68
Corus, 27
  (result of merger between British Steel and Hoogovens)
Creyf's Interim, 31, 161

Daewoo, 115
DAF Trucks, 30–1, 39, 62, 87, 109, 163
DaimlerChrysler, 115, 157, 158, 159
Dell, 31, 79
Deloitte (and Touche), 9
Deutsche Bank, 32, 164
Deutsche Telekom, 41, 50, 68, 69
  T-Online, 50
DHL, 93
Dressmart.com, 52

eBay, 42
Electrabel, 123, 171
Electricité de France (EdF), 124
Electrolux, 27
Elf, 38
Eli Lilly, 30, 169–70
EMI, 48, 109–10
Eureko (Alliance), 39, 70, 96, 109, 131, 157, 166, 168

Federal Express (FedEx), 93
Ferrari, 67
Financial Times, 70
First Direct, 91
Ford, 8, 71, 76, 80, 84, 162, 176, 178
Fortis, 61, 71

GB, 40
General Electric (GE), 6, 153
General Motors (GM), 6, 115
Generali, 91
Gillette, 26, 71, 88–9, 160–1
GlobalnetXchange, 103
Goodyear, 172
Grupo Prisa, 27

Hewlett-Packard (HP), 79
Hilton, 69
Honda, 109
Hoogovens
  see Corus
HSBC, 46, 68, 70

IBM, 6, 79, 124–5, 142, 155, 170
ICL, 86
Ikea, 72
ING (Group), 8, 47, 129, 164
Interbrew, 43, 109
ISS, 26

Johnson & Johnson, 36
Jolibee, 42

Kinepolis, 8, 66–7, 89
Kingfisher, 8, 80
K-Mart, 43
Kodak, 41
KPN, 41, 50

Lernout and Hauspie Speech Products (LHSP), 8, 51, 129
Leyland, 31, 62, 109

Mannesmann, 41
Marks & Spencer (M&S), 8, 173
Marlboro, 72
Matsushita, 7, 83, 84, 90, 119, 134, 178
Maxdata, 31, 79
McDonald's, 7, 42, 46, 66–7, 69, 89, 113, 133
McDonnell Douglas, 27
McKinsey and Company, 128
Merck, 30
Mitsubishi, 115
Morgan Stanley, 34
Motorola, 34
Mr. Minit, 66–7, 113
MTV, 133

Nestlé, 98, 132, 178
  Nestec, 98
Nexia, 70, 109
Nissan, 115, 158
Nokia, 153
Novotel, 69, 75

One Swoop, 52
One2One, 41
Orange, 41
Otis, 133

Paccar, 31, 62, 109
Packard Bell, 79
Paribas, 38
Pharmacia & Upjohn, 30, 82, 158
Philip Morris, 113
Philips, 6, 119, 142, 155, 158, 178
Pinault Printemps Redoute, 27
Porsche, 67
Price Waterhouse, 128
  (now PricewaterhouseCoopers)
Procter & Gamble (P&G), 83, 130, 143, 147, 152, 154, 163, 178
Publicis, 174

Ranbaxy, 96
Randstad Group, 31
Real Software, 8, 129
Recipeweb, 52
Renault, 34, 115, 158
Royal and Sun Alliance, 91

Saatchi & Saatchi (S&S), 2, 5, 47, 71, 87, 94, 104, 164, 174
Sabena, 8, 42
SAir Group, 8, 42
  see also Swissair
Samsung, 25
SAP, 124
Scania, 37, 115
Sears, 103
Selection, 31
Shell, 6

Skandia, 91, 128
Societé Générale, 38
Solvay Chemicals, 111
Sonera, 42, 107, 117
Spector, 8
Statoil (Norway), 63
Sulzer, 43
Swissair, 42
  *see also* SAir Group
Telefonica, 50, 96
Texas Instruments, 151
Time Warner, 50
Tiny, 31, 79
TotalFina, 38
Toyota, 6, 8, 83–4, 113,
  133–4, 178
Tractebel (Group), 91, 95,
  110–1, 123, 144, 150, 160,
  162, 166, 171
  Powerfin, 123, 144
Unilever, 61, 72, 89, 156, 178
UPS, 93
Van Hool, 31
Vedior (International), 31, 36,
  120, 122, 161
Virgin, 91
Vodafone, 32, 38, 41, 47, 50
VoiceStreamWirelessCorp, 41
Volkswagen (VW), 37, 115
Volvo, 37
*Wall Street Journal, The*, 70
Wal-Mart, 8, 43, 96, 169
Whirlpool, 80, 158
Whitbread, 44
WPP, 5, 94
Yahoo!, 29, 50–1

## Subject Index

### A
acquisitions, 111–17
  *see also* mergers &
    acquisitions
ad hoc teams, 145–6
advertising industry, 47, 87
aircraft manufacturing industry,
  39, 27, 58, 78
airline industry, 50
alliances, 39, 42, 50, 70, 90,
  93, 96, 109, 111–17, 109,
  131, 160, 164, 168, 171
  cynical, 115
ambition, 34–7, 44–52, 57–9,
  68
  *see also* strategic ambition

### B
bakery industry, 79–80
barriers to globalization
  external, *see* market *or*
    globalization limits

internal, 73, 83, 119,
  135–7, 139–49, 171,
  177–9, 181–2, 185
  overcoming, 136–7,
    149–57, 162, 186–7
beer industry, 72
brain power, 119

### C
capacity
  trap, 62–3
  utilization, 62–3, 65, 78,
    80, 108, 112
car industry, 29–30, 61, 64, 78
catering services, 78
centralization, 44–7, 100,
  128–31, 156, 143
Centres of Excellence, 132
  *see also* Competence Centres
comparative advantage, 49,
  53–4, 99
Competence Centres, 98
  *see also* Centres of
    Excellence
competitive advantage (edge),
  34–5, 39–40, 40–2, 50–1,
  65, 97, 116–17, 127–8,
  173–4
concepts, 60, 66–8, 75, 94, 97,
  99, 110, 113–15
Conelearn framework, 59,
  100–2
coordination mechanisms
  informal, 120–1, 125–6,
    130
  formal, 120–1, 125–6, 130
cost advantages, 60–8, 108–9

### D
decentralization
  *see* centralization
diversity, 94–8, 109
dominant strategic logic,
  119–21

### E
economic value added (EVA),
  139, 168
economies of scale (EOS),
  33–4, 46, 60–2, 74–5,
  78–80, 83, 87, 99, 108, 112,
  173
  minimum efficient scale
    (MES), 33, 44, 61, 78,
    180
  *see also* cost advantages
electricity industry, 91, 95, 110
endgame, 34
entry mode, 14–15, 58–9, 104,
  107–17
ethnocentric, 152
Euro, 8, 35–6, 92–4, 171
Euro-pricing
  *see* pricing

European Single Market
  Programme, 8, 34–5, 90–4,
  161–3, 171
expatriation, 147, 178
expertise, 65, 97, 115, 119,
  132, 168, 176
export, 63, 96, 109, 111–17

### F
financial services, 35, 38, 46
first mover advantages, 34
foreign direct investments
  (FDI), 111–17, 184
franchising, 66, 111–17

### G
game theory, 39, 41
geocentric, 152
geographic diversification,
  53–4
global
  account programmes,
    *see* key account
    management
  brand, 7, 66–7
  company, 5–7, 16–17, 25,
    82–5, 158–9
  consolidation, 14, 29–33,
    34–6, 78–9, 115
  industry, 6–7, 25–6, 88
  sourcing, 143–4
globalization
  limits, 76–82, 85–6, *see
    also* market limits
  potential, 74–8, 79–89,
    119–26, 141, 161–3
greenfield, 111–13
  *see also* FDI

### H
headquarters
  global, 131, 133–4, 140
  regional, *see* regional
    headquarters
hedging, 53
home country bias, 2, 5–6, 10,
  111
horizontal (market) segments,
  66–8, 68–71

### I
industry
  clusters, 48–9, 65, *see also*
    valley
  verticals, 124–5, 170
information, 65, 73, 128, 130,
  174, 176
input factors, 49, 63–5, 108–9,
  113, 115
insurance services, 39, 62, 91
integrated market
  *see* European Single Market
    Programme

Integration-Responsiveness
  (-Learning) (IR- and IRL-
  grid), 99 (note), 191
international
  account management, *see*
    key account
    management
  division, 16–17, 28, 123–4,
    140, 144, 150, 168–9
  playing field, 74–8, 85–6,
    89, 91
  training, *see* expatriation
internationalization
  decision tree, 100 (note),
    191
  loop, 11–14, 54, 135–7,
    163–6, 177
internet business (dotcom
  companies), 51–2

**J**
joint venture, 103, 111–17,
  150, 160, 164

**K**
key
  account management, 125
  supplier management, 44–7
knowledge (management), 4,
  64, 94–8, 111–15, 118–19,
  123, 125–8, 159–60, 167,
  174–7

**L**
learning
  curve, 65–6, 74–5, 78, 108,
    112
  opportunities, 94–8, 122,
    167, 169–71, 173–7
leverage, 12, 46, 66–8, 69,
  95–6, 98–9, 108, 175–7,
  187–8
liability of foreignness, 46
licensing, 111–17
local
  differences, *see* regional
    differences
  brand, 70, 80, 89
  location, 48–9, 63–5, 113, 142,
    175–7
low hanging fruit
  *see* quick wins

**M**
market
  blunders, 71–2
  convergence, 1–2, 83, 85,
    90–4, 183
  limits (limitations), 2, 4,
    61, 63, 65, 73, 83–4,
    90–4, 112, 119, 123,
    141, 183–4,
    *see also* globalization limits
  saturation, 42–4

matrix (organization), 119,
  128–31, 155, 178
merger, 111–17
mergers & acquisitions (M&A)
  20, 30, 39, 50, 82, 111–17,
  171
metanational, 120–1

**N**
negotiation power, 102–5
network benefits, 68–71, 109,
  173–4
not-invented-here syndrome
  (NIH), 147, 176

**O**
oil industry, 29, 38, 63
organization
  global, 71–4, 122–3
  multinational, 71–4, 122–3
organizational
  blueprint, 12, 15, 98, 105,
    118–34, 142–4, 181, 184
  culture, 96–7, 125–8,
    141–2, 149–57
  dimensions, 119, 122–6,
    159, 184
  structure, *see* organizational
    blueprint
overglobalization, 87–8, 161–3
overlay structures, 145–6

**P**
parcel delivery services, 93
PC industry, 31, 61, 75, 79
pharmaceutical industry, 30,
  61, 82
polycentric, 152
pricing, 3, 7–9, 26, 47, 50,
  66–9, 71–3, 75, 90–4, 140

**Q**
quick wins, 116, 172, 186

**R**
regional
  brand, *see* local brand
  differences, 2, 8, 82–5
  headquarters, 119, 133–4,
    140, 178
  strategy, 78, 82–5, 133–4
  structure, 45, 124–5, 160
regionalization
  *see* regional strategy
relocation, 63–4
reporting lines, 142
  *modus operandi*, 142
  systems and processes,
    143, 152
  profit–loss responsibility
    (P&L), 143–4, 152

**S**
scale economies
  *see* economies of scale

segmentation, 94, 170
self-fulfilling prophecy, 88–9
silos, 126–7, 147
single currency
  *see* Euro
spiderweb, 78 (note), 99–100
  (notes), 191
steel industry, 61, 63, 113
strategic
  ambition, 169
  innovation (management),
    167
  investments, 28–9
strategy paradox, 181
stuck in the middle, 154–8
supranational, 120–1
subsidiaries, 16–17, 44–7, 83,
  90, 119–20, 128–32, 140,
  152, 163–5, 175–7
  black hole, 131–2
  contributor, 131–2
  implementer, 131–2
  strategic leader, 131–2

**T**
target market, 36–7, 69, 99,
  108–11, 114, 116
telecom industry, 32, 37–8,
  41–2, 45, 50
temporary work services, 31,
  46–8, 58, 165
textile industry, 63–4, 113
timing
  of internationalization, 5,
    58, 87–8, 161–3, 166–7
  of global transformations,
    141, 146, 154–7
transition, 118–21, 123, 146,
  185–7
transnational, 5–7, 9–10, 120–1
transnationality index, 6
truck manufacturing industry,
  30–1, 37
TV broadcasting, 69

**U**
UNCTAD (World Investment
  Report), 6
underglobalization, 87–8

**V**
valley, 48–9, 65
  *see also* industry clusters
value chain, 34, 46, 74, 80–1,
  84, 86, 111, 125, 127, 169
vision, 4–5, 73, 88–9, 161–3,
  182–3

**W**
WTO, 41